HOW
DEMOCRACIES
DIE

HOW
DEMOCRACIES
DIE

STEVEN LEVITSKY &
DANIEL ZIBLATT

 CROWN
NEW YORK

CROWN and the Crown colophon are registered trademarks
of Penguin Random House LLC.

Library of Congress Cataloging-in-Publication Data
Names: Levitsky, Steven, author. | Ziblatt, Daniel, 1972–
    author.
Title: How democracies die / Steven Levitsky and Daniel
    Ziblatt.
Description: First edition. | New York : Crown Publishing,
    [2018] | Includes bibliographical references.
Identifiers: LCCN 2017045872| ISBN 9781524762933 |
    ISBN 9781524762940 (pbk.) | ISBN 9781524762957 (ebook)
Subjects: LCSH: Democracy. | Political culture. |
    Democracy—United States. | Political culture—United
    States. | United States—Politics and government—2017–
Classification: LCC JC423 .L4855 2018 | DDC 321.8—
    dc23
LC record available at https://lccn.loc.gov/2017045872

ISBN 978-1-5247-6293-3
Ebook ISBN 978-1-5247-6295-7
International edition ISBN 978-0-525-57453-8

Printed in the United States of America

Jacket design by Christopher Brand

10 9 8 7 6 5 4 3 2

First Edition

To our families:

Liz Mineo and Alejandra Mineo-Levitsky

& Suriya, Lilah, and Talia Ziblatt

CONTENTS

∎

Introduction

Is our democracy in danger? It is a question we never thought we'd be asking. We have been colleagues for fifteen years, thinking, writing, and teaching students about failures of democracy in other places and times—Europe's dark 1930s, Latin America's repressive 1970s. We have spent years researching new forms of authoritarianism emerging around the globe. For us, how and why democracies die has been an occupational obsession.

But now we find ourselves turning to our own country. Over the past two years, we have watched politicians say and do things that are unprecedented in the United States—but that we recognize as having been the precursors of democratic crisis in other places. We feel dread, as do so many other Americans, even as we try to reassure ourselves that *things can't really be that bad here.* After all, even though we know democracies are always fragile, the one in which we live has somehow managed to defy gravity. Our Constitution, our national creed of freedom and equality, our historically robust middle class, our high levels of wealth and education, and our large, diversified private sector—all these should inoculate us from the kind of democratic breakdown that has occurred elsewhere.

Yet, we worry. American politicians now treat their rivals as enemies, intimidate the free press, and threaten to reject the results of elections. They try to weaken the institutional buffers of our democracy, including the courts, intelligence services, and ethics offices. American states, which were once praised by the great jurist Louis Brandeis as "laboratories of democracy," are in danger of becoming laboratories of authoritarianism as those in power rewrite electoral rules, redraw constituencies, and even rescind voting rights to ensure that they do not lose. And in 2016, for the first time in U.S. history, a man with no experience in public office, little observable commitment to constitutional rights, and clear authoritarian tendencies was elected president.

What does all this mean? Are we living through the decline and fall of one of the world's oldest and most successful democracies?

At midday on September 11, 1973, after months of mounting tensions in the streets of Santiago, Chile, British-made Hawker Hunter jets swooped overhead, dropping bombs on La Moneda, the neoclassical presidential palace in the center of the city. As the bombs continued to fall, La Moneda burned. President Salvador Allende, elected three years earlier at the head of a leftist coalition, was barricaded inside. During his term, Chile had been wracked by social unrest, economic crisis, and political paralysis. Allende had said he would not leave his post until he had finished his job—but now the moment of truth had arrived. Under the command of General Augusto Pinochet, Chile's armed forces were seizing control of the country.

Early in the morning on that fateful day, Allende offered defiant words on a national radio broadcast, hoping that his many supporters would take to the streets in defense of democracy. But the resistance never materialized. The military police who guarded the palace had abandoned him; his broadcast was met with silence. Within hours, President Allende was dead. So, too, was Chilean democracy.

This is how we tend to think of democracies dying: at the hands of men with guns. During the Cold War, coups d'état accounted for nearly three out of every four democratic breakdowns. Democracies in Argentina, Brazil, the Dominican Republic, Ghana, Greece, Guatemala, Nigeria, Pakistan, Peru, Thailand, Turkey, and Uruguay all died this way. More recently, military coups toppled Egyptian President Mohamed Morsi in 2013 and Thai Prime Minister Yingluck Shinawatra in 2014. In all these cases, democracy dissolved in spectacular fashion, through military power and coercion.

But there is another way to break a democracy. It is less dramatic but equally destructive. Democracies may die at the hands not of generals but of elected leaders—presidents or prime ministers who subvert the very process that brought them to power. Some of these leaders dismantle democracy quickly, as Hitler did in the wake of the 1933 Reichstag fire in Germany. More often, though, democracies erode slowly, in barely visible steps.

In Venezuela, for example, Hugo Chávez was a political outsider who railed against what he cast as a corrupt governing elite, promising to build a more "authentic" democracy that used the country's vast oil wealth to improve the lives of the poor. Skillfully tapping into the anger of ordinary Venezuelans, many of whom felt ignored or mistreated by the established political parties, Chávez was elected president in 1998. As a woman in Chávez's home state of Barinas put it on election night, "Democracy is infected. And Chávez is the only anti-biotic we have."

When Chávez launched his promised revolution, he did so democratically. In 1999, he held free elections for a new constituent assembly, in which his allies won an overwhelming majority. This allowed the *chavistas* to single-handedly write a new constitution. It was a democratic constitution, though, and to reinforce its legitimacy, new presidential and legislative elections were held in 2000. Chávez and his allies won those, too. Chávez's populism triggered intense opposition, and in April 2002, he was briefly toppled by the military. But the coup failed, allowing a triumphant Chávez to claim for himself even more democratic legitimacy.

It wasn't until 2003 that Chávez took his first clear steps toward authoritarianism. With public support fading, he stalled an opposition-led referendum that would have recalled him from office—until a year later, when soaring oil prices had boosted his standing enough for him to win. In 2004, the government blacklisted those who had signed the recall petition and packed the supreme court, but Chávez's landslide reelection in 2006 allowed him to maintain a democratic veneer. The *chavista* regime grew more repressive after 2006, closing a major television station, arresting or exiling opposition politicians, judges, and media figures on dubious charges, and eliminating presidential term limits so that Chávez could remain in power indefinitely. When Chávez, now dying of cancer, was reelected in 2012, the contest was free but not fair: *Chavismo* controlled much of the media and deployed the vast machinery of the government in its favor. After Chávez's death a year later, his successor, Nicolás Maduro, won another questionable reelection, and in 2014, his government imprisoned a major opposition leader. Still, the opposition's landslide victory in the 2015 legislative elections seemed to belie critics' claims that Venezuela was no longer democratic. It was only when a new single-party constituent assembly usurped the power of Congress in 2017, nearly two decades after Chávez first won the presidency, that Venezuela was widely recognized as an autocracy.

This is how democracies now die. Blatant dictatorship—in the form of fascism, communism, or military rule—has disappeared across much of the world. Military coups and other violent seizures of power are rare. Most countries hold regular elections. Democracies still die, but by different means. Since the end of the Cold War, most democratic breakdowns have been caused not by generals and soldiers but by elected governments themselves. Like Chávez in Venezuela, elected leaders have subverted democratic institutions in Georgia, Hungary, Nicaragua, Peru, the Philippines, Poland, Russia, Sri Lanka, Turkey, and Ukraine. Democratic backsliding today begins at the ballot box.

The electoral road to breakdown is dangerously deceptive. With a classic coup d'état, as in Pinochet's Chile, the death of a democracy is immediate and evident to all. The presidential palace burns. The president is killed, imprisoned, or shipped off into exile. The constitution is suspended or scrapped. On the electoral road, none of these things happen. There are no tanks in the streets. Constitutions and other nominally democratic institutions remain in place. People still vote. Elected autocrats maintain a veneer of democracy while eviscerating its substance.

Many government efforts to subvert democracy are "legal," in the sense that they are approved by the legislature or accepted by the courts. They may even be portrayed as efforts to *improve* democracy—making the judiciary more efficient, combating corruption, or cleaning up the electoral process.

Newspapers still publish but are bought off or bullied into self-censorship. Citizens continue to criticize the government but often find themselves facing tax or other legal troubles. This sows public confusion. People do not immediately realize what is happening. Many continue to believe they are living under a democracy. In 2011, when a Latinobarómetro survey asked Venezuelans to rate their own country from 1 ("not at all democratic") to 10 ("completely democratic"), 51 percent of respondents gave their country a score of 8 or higher.

Because there is no single moment—no coup, declaration of martial law, or suspension of the constitution—in which the regime obviously "crosses the line" into dictatorship, nothing may set off society's alarm bells. Those who denounce government abuse may be dismissed as exaggerating or crying wolf. Democracy's erosion is, for many, almost imperceptible.

How vulnerable is American democracy to this form of backsliding? The foundations of our democracy are certainly stronger than those in Venezuela, Turkey, or Hungary. But are they strong enough?

Answering such a question requires stepping back from daily headlines and breaking news alerts to widen our view, drawing lessons from the experiences of other democracies around the world and throughout history. Studying other democracies in crisis allows us to better understand the challenges facing our own democracy. For example, based on the historical experiences of other nations, we have developed a litmus test to help identify would-be autocrats before they come to power. We can learn from the mistakes that past democratic leaders have made in opening the door to would-be authoritarians—and, conversely, from the ways that other democracies have kept extremists out of power. A comparative approach also reveals how elected autocrats in different parts of the world employ remarkably similar strategies to subvert democratic institutions. As these patterns become visible, the steps toward breakdown grow less ambiguous—and easier to combat. Knowing how citizens in other democracies have successfully resisted elected autocrats, or why they tragically failed to do so, is essential to those seeking to defend American democracy today.

We know that extremist demagogues emerge from time to time in all societies, even in healthy democracies. The United States has had its share of them, including Henry Ford, Huey Long, Joseph McCarthy, and George Wallace. An essential test for democracies is not whether such figures emerge but whether political leaders, and especially political parties, work to prevent them from gaining power in the first place—by keeping them off mainstream party tickets, refusing to endorse or align with them, and when necessary, making common cause with rivals in support of democratic candidates. Isolating popular extremists requires political courage. But when fear, opportunism, or miscalculation leads established parties to bring extremists into the mainstream, democracy is imperiled.

Once a would-be authoritarian makes it to power, democracies face a second critical test: Will the autocratic leader subvert democratic institutions or be constrained by them? Institutions alone are not enough to rein in elected autocrats. Constitutions must be defended—by political parties and organized citizens, but also by democratic norms. Without robust norms, constitutional checks and balances do not serve as the bulwarks of democracy we imagine them to be. Institutions become political weapons, wielded forcefully by those who control them against those who do not. This is how elected autocrats subvert democracy—packing and "weaponizing" the courts and other neutral agencies, buying off the media and the private sector (or bullying them into silence), and rewriting the rules of politics to tilt the playing field against opponents. The tragic paradox of the electoral route to authoritarianism is that democracy's assassins use the very institutions of democracy—gradually, subtly, and even legally—to kill it.

America failed the first test in November 2016, when we elected a president with a dubious allegiance to democratic norms. Donald Trump's surprise victory was made possible not only by public disaffection but also by the Republican Party's failure to keep an extremist demagogue within its own ranks from gaining the nomination.

How serious is the threat now? Many observers take comfort in our Constitution, which was designed precisely to thwart and contain demagogues like Donald Trump. Our Madisonian system of checks and balances has endured for more than two centuries. It survived the Civil War, the Great Depression, the Cold War, and Watergate. Surely, then, it will be able to survive Trump.

We are less certain. Historically, our system of checks and balances *has* worked pretty well—but not, or not entirely, because of the constitutional system designed by the founders. Democracies work best—and survive longer—where constitutions are reinforced by unwritten democratic norms. Two basic norms have preserved America's checks and balances in ways we have come to take for granted: mutual toleration, or the understanding that competing parties accept one another as legitimate rivals, and forbearance, or the idea that politicians should exercise restraint in deploying their institutional prerogatives. These two norms undergirded American democracy for most of the twentieth century. Leaders of the two major parties accepted one another as legitimate and resisted the temptation to use their temporary control of institutions to maximum partisan advantage. Norms of toleration and restraint served as the soft guardrails of American democracy, helping it avoid the kind of partisan fight to the death that has destroyed democracies elsewhere in the world, including Europe in the 1930s and South America in the 1960s and 1970s.

Today, however, the guardrails of American democracy are weakening. The erosion of our democratic norms began in the 1980s and 1990s and accelerated in the 2000s. By the time Barack Obama became president, many Republicans, in particular, questioned the legitimacy of their Democratic rivals and had abandoned forbearance for a strategy of winning by any means necessary. Donald Trump may have accelerated this process, but he didn't cause it. The challenges facing American democracy run deeper. The weakening of our democratic norms is rooted in extreme partisan polarization—one that extends beyond policy differences into an existential conflict over race and culture. America's efforts to achieve racial equality as our society grows increasingly diverse have fueled an insidious reaction and intensifying polarization. And if one thing is clear from studying breakdowns throughout history, it's that extreme polarization can kill democracies.

There are, therefore, reasons for alarm. Not only did Americans elect a demagogue in 2016, but we did so at a time when the norms that once protected our democracy were already coming unmoored. But if other countries' experiences teach us that that polarization can kill democracies, they also teach us that breakdown is neither inevitable nor irreversible. Drawing lessons from other democracies in crisis, this book suggests strategies that citizens should, and should *not*, follow to defend our democracy.

Many Americans are justifiably frightened by what is happening to our country. But protecting our democracy requires more than just fright or outrage. We must be humble *and* bold. We must learn from other countries to see the warning signs— and recognize the false alarms. We must be aware of the fateful missteps that have wrecked other democracies. And we must see how citizens have risen to meet the great democratic crises of the past, overcoming their own deep-seated divisions to avert breakdown. History doesn't repeat itself. But it rhymes. The promise of history, and the hope of this book, is that we can find the rhymes before it is too late.

1

Fateful Alliances

A quarrel had arisen between the Horse and the Stag, so the Horse came to a Hunter to ask his help to take revenge on the Stag. The Hunter agreed but said: "If you desire to conquer the Stag, you must permit me to place this piece of iron between your jaws, so that I may guide you with these reins, and allow this saddle to be placed upon your back so that I may keep steady upon you as we follow the enemy." The Horse agreed to the conditions, and the Hunter soon saddled and bridled him. Then, with the aid of the Hunter, the Horse soon overcame the Stag and said to the Hunter: "Now get off, and remove those things from my mouth and back." "Not so fast, friend," said the Hunter. "I have now got you under bit and spur and prefer to keep you as you are at present."

—"The Horse, the Stag, and the Hunter," *Aesop's Fables*

On October 30, 1922, Benito Mussolini arrived in Rome at 10:55 A.M. in an overnight sleeping car from Milan. He had been invited to the capital city by the king to accept Italy's premiership and form a new cabinet. Accompanied by a small group of guards, Mussolini first stopped at the Hotel Savoia and then, wearing a black suit jacket, black shirt, and matching black bowler hat, walked triumphantly to the king's Quirinal Palace. Rome was filled with rumors of unrest. Bands of Fascists—many in mismatched uniforms—roamed the city's streets. Mussolini, aware of the power of the spectacle, strode into the king's marble-floored residential palace and greeted him, "Sire, forgive my attire. I come from the battlefield."

This was the beginning of Mussolini's legendary "March on Rome." The image of masses of Blackshirts crossing the Rubicon to seize power from Italy's Liberal state became fascist canon, repeated on national holidays and in children's schoolbooks throughout the 1920s and 1930s. Mussolini did his part to enshrine the myth. At the last train stop before entering Rome that day, he had considered disembarking to ride into the city on horseback surrounded by his guards. Though the plan was ultimately abandoned, afterward he did all he could to bolster the legend of his rise to power as, in his own words, a "revolution" and "insurrectional act" that launched a new fascist epoch.

The truth was more mundane. The bulk of Mussolini's Blackshirts, often poorly fed and unarmed, arrived only after he had been invited to become prime minister. The squads of Fascists around the country were a menace, but Mussolini's machinations to take the reins of state were no revolution. He used his party's 35 parliamentary votes (out of 535), divisions among establishment politicians, fear of socialism, and the threat of violence by 30,000 Blackshirts to capture the attention of the timid King Victor Emmanuel III, who saw in

Mussolini a rising political star and a means of neutralizing unrest.

With political order restored by Mussolini's appointment and socialism in retreat, the Italian stock market soared. Elder statesmen of the Liberal establishment, such as Giovanni Giolitti and Antonio Salandra, found themselves applauding the turn of events. They regarded Mussolini as a useful ally. But not unlike the horse in Aesop's fable, Italy soon found itself under "bit and spur."

Some version of this story has repeated itself throughout the world over the last century. A cast of political outsiders, including Adolf Hitler, Getúlio Vargas in Brazil, Alberto Fujimori in Peru, and Hugo Chávez in Venezuela, came to power on the same path: from the inside, via elections or alliances with powerful political figures. In each instance, elites believed the invitation to power would *contain* the outsider, leading to a restoration of control by mainstream politicians. But their plans backfired. A lethal mix of ambition, fear, and miscalculation conspired to lead them to the same fateful mistake: willingly handing over the keys of power to an autocrat-in-the-making.

Why do seasoned elder statesmen make this mistake? There are few more gripping illustrations than the rise of Adolf Hitler in January 1933. His capacity for violent insurrection was on display as early as Munich's Beer Hall Putsch of 1923—a surprise evening strike in which his group of pistol-bearing loyalists took control of several government buildings and a Munich beer hall where Bavarian officials were meeting. The ill-conceived attack was halted by the authorities, and Hitler spent nine months in jail, where he wrote his infamous personal testament, *Mein*

Kampf. Thereafter, Hitler publicly committed to gaining power via elections. Initially, his National Socialist movement found few votes. The Weimar political system had been founded in 1919 by a prodemocratic coalition of Catholics, Liberals, and Social Democrats. But beginning in 1930, with the German economy reeling, the center-right fell prey to infighting, and the Communists and Nazis grew in popularity.

The elected government collapsed in March 1930 amid the pain of the Great Depression. With political gridlock blocking government action, the figurehead president, World War I hero Paul von Hindenburg, took advantage of a constitutional article giving the head of state the authority to name chancellors in the exceptional circumstance that parliament failed to deliver governing majorities. The aim of these unelected chancellors—and the president—was not only to govern but to sideline radicals on the left and right. First, Center Party economist Heinrich Brüning (who would later flee Germany to become a professor at Harvard) attempted, but failed, to restore economic growth; his time as chancellor was short-lived. President von Hindenburg turned next to nobleman Franz von Papen, and then, in growing despondency, to von Papen's close friend and rival, former defense minister General Kurt von Schleicher. But without parliamentary majorities in the Reichstag, stalemate persisted. Leaders, for good reason, feared the next election.

Convinced that "something must finally give," a cabal of rivalrous conservatives convened in late January 1933 and settled on a solution: A popular outsider should be placed at the head of the government. They despised him but knew that at least he had a mass following. And, most of all, they thought they could control him.

On January 30, 1933, von Papen, one of the chief architects of the plan, dismissed worries over the gamble that would make Adolf Hitler chancellor of a crisis-ridden Germany with the reassuring words: "We've engaged him for ourselves. . . . Within two months, we will have pushed [him] so far into a corner that he'll squeal." A more profound miscalculation is hard to imagine.

The Italian and German experiences highlight the type of "fateful alliance" that often elevates authoritarians to power. In any democracy, politicians will at times face severe challenges. Economic crisis, rising public discontent, and the electoral decline of mainstream political parties can test the judgment of even the most experienced insiders. If a charismatic outsider emerges on the scene, gaining popularity as he challenges the old order, it is tempting for establishment politicians who feel their control is unraveling to try to co-opt him. If an insider breaks ranks to embrace the insurgent before his rivals do, he can use the outsider's energy and base to outmaneuver his peers. And then, establishment politicians hope, the insurgent can be redirected to support their own program.

This sort of devil's bargain often mutates to the benefit of the insurgent, as alliances provide outsiders with enough respectability to become legitimate contenders for power. In early 1920s Italy, the old Liberal order was crumbling amid growing strikes and social unrest. The failure of traditional parties to forge solid parliamentary majorities left the elderly fifth-term prime minister Giovanni Giolitti desperate, and against the wishes of advisors he called early elections in May 1921. With the aim of tapping into the Fascists' mass appeal, Giolitti decided to offer Mussolini's upstart movement a place on his electoral group's "bourgeois bloc" of Nationalists, Fascists, and Liberals. This strategy failed—the bourgeois bloc won less than 20 percent of the vote, leading to Giolitti's resignation. But Mussolini's place on the ticket gave his ragtag group the legitimacy it would need to enable its rise.

Such fateful alliances are hardly confined to interwar Europe. They also help to explain the rise of Hugo Chávez. Venezuela had prided itself on being South America's oldest democracy, in place since 1958. Chávez, a junior military officer and failed coup leader who had never held public office, was a political outsider. But his rise to power was given a critical boost from a consummate insider: ex-president Rafael Caldera, one of the founders of Venezuelan democracy.

Venezuelan politics was long dominated by two parties, the center-left Democratic Action and Caldera's center-right Social Christian Party (known as COPEI). The two alternated in power peacefully for more than thirty years, and by the 1970s, Venezuela was viewed as a model democracy in a region plagued by coups and dictatorships. During the 1980s, however, the country's oil-dependent economy sank into a prolonged slump, a crisis that persisted for more than a decade, nearly doubling the poverty rate. Not surprisingly, Venezuelans grew disaffected. Massive riots in February 1989 suggested that the established parties were in trouble. Three years later, in February 1992, a group of junior military officers rose up against President Carlos Andrés Pérez. Led by Hugo Chávez, the rebels called themselves "Bolivarians," after revered independence hero Simón Bolívar. The coup failed. But when the now-detained Chávez appeared on live television to tell his supporters to lay down their arms (declaring, in words that would become legendary, that their mission had failed "for now"), he became a hero in the eyes of many Venezuelans, particularly poorer ones. Following a second failed coup in November 1992, the imprisoned Chávez changed course, opting to pursue power via elections. He would need help.

Although ex-president Caldera was a well-regarded elder statesman, his political career was waning in 1992. Four years earlier, he had failed to secure his party's presidential nomination, and he was now considered a political relic. But the seventy-six-year-old senator still dreamed of returning to the presidency, and Chávez's emergence provided him with a lifeline. On the night of Chávez's initial coup, the former president stood up during an emergency joint session of congress and embraced the rebels' cause, declaring:

> It is difficult to ask the people to sacrifice themselves for freedom and democracy when they think that freedom and democracy are incapable of giving them food to eat, of preventing the astronomical rise in the cost of subsistence, or of placing a definitive end to the terrible scourge of corruption that, in the eyes of the entire world, is eating away at the institutions of Venezuela with each passing day.

The stunning speech resurrected Caldera's political career. Having tapped into Chávez's antisystem constituency, the ex-president's public support swelled, which allowed him to make a successful presidential bid in 1993.

Caldera's public flirtation with Chávez did more than boost his own standing in the polls; it also gave Chávez new credibility. Chávez and his comrades had sought to destroy their country's thirty-four-year-old democracy. But rather than denouncing the coup leaders as an extremist threat, the former president offered them public sympathy—and, with it, an opening to mainstream politics.

Caldera also helped open the gates to the presidential palace for Chávez by dealing a mortal blow to Venezuela's established parties. In a stunning about-face, he abandoned COPEI, the party he had founded nearly half a century earlier, and launched an independent presidential bid. To be sure, the parties were already in crisis. But Caldera's departure and subsequent anti-establishment campaign helped bury them. The party system collapsed after Caldera's 1993 election as an antiparty independent, paving the way for future outsiders. Five years later, it would be Chávez's turn.

But back in 1993, Chávez still had a major problem. He was in jail, awaiting trial for treason. However, in 1994, now-President Caldera dropped all charges against him. Caldera's final act in enabling Chávez was literally opening the gates—of prison—for him. Immediately after Chávez's release, a reporter asked him where he was going. "To power," he replied. Freeing Chávez was popular, and Caldera had promised such a move during the campaign. Like most Venezuelan elites, he viewed Chávez as a passing fad—someone who would likely fall out of public favor by the time of the next election. But in dropping all charges, rather than allowing Chávez to stand trial and then pardoning him, Caldera elevated him, transforming the former coup leader overnight into a viable presidential candidate. On December 6, 1998, Chávez won the presidency, easily defeating an establishment-backed candidate. On inauguration day, Caldera, the outgoing president, could not bring himself to deliver the oath of office to Chávez, as tradition dictated. Instead, he stood glumly off to one side.

Despite their vast differences, Hitler, Mussolini, and Chávez followed routes to power that share striking similarities. Not only were they all outsiders with a flair for capturing public attention, but each of them rose to power because establishment politicians overlooked the warning signs and either handed over power to them (Hitler and Mussolini) or opened the door for them (Chávez).

The abdication of political responsibility by existing leaders often marks a nation's first step toward authoritarianism. Years after Chávez's presidential victory, Rafael Caldera explained his mistakes simply: "Nobody thought that Mr. Chávez had even the remotest chance of becoming president." And merely a day after Hitler became chancellor, a prominent conservative who aided him admitted, "I have just committed the greatest stupidity of my life; I have allied myself with the greatest demagogue in world history."

Not all democracies have fallen into this trap. Some—including Belgium, Britain, Costa Rica, and Finland—have faced challenges from demagogues but also have managed to keep them out of power. How have they done it? It is tempting to think this survival is rooted in the collective wisdom of voters. Maybe Belgians and Costa Ricans were simply more democratic than their counterparts in Germany or Italy. After all, we like to believe that the fate of a government lies in the hands of its citizens. If the people hold democratic values, democracy will be safe. If citizens are open to authoritarian appeals, then, sooner or later, democracy will be in trouble.

This view is wrong. It assumes too much of democracy—that "the people" can shape at will the kind of government they possess. It's hard to find any evidence of majority support for authoritarianism in 1920s Germany and Italy. Before the Nazis and Fascists seized power, less than 2 percent of the population were party members, and neither party achieved anything close to a majority of the vote in free and fair elections. Rather, solid electoral majorities opposed Hitler and Mussolini—before both men achieved power with the support of political insiders blind to the danger of their own ambitions.

Hugo Chávez was elected by a majority of voters, but there is little evidence that Venezuelans were looking for a strongman. At the time, public support for democracy was higher there than in Chile—a country that was, and remains, stably democratic. According to the 1998 Latinobarómetro survey, 60 percent of Venezuelans agreed with the statement "Democracy is always the best form of government," while only 25 percent agreed that "under some circumstances, an authoritarian government can be preferable to a democratic one." By contrast, only 53 percent of respondents in Chile agreed that "democracy is always the best form of government."

Potential demagogues exist in all democracies, and occasionally, one or more of them strike a public chord. But in some democracies, political leaders heed the warning signs and take steps to ensure that authoritarians remain on the fringes, far from the centers of power. When faced with the rise of extremists or demagogues, they make a concerted effort to isolate and defeat them. Although mass responses to extremist appeals matter, what matters more is whether political elites, and especially parties, serve as filters. Put simply, political parties are democracy's gatekeepers.

If authoritarians are to be kept out, they first have to be identified. There is, alas, no foolproof advance warning system. Many authoritarians can be easily recognized before they come to power. They have a clear track record: Hitler led a failed putsch; Chávez led a failed military uprising; Mussolini's Blackshirts engaged in paramilitary violence; and in Argentina in the mid–twentieth century, Juan Perón helped lead a successful coup two and a half years before running for president.

But politicians do not always reveal the full scale of their authoritarianism before reaching power. Some adhere to democratic norms early in their careers, only to abandon them later. Consider Hungarian Prime Minister Viktor Orbán. Orbán and his Fidesz party began as liberal democrats in the late 1980s, and in his first stint as prime minister between 1998 and 2002, Orbán governed democratically. His autocratic about-face after returning to power in 2010 was a genuine surprise.

So how do we identify authoritarianism in politicians who don't have an obvious antidemocratic record? Here we turn to the eminent political scientist Juan Linz. Born in Weimar Germany and raised amid Spain's civil war, Linz knew all too well the perils of losing a democracy. As a professor at Yale, he devoted much of his career to trying to understand how and why democracies die. Many of Linz's conclusions can be found in a small but seminal book called *The Breakdown of Democratic Regimes*. Published in 1978, the book highlights the role of politicians, showing how their behavior can either reinforce democracy or put it at risk. He also proposed, but never fully developed, a "litmus test" for identifying antidemocratic politicians.

Building on Linz's work, we have developed a set of four behavioral warning signs that can help us know an authoritarian when we see one. We should worry when a politician 1) rejects, in words or action, the democratic rules of the game, 2) denies the legitimacy of opponents, 3) tolerates or encourages violence, or 4) indicates a willingness to curtail the civil liberties of opponents, including the media. Table 1 shows how to assess politicians in terms of these four factors.

A politician who meets even one of these criteria is cause for concern. What kinds of candidates tend to test positive on a litmus test for authoritarianism? Very often, populist outsiders do. Populists are antiestablishment politicians—figures who, claiming to represent the voice of "the people," wage war on what they depict as a corrupt and conspiratorial elite. Populists tend to deny the legitimacy of established parties, attacking them as undemocratic and even unpatriotic. They tell voters that the existing system is not really a democracy but instead has been hijacked, corrupted, or rigged by the elite. And they promise to bury that elite and return power to "the people." This discourse should be taken seriously. When populists win elections, they often assault democratic institutions. In Latin America, for example, of all fifteen presidents elected in Bolivia, Ecuador, Peru, and Venezuela between 1990 and 2012, five were populist outsiders: Alberto Fujimori, Hugo Chávez, Evo Morales, Lucio Gutiérrez, and Rafael Correa. All five ended up weakening democratic institutions.

Table 1: Four Key Indicators of Authoritarian Behavior

1. Rejection of (or weak commitment to) democratic rules of the game	Do they reject the Constitution or express a willingness to violate it? Do they suggest a need for antidemocratic measures, such as canceling elections, violating or suspending the Constitution, banning certain organizations, or restricting basic civil or political rights? Do they seek to use (or endorse the use of) extraconstitutional means to change the government, such as military coups, violent insurrections, or mass protests aimed at forcing a change in the government? Do they attempt to undermine the legitimacy of elections, for example, by refusing to accept credible electoral results?
2. Denial of the legitimacy of political opponents	Do they describe their rivals as subversive, or opposed to the existing constitutional order? Do they claim that their rivals constitute an existential threat, either to national security or to the prevailing way of life? Do they baselessly describe their partisan rivals as criminals, whose supposed violation of the law (or potential to do so) disqualifies them from full participation in the political arena? Do they baselessly suggest that their rivals are foreign agents, in that they are secretly working in alliance with (or the employ of) a foreign government—usually an enemy one?

3. Toleration or encouragement of violence	Do they have any ties to armed gangs, paramilitary forces, militias, guerrillas, or other organizations that engage in illicit violence?
	Have they or their partisan allies sponsored or encouraged mob attacks on opponents?
	Have they tacitly endorsed violence by their supporters by refusing to unambiguously condemn it and punish it?
	Have they praised (or refused to condemn) other significant acts of political violence, either in the past or elsewhere in the world?
4. Readiness to curtail civil liberties of opponents, including media	Have they supported laws or policies that restrict civil liberties, such as expanded libel or defamation laws, or laws restricting protest, criticism of the government, or certain civic or political organizations?
	Have they threatened to take legal or other punitive action against critics in rival parties, civil society, or the media?
	Have they praised repressive measures taken by other governments, either in the past or elsewhere in the world?

Keeping authoritarian politicians out of power is more easily said than done. Democracies, after all, are not supposed to ban parties or prohibit candidates from standing for election—and we do not advocate such measures. The responsibility for filtering out authoritarians lies, rather, with political parties and party leaders: democracy's gatekeepers.

Successful gatekeeping requires that mainstream parties isolate and defeat extremist forces, a behavior political scientist Nancy Bermeo calls "distancing." Prodemocratic parties may engage in distancing in several ways. First, they can keep would-be authoritarians off party ballots at election time. This requires that they resist the temptation to nominate these extremists for higher office even when they can potentially deliver votes.

Second, parties can root out extremists in the grass roots of their own ranks. Take the Swedish Conservative Party (AVF) during the perilous interwar period. The AVF's youth group (an organization of voting-age activists), called the Swedish Nationalist Youth Organization, grew increasingly radical in the early 1930s, criticizing parliamentary democracy, openly supporting Hitler, and even creating a group of uniformed storm troopers. The AVF responded in 1933 by expelling the organization. The loss of 25,000 members may have cost the AVF votes in the 1934 municipal elections, but the party's distancing strategy reduced the influence of antidemocratic forces in Sweden's largest center-right party.

Third, prodemocratic parties can avoid all alliances with antidemocratic parties and candidates. As we saw in Italy and Germany, prodemocratic parties are sometimes tempted to align with extremists on their ideological flank to win votes or, in parliamentary systems, form governments. But such alliances can have devastating long-term consequences. As Linz wrote, the demise of many democracies can be traced to a party's "greater affinity for extremists on its side of the political spectrum than for [mainstream] parties close to the opposite side."

Fourth, prodemocratic parties can act to systematically isolate, rather than legitimize, extremists. This requires that politicians avoid acts—such as German Conservatives' joint rallies with Hitler in the early 1930s or Caldera's speech sympathizing with Chávez—that help to "normalize" or provide public respectability to authoritarian figures.

Finally, whenever extremists emerge as serious electoral contenders, mainstream parties must forge a united front to defeat them. To quote Linz, they must be willing to "join with opponents ideologically distant but committed to the survival of the democratic political order." In normal circumstances, this is almost unimaginable. Picture Senator Edward Kennedy and other liberal Democrats campaigning for Ronald Reagan, or the British Labour Party and their trade union allies endorsing Margaret Thatcher. Each party's followers would be infuriated at this seeming betrayal of principles. But in extraordinary times, courageous party leadership means putting democracy and country before party and articulating to voters what is at stake. When a party or politician that tests positive on our litmus test emerges as a serious electoral threat, there is little alternative. United democratic fronts can prevent extremists from winning power, which can mean saving a democracy.

Although the failures are more memorable, some European democracies practiced successful gatekeeping between the wars. Surprisingly big lessons can be drawn from small countries. Consider Belgium and Finland. In Europe's years of political and economic crisis in the 1920s and 1930s, both countries experienced an early warning sign of democratic decay—the rise of antisystem extremists—but, unlike Italy and Germany, they were saved by political elites who defended democratic institutions (at least until Nazi invasion several years later).

During Belgium's 1936 general election, as the contagion of fascism was spreading from Italy and Germany across Europe, voters delivered a jarring result. Two authoritarian far-right parties—the Rex Party and the Flemish nationalist party, or Vlaams Nationaal Verbond (VNV)—surged in the polls, capturing almost 20 percent of the popular vote and challenging the historical dominance of three establishment parties: the center-right Catholic Party, the Socialists, and the Liberal Party. The challenge from the leader of the Rex Party, Léon Degrelle, a Catholic journalist who would become a Nazi collaborator, was especially strong. Degrelle, a virulent critic of parliamentary democracy, had departed from the right edges of the Catholic Party and now attacked its leaders as corrupt. He received encouragement and financial support from both Hitler and Mussolini.

The 1936 election shook the centrist parties, which suffered losses across the board. Aware of the antidemocratic movements in nearby Italy and Germany and fearful for their own survival, they confronted the daunting task of deciding how to respond. The Catholic Party, in particular, faced a difficult dilemma: collaborate with their longtime rivals, the Socialists and Liberals, or forge a right-wing alliance that included the Rexists, a party with whom they shared some ideological affinity but that rejected the value of democratic politics.

Unlike the retreating mainstream politicians of Italy and Germany, the Belgian Catholic leadership declared that any cooperation with the Rexists was incompatible with party membership and then pursued a two-pronged strategy to combat the movement. Internally, Catholic Party leaders heightened discipline by screening candidates for pro-Rexist sympathies and expelling those who expressed extremist views. In addition, the party leadership took a strong stance against cooperation with the far right. Externally, the Catholic Party fought Rex on its own turf. The Catholic Party adopted new propaganda and campaign tactics that targeted younger Catholics, who had formerly been part of the Rexist base. They created the Catholic Youth Front in December 1935 and began to run former allies against Degrelle.

The final clash between Rex and the Catholic Party, in which Rex was effectively sidelined (until the Nazi occupation), centered around the formation of a new government after the 1936 election. The Catholic Party supported the incumbent Catholic prime minister Paul van Zeeland. After van Zeeland regained the premiership, there were two chief options for forming a government: The first was an alliance with the rival Socialists, along the lines of France's "Popular Front," which van Zeeland and other Catholic leaders had initially hoped to avoid. The second was a right-wing alliance of antisocialist forces that would include Rex and VNV. The choice was not easy; the second option was supported by a traditionalist faction that sought to upset the fragile van Zeeland cabinet by rallying the Catholic rank and file, organizing a "March on Brussels," and forcing a by-election in which Rex leader Degrelle would run against van Zeeland. These plans were thwarted in 1937 when Degrelle lost the by-election, largely because the Catholic Party MPs had taken a stand: They refused to go with the traditionalists' plan and instead united with the Liberals and Socialists behind van Zeeland. This was the Catholic Party's most important gatekeeping act.

The Catholic Party's stand on the right was also made possible by King Leopold III and the Socialist Party. The election of 1936 had left the Socialist Party as the largest party in the legislature, which gave it the prerogative to form a government. However, when it became evident that the Socialists could not gain enough parliamentary support, rather than call a new election—which may have handed even more seats to extremist parties—the king met with leaders of the largest parties to talk them into a power-sharing cabinet, led by incumbent prime minister van Zeeland, which would include both the conservative Catholics and the Socialists but exclude antisystem parties on both sides. Although the Socialists distrusted van Zeeland, a Catholic Party man, they nevertheless put democracy ahead of their own interests and endorsed the grand coalition.

A similar dynamic unfolded in Finland, where the extreme-right Lapua Movement burst onto the political stage in 1929, threatening the country's fragile democracy. The movement sought the destruction of communism by any means necessary. It threatened violence if its demands were not met and attacked mainstream politicians whom it deemed collaborators with Socialists. At first, politicians from the governing center-right Agrarian Union flirted with the Lapua Movement, finding its anticommunism politically useful; they met the movement's demands to deny communist political rights while tolerating extreme-right violence. In 1930, P. E. Svinhufvud, a conservative whom the Lapua leaders considered "one of their own," became prime minister, and he offered them two cabinet posts. A year later, Svinhufvud became president. Yet the Lapua Movement continued its extremist behavior; with the communists banned, it targeted the more moderate Social Democratic Party. Lapua thugs abducted more than a thousand Social Democrats, including union leaders and members of parliament. The Lapua Movement also organized a 12,000-person march on Helsinki (modeled on the mythical March on Rome), and in 1932, it backed a failed putsch aimed at replacing the government with one that was "apolitical" and "patriotic."

As the Lapua Movement grew more radical, however, Finland's traditional conservative parties broke decisively with it. In late 1930, the bulk of the Agrarian Union, the liberal Progress Party, and much of the Swedish Peoples Party joined their main ideological rival, the Social Democrats, in the so-called Lawfulness Front to defend democracy against violent extremists. Even the conservative president, Svinhufvud, force-fully rejected—and eventually banned—his former allies. The Lapua Movement was left isolated, and Finland's brief burst of fascism was aborted.

It is not only in distant historical cases that one finds successful gatekeeping. In Austria in 2016, the main center-right party (the Austrian People's Party, ÖVP) effectively kept the radical-right Freedom Party (FPÖ) out of the presidency. Austria has a long history of extreme right politics, and the FPÖ is one of Europe's strongest far-right parties. Austria's political system was growing vulnerable because the two main parties, the Social Democratic SPÖ and the Christian Democratic ÖVP, which had alternated in the presidency throughout the postwar period, were weakening. In 2016, their dominance was challenged by two upstarts—the Green Party's former chairman, Alexander Van der Bellen, and the extremist FPÖ leader Norbert Hofer.

To the surprise of most analysts, the first round left Van der Bellen and the right-wing outsider Hofer as the two candidates in a second-round runoff. After a procedural error in October 2016, the runoff was held in December. At this point, several leading politicians, including some from the conservative ÖVP, argued that Hofer and his Freedom Party had to be defeated. Hofer had appeared to encourage violence against immigrants, and many questioned whether an elected Hofer would privilege his party in ways that violated long-standing norms of the president remaining above politics. In the face of this threat, some important ÖVP leaders worked to defeat Hofer by supporting their ideological rival, the left-leaning Green candidate, Van der Bellen. The ÖVP's presidential candidate, Andreas Khol, endorsed Van der Bellen, as did Chairman Reinhold Mitterlehner, Cabinet Minister Sophie Karmasin, and dozens of ÖVP mayors in the Austrian countryside. In one letter, former chairman Erhard Busek wrote that he endorsed Van der Bellen "not with passion but after careful deliberation," and that, furthermore, the decision was motivated by the sentiment that "we don't want congratulations from Le Pen, Jobbik, Wilders and the AfD [and other extremists] after our presidential elections." Van der Bellen won by a mere 300,000 votes.

This stance took considerable political courage. According to one Catholic Party mayor of a small city outside Vienna, Stefan Schmuckenschlager, who endorsed the Green Party candidate, it was a decision that split families. His twin brother, another party leader, had supported Hofer. As Schmuckenschlager explained it, power politics sometimes has to be put aside to do the right thing.

Did the endorsements from the ÖVP help? There is evidence that they did. According to exit polls, 55 percent of respondents who identified as ÖVP supporters said they voted for Van der Bellen, and 48 percent of Van der Bellen voters said they had voted for him to prevent Hofer from winning. In addition, the strong urban/rural division that has always marked Austrian politics (between left-wing urban areas and right-wing rural areas) was dramatically diminished in the second round in December 2016, with a surprising number of traditional rural conservative states switching to vote for Van der Bellen.

In short, in 2016, responsible leaders in the ÖVP resisted the temptation to ally with an extremist party on their own ideological flank, and the result was that party's defeat. The FPÖ's strong performance in the 2017 parliamentary elections, which positioned it to become a junior partner in a new right-wing government, made it clear that the dilemma facing Austrian conservatives persists. Still, their effort to keep an extremist out of the presidency provides a useful model of contemporary gatekeeping.

For its part, the United States has an impressive record of gatekeeping. Both Democrats and Republicans have confronted extremist figures on their fringes, some of whom enjoyed considerable public support. For decades, both parties succeeded in keeping these figures out of the mainstream. Until, of course, 2016.

Gatekeeping in America

In *The Plot Against America*, American novelist Philip Roth builds on real historical events to imagine what fascism might have looked like in prewar America.

An early American mass-media hero, Charles Lindbergh, is the novel's central figure: He skyrockets to fame with his 1927 solo flight across the Atlantic and later becomes a vocal isolationist and Nazi sympathizer. But here is where history takes a fantastic turn in Roth's hands: Rather than fading into obscurity, Lindbergh arrives by plane at the 1940 Republican Party convention in Philadelphia at 3:14 A.M., as a packed hall finds itself deadlocked on the twentieth ballot. Cries of "Lindy! Lindy! Lindy!" erupt for thirty uncontained minutes on the convention floor, and in a moment of intense collective fervor, his name is proposed, seconded, and approved by acclamation as the party's nominee for president. Lindbergh, a man with no political experience but unparalleled media savvy, ignores the advice of his advisors and campaigns by piloting his iconic solo aircraft, *Spirit of St. Louis*, from state to state, wearing his flight goggles, high boots, and jumpsuit.

In this world turned upside down, Lindbergh beats Franklin Delano Roosevelt, the incumbent, to become president. And Lindbergh, whose campaign is later revealed to be linked to Hitler, goes on to sign peace treaties with America's enemies. A wave of anti-Semitism and violence is unleashed across America.

Many Americans have found parallels between the 2016 presidential election and Roth's work of fiction. The premise—an outsider with dubious democratic credentials comes to power with the aid of a foreign nation—cannot help but resonate. But the comparison raises another striking question: Given the severity of the economic crisis in 1930s America, why *didn't* this happen here?

The reason no extremist demagogue won the presidency before 2016 is not the absence of contenders for such a role. Nor is it the lack of public support for them. To the contrary, extremist figures have long dotted the landscape of American politics. In the 1930s alone, as many as eight hundred right-wing extremist groups existed in the United States. Among the most important figures to emerge during this period was Father Charles Coughlin, an anti-Semitic Catholic priest whose fiery nationalist radio program reached up to forty million listeners a week. Father Coughlin was openly antidemocratic, calling for the abolition of political parties and questioning the value of elections. His newspaper, *Social Justice*, adopted profascist positions in the 1930s, naming Mussolini its "Man of the Week" and often defending the Nazi regime. Despite his extremism, Father Coughlin was immensely popular. *Fortune* magazine called him "just about the biggest thing ever to happen to radio." He delivered speeches to packed stadiums and auditoriums across the country; as he traveled from city to city, fans lined his route to see him passing by. Some contemporary observers called him the most influential figure in the United States after Roosevelt.

The Depression also gave rise to Louisiana governor and senator Huey Long, who called himself "the Kingfish." Long was described by the historian Arthur M. Schlesinger Jr. as "the great demagogue of the day, a man who resembled . . . a Latin American dictator, a Vargas or a Perón." The Kingfish was a gifted stump speaker, and he routinely flouted the rule of law. As governor, Long built what Schlesinger described as "the nearest approach to a totalitarian state the American republic has ever seen," using a mix of bribes and threats to bring the state's legislature, judges, and press to heel. Asked by an opposition legislator if he had heard of the state constitution, Long replied, "I'm the constitution just now." Newspaper editor Hodding Carter called Long "the first true dictator out of the soil of America." When Franklin Roosevelt's campaign manager, James A. Farley, met Mussolini in Rome in 1933, he wrote that the Italian dictator "reminded me of Huey Long."

Long built a massive following with his call to redistribute wealth. In 1934, he was said to have "received more mail than all other senators combined, more even than the president." By then his Share Our Wealth movement had more than 27,000 cells across the country and a mailing list of nearly eight million names. Long planned a presidential run, telling a *New York Times* reporter, "I can take this Roosevelt. . . . I can out-promise him. And he knows it." Roosevelt viewed Long as a serious threat but was spared when Long was assassinated in September 1935.

America's authoritarian tendency persisted through the post–World War II golden age. Senator Joseph McCarthy, who used the Cold War fear of communist subversion to promote blacklisting, censorship, and book banning, enjoyed wide backing among the American public. At the height of McCarthy's political power, polls showed that nearly half of all Americans approved of him. Even after the Senate's 1954 censure of him, McCarthy enjoyed 40 percent support in Gallup polls.

A decade later, Alabama governor George Wallace's defiant segregationist stance vaulted him to national prominence, leading to surprisingly vigorous bids for the presidency in 1968 and 1972. Wallace engaged in what journalist Arthur Hadley called the "old and honorable American tradition of hate the powerful." He was, Hadley wrote, a master at exploiting "plain old American rage." Wallace often encouraged violence and displayed a casual disregard for constitutional norms, declaring:

> There is one thing more powerful than the Constitution. . . . That's the will of the people. What is a Constitution anyway? They're the products of the people, the people are the first source of power, and the people can abolish a Constitution if they want to.

Wallace's message, which mixed racism with populist appeals to working-class whites' sense of victimhood and economic anger, helped him make inroads into the Democrats' traditional blue-collar base. Polls showed that roughly 40 percent of Americans approved of Wallace in his third-party run in 1968, and in 1972 he shocked the establishment by emerging as a serious contender in the Democratic primaries. When Wallace's campaign was derailed by an assassination attempt in May 1972, he was leading George McGovern by more than a million votes in the primaries.

In short, Americans have long had an authoritarian streak.

It was not unusual for figures such as Coughlin, Long, McCarthy, and Wallace to gain the support of a sizable minority—30 or even 40 percent—of the country. We often tell ourselves that America's national political culture in some way immunizes us from such appeals, but this requires reading history with rose-colored glasses. The real protection against would-be authoritarians has not been Americans' firm commitment to democracy but, rather, the gatekeepers—our political parties.

On June 8, 1920, as Woodrow Wilson's presidency was winding down, Republican delegates gathered to choose their nominee in the flag-draped but poorly ventilated Chicago Coliseum, where the withering heat reached over one hundred degrees. After nine ballots over four days, the convention remained undecided. On Friday evening, in Suite 404 on the thirteenth floor of the nearby Blackstone Hotel, Republican National Committee Chairman Will Hays and George Harvey, the powerful publisher of *Harvey's Weekly*, hosted a rotating group of U.S. senators and party leaders in the original "smoke-filled back room." The Old Guard, as journalists called them, poured themselves drinks, smoked cigars, and talked late into the night about how to break the deadlock to get a candidate the 493 delegates needed for the nomination.

The leading contender on the convention floor was Major General Leonard Wood, an old ally of Theodore Roosevelt who had generated popular enthusiasm in the primaries and dominated the ballot earlier in the week, with 287 delegates. He was followed by Illinois governor Frank Lowden, California senator Hiram Johnson, and Ohio senator Warren G. Harding, trailing in a distant fourth place with only 65½ delegates. From the convention floor, reporters wrote, "Nobody is talking

Harding . . . [He is] not even considered as among the most promising dark horses." But as reporters heard rumors about the discussions taking place at the Blackstone, the most motivated of them found their way to the thirteenth floor of the hotel and quietly gathered in the hallways outside Suite 404 to catch a glimpse as leading senators—including Henry Cabot Lodge of Massachusetts, McCormick of Illinois, Phipps of Colorado, Calder of New York, former senator Crane of Massachusetts, and others—came and went.

Inside Suite 404, the upsides and downsides of each candidate were carefully reviewed and debated (Knox was too old; Lodge didn't like Coolidge). At one in the morning, seven members of the Old Guard remained in the room and took a "standing vote." Called in at 2:11 A.M. by George Harvey, a stunned Harding was informed that *he* had been selected. Word spread. By the next evening, on the tenth ballot and to the great relief of the sweltering delegates, Warren G. Harding received an overwhelming 692½ convention delegates amid rousing cheers. Though he garnered just over 4 percent of the primary vote, he was now the Republican Party's 1920 presidential nominee.

Nobody likes smoke-filled rooms today—and for good reason. They were not very democratic. Candidates were chosen by a small group of power brokers who were not accountable to the party rank and file, much less to average citizens. And smoke-filled rooms did not always produce good presidents—Harding's term, after all, was marked by scandal. But backroom candidate selection had a virtue that is often forgotten today: It served a gatekeeping function, keeping demonstrably unfit figures off the ballot and out of office. To be sure, the reason for this was not the high-mindedness of party leaders. Rather, party "bosses," as their opponents called them, were most interested in picking safe candidates who could win. It was, above all, their risk aversion that led them to avoid extremists.

Gatekeeping institutions go back to the founding of the American republic. The 1787 Constitution created the world's first presidential system. Presidentialism poses distinctive challenges for gatekeeping. In parliamentary democracies, the prime minister is a member of parliament and is selected by the leading parties in parliament, which virtually ensures that he or she will be acceptable to political insiders. The very process of government formation serves as a filter. Presidents, by contrast, are not sitting members of Congress, nor are they elected by Congress. At least in theory, they are elected by the people, and anyone can run for president and—if he or she earns enough support—win.

Our founders were deeply concerned with gatekeeping. In designing the Constitution and electoral system, they grappled with a dilemma that, in many respects, remains with us today. On the one hand, they sought not a monarch but an elected president—one who conformed to their idea of a republican popular government, reflecting the will of the people. On the other, the founders did not fully trust the people's ability to judge candidates' fitness for office. Alexander Hamilton worried that a popularly elected presidency could be too easily captured by those who would play on fear and ignorance to win elections and then rule as tyrants. "History will teach us," Hamilton wrote in the *Federalist Papers*, that "of those men who have overturned the liberties of republics, the great number have begun their career by paying an obsequious court to the people; commencing demagogues, and ending tyrants." For Hamilton and his colleagues, elections required some kind of built-in screening device.

The device the founders came up with was the Electoral

College. Article II of the Constitution created an indirect election system that reflected Hamilton's thinking in Federalist 68:

> The immediate election should be made by men most capable of analyzing the qualities adapted to the station, and acting under the circumstances favorable to deliberation, and to a judicious combination of all the reasons and inducements which were proper to govern them.

The Electoral College, made up of locally prominent men in each state, would thus be responsible for choosing the president. Under this arrangement, Hamilton reasoned, "the office of president will seldom fall to the lot of any man who is not in an eminent degree endowed with the requisite qualifications." Men with "talents for low intrigue, and the little arts of popularity" would be filtered out. The Electoral College thus became our original gatekeeper.

This system proved short-lived, however, due to two shortcomings in the founders' original design. First, the Constitution is silent on the question of how presidential candidates are to be selected. The Electoral College goes into operation *after* the people vote, playing no role in determining who seeks the presidency in the first place. Second, the Constitution never mentions political parties. Though Thomas Jefferson and James Madison would go on to pioneer our two-party system, the founders did not seriously contemplate those parties' existence.

The rise of parties in the early 1800s changed the way our electoral system worked. Instead of electing local notables as delegates to the Electoral College, as the founders had envisioned, each state began to elect party loyalists. Electors became party agents, which meant that the Electoral College surrendered its gatekeeping authority to the parties. The parties have retained it ever since.

Parties, then, became the stewards of American democracy. Because they select our presidential candidates, parties have the ability—and, we would add, the responsibility—to keep dangerous figures out of the White House. They must, therefore, strike a balance between two roles: a democratic role, in which they choose the candidates that best represent the party's voters; and what political scientist James Ceaser calls a "filtration" role, in which they screen out those who pose a threat to democracy or are otherwise unfit to hold office.

These dual imperatives—choosing a popular candidate and keeping out demagogues—may, at times, conflict with each other. What if the people choose a demagogue? This is the recurring tension at the heart of the presidential nomination process, from the founders' era through today. An overreliance on gatekeeping is, in itself, undemocratic—it can create a world of party bosses who ignore the rank and file and fail to represent the people. But an overreliance on the "will of the people" can also be dangerous, for it can lead to the election of a demagogue who threatens democracy itself. There is no escape from this tension. There are always trade-offs.

For most of American history, political parties prioritized gatekeeping over openness. There was always some form of a smoke-filled room. In the early nineteenth century, presidential candidates were chosen by groups of congressmen in Washington, in a system known as Congressional Caucuses. The system was soon criticized as too closed, so beginning in the 1830s, candidates were nominated in national party conventions made up of delegates from each state. Delegates were not popularly elected; they were chosen by state and local political party committees, and they were not bound to support particular candidates. They generally followed the instructions of the state party leaders who sent them to the convention. The system thus favored insiders, or candidates backed by the party leaders who controlled the delegates. Candidates who lacked support among their party's network of state and local politicians had no chance of success.

The convention system was also criticized for being closed and undemocratic, and there was no shortage of efforts to reform it. Primary elections were introduced during the Progressive era; the first was held in Wisconsin in 1901, and in 1916, primaries were held in two dozen states. Yet these brought little change—in part because many states didn't use them, but mostly because elected delegates were not required to support the candidate who won the primary. They remained "unpledged," free to negotiate their vote on the convention floor. Party leaders—with their control over government jobs, perks, and other benefits—were well-positioned to broker these deals, so they remained the presidency's gatekeepers. Because primaries had no binding impact on presidential nominations, they were little more than beauty contests. Real power remained in the hands of party insiders, or what contemporaries called "organization men." For prospective candidates, securing the backing of the organization men was the only viable road to the nomination.

The old convention system highlights the trade-offs inherent to gatekeeping. On the one hand, the system wasn't very democratic. The organization men were hardly representative of American society. Indeed, they were the very definition of an "old boys" network. Most rank-and-file party members, especially the poor and politically unconnected, women, and minorities, were not represented in the smoke-filled rooms and were thus excluded from the presidential nomination process.

On the other hand, the convention system was an effective gatekeeper, in that it systematically filtered out dangerous candidates. Party insiders provided what political scientists called "peer review." Mayors, senators, and congressional representatives knew the candidates personally. They had worked with them, under diverse conditions, over the years and were thus well-positioned to evaluate their character, judgment, and ability to operate under stress. Smoke-filled back rooms therefore served as a screening mechanism, helping to keep out the kind of demagogues and extremists who derailed democracy elsewhere in the world. American party gatekeeping was so effective that outsiders simply couldn't win. As a result, most didn't even try.

Consider Henry Ford, the founder of the Ford Motor Company. One of the richest men in the world in the early twentieth century, Ford was a modern version of the kind of extremist demagogue Hamilton had warned against. Using his *Dearborn Independent* as a megaphone, he railed against bankers, Jews, and Bolsheviks, publishing articles claiming that Jewish banking interests were conspiring against America. His views attracted praise from racists worldwide. He was mentioned with admiration by Adolf Hitler in *Mein Kampf* and described by future Nazi leader Heinrich Himmler as "one of our most valuable, important, and witty fighters." In 1938, the Nazi government awarded him the Grand Cross of the German Eagle.

Yet Ford was also a widely admired, even beloved, figure in the United States, especially in the Midwest. A "poor farm boy who made good," the plainspoken businessman was revered by many rural Americans as a folk hero, alongside such presidents as Washington and Lincoln.

Ford's restless imperiousness eventually lured him into politics. He began with opposition to World War I, launching an amateurish but high-profile "peace mission" to Europe. He dipped in and out of politics after the Great War, nearly winning a Senate seat in 1918 and then flirting with the idea of running for president (as a Democrat) in 1924. The idea quickly generated enthusiasm, especially in rural parts of the country. Ford for President clubs sprang up in 1923, and the press began to write of a "Ford Craze."

That summer, the popular magazine *Collier's* began a weekly national poll of its readers, which suggested that Ford's celebrity, reputation for business acumen, and unremitting media attention could translate into a popular presidential candidacy. As the results rolled in each week, they were accompanied by increasingly reverential headlines: "Politics in Chaos as Ford Vote Grows" and "Ford Leads in Presidential Free-for-All." By the end of the two-month straw poll of upward of 250,000 readers, Henry Ford ran away from the competition, outpacing all twelve contenders, including President Warren Harding and future president Herbert Hoover. With these results, *Collier's* editors concluded, "Henry Ford has become *the* issue in American politics."

But if Ford harbored serious presidential ambitions, he was born a century too soon. What mattered far more than public opinion was the opinion of party leaders, and party leaders soundly rejected him. A week after publishing the results of its readers' poll, in a series of articles, including one titled "The Politicians Pick a President," *Collier's* reported the results of its poll of the ultimate insiders—a group of 116 party leaders in both parties, including all members of the Republican and Democratic Party National Committees, 14 leading governors, and senators and congressmen in each party. Among these kingmakers, Ford lagged in a distant fifth position. The *Collier's* editors observed that fall:

> When Democratic [Party] chieftains are asked: "What about Ford?" they all shrug their shoulders. Almost without a single exception the men who constitute what is usually known as the "organization" in every State are opposed to Ford. *In all the States except where there are presidential primaries these men practically hand-pick the delegates to the national conventions.* . . . Nobody denies the amount of Ford sentiment among the masses of the people—Democratic and Republican. Every Democratic leader knows his State is full of it—and he is afraid of it. He thinks, however, that because of the machinery of selection of delegates there is little likelihood that Ford will make much of a showing.

Despite popular enthusiasm for his candidacy, Ford was effectively locked out of contention. Senator James Couzens called the idea of his candidacy ridiculous. "How can a man over sixty years old, who . . . has no training, no experience, aspire to such an office?" he asked. "It is most ridiculous."

It is, therefore, not surprising that when Ford was interviewed for *Collier's* at the end of that long summer, his presidential ambitions were tempered:

> I can't imagine myself today accepting any nomination. Of course, I can't say . . . what I will do tomorrow. There might be a war or some crisis of the sort,

in which legalism and constitutionalism and all that wouldn't figure, and the nation wanted some person who could do things and do them quick.

What Ford was saying, in effect, was that he would only consider running if the gatekeeping system blocking his path were somehow removed. So, in reality, he never stood a chance.

Huey Long didn't live long enough to test the presidential waters, but despite his extraordinary political skills, popularity, and ambition, there is good reason to think that he, too, would have been stopped by the partisan gatekeepers. When he was elected to the Senate in 1932, Long's norm-breaking behavior quickly isolated him from his peers. Lacking support among Democratic Party leaders, Long would have stood no chance of defeating Roosevelt at the 1936 convention. He would have had to mount an independent presidential bid, which would have been extraordinarily difficult. Polls suggested that a Long candidacy could divide the Democratic vote and throw the 1936 race to the Republicans but that Long himself had little chance of winning.

Party gatekeeping also helped confine George Wallace to the margins of politics. The segregationist governor participated in a few Democratic primaries in 1964, performing surprisingly well. Running against civil rights and under the slogan "Stand Up for America," Wallace shocked the pundits by winning nearly a third of the vote in Wisconsin and Indiana and a stunning 43 percent in Maryland. But primaries mattered little in 1964, and Wallace soon bowed out in the face of an inevitable Lyndon Johnson candidacy. Over the next four years, however, Wallace campaigned across the country in anticipation of the 1968 presidential race. His mix of populism and white nationalism earned him strong support among some white working-class voters. By 1968, roughly 40 percent of Americans approved of him. In other words, Wallace made a Trump-like appeal in 1968, and he enjoyed Trump-like levels of public support.

But Wallace operated in a different political world. Knowing that the Democratic Party establishment would never back his candidacy, he ran as the candidate of the American Independence Party, which doomed him. Wallace's performance—13.5 percent of the vote—was strong for a third-party candidate, but it left him far from the White House.

We can now grasp the full scale of Philip Roth's imaginative leap in his novel *The Plot Against America*. The Lindbergh phenomenon was not entirely a figment of Roth's imagination. Lindbergh—an advocate of "racial purity" who toured Nazi Germany in 1936 and was awarded a medal of honor by Hermann Göring—emerged as one of America's most prominent isolationists in 1939 and 1940, speaking nationwide on behalf of the America First Committee. And he was extraordinarily popular. His speeches drew large crowds, and in 1939, according to *Reader's Digest* editor Paul Palmer, his radio addresses generated more mail than those of any other person in America. As one historian put it, "Conventional wisdom had had it that Lindbergh would eventually run for public office," and in 1939, Idaho senator William Borah suggested that Lindbergh would make a good presidential candidate. But here is where we return to reality. The Republican Party's 1940 convention was not even remotely like the fictionalized one described in *The Plot Against America*. Not only did Lindbergh not appear at the convention, but his name never even came up. Gatekeeping worked.

In the conclusion of their history of radical-right politics in the United States, *The Politics of Unreason*, Seymour Martin

Lipset and Earl Raab described American parties as the "chief practical bulwark" against extremists. They were correct. But Lipset and Raab published their book in 1970, just as the parties were embarking on the most dramatic reform of their nomination systems in well over a century. Everything was about to change, with consequences far beyond what anyone might have imagined.

The turning point came in 1968. It was a heart-wrenching year for Americans. President Lyndon Johnson had escalated the war in Vietnam, which was now spiraling out of control—16,592 Americans died in Vietnam in 1968 alone, more than in any previous year. American families sat in their living rooms each evening watching the TV nightly news, assaulted with ever more graphic scenes of combat. In April 1968, an assassin gunned down Martin Luther King Jr. Then, in June, within hours of his winning the California Democratic presidential primary, Robert F. Kennedy's presidential campaign—centered on opposition to Johnson's escalating war—was abruptly halted by a second assassin's gun. The cries of despair in Los Angeles's Ambassador Hotel ballroom that night were given expression by novelist John Updike, who wrote that it felt as if "God might have withdrawn His blessing from America."

Meanwhile, the Democrats grew divided between supporters of Johnson's foreign policy and those who had embraced Robert Kennedy's antiwar position. This split played out in a particularly disruptive manner at the Democratic convention in Chicago. With Kennedy tragically gone, the traditional party organization stepped into the breach. The party insiders who dominated on the convention floor favored Vice President Hubert Humphrey, but Humphrey was deeply unpopular among antiwar delegates because of his association with President Johnson's Vietnam policies. Moreover, Humphrey had not run in a single primary. His campaign, as one set of analysts put it, was limited to "party leaders, union bosses, and other insiders." Yet, with the backing of the party regulars, including the machine of powerful Chicago mayor Richard Daley, he won the nomination on the first ballot.

Humphrey was hardly the first presidential candidate to win the nomination without competing in primaries. He would, however, be the last. The events that unfolded in Chicago—displayed on television screens across America—mortally wounded the party-insider presidential selection system. Even before the convention began, the crushing blow of Robert Kennedy's assassination, the escalating conflict over Vietnam, and the energy of the antiwar protesters in Chicago's Grant Park sapped any remaining public faith in the old system. On August 28, the protesters turned to march on the convention: Blue-helmeted police attacked protesters and bystanders, and bloodied men, women, and children sought refuge in nearby hotels. The so-called Battle of Michigan Avenue then spilled over into the convention hall itself. Senator Abraham Ribicoff of Connecticut, in his nomination speech for antiwar candidate George McGovern, decried "the gestapo tactics" of the Chicago police, looking—on live television—directly at Mayor Daley. As confrontations exploded on the convention floor, uniformed police officers dragged several delegates from the auditorium. Watching in shock, NBC anchor Chet Huntley observed, "This surely is the first time policemen have ever entered the floor of a convention." His coanchor, David Brinkley, wryly added, "In the United States."

The Chicago calamity triggered far-reaching reform. Following Humphrey's defeat in the 1968 election, the Democratic

Party created the McGovern–Fraser Commission and gave it the job of rethinking the nomination system. The commission's final report, published in 1971, cited an old adage: "The cure for the ills of democracy is more democracy." With the legitimacy of the political system at stake, party leaders felt intense pressure to open up the presidential nomination process. As George McGovern put it, "Unless changes are made, the next convention will make the last look like a Sunday-school picnic." If the people were not given a real say, the McGovern–Fraser report darkly warned, they would turn to "the anti-politics of the street."

The McGovern–Fraser Commission issued a set of recommendations that the two parties adopted before the 1972 election. What emerged was a system of binding presidential primaries. Beginning in 1972, the vast majority of the delegates to both the Democratic and Republican conventions would be elected in state-level primaries and caucuses. Delegates would be preselected by the candidates themselves to ensure their loyalty. This meant that for the first time, the people who chose the parties' presidential candidates would be neither beholden to party leaders nor free to make backroom deals at the convention; rather, they would faithfully reflect the will of their state's primary voters. There were differences between the parties, such as the Democrats' adoption of proportional rules in many states and mechanisms to enhance the representation of women and minorities. But in adopting binding primaries, both parties substantially loosened their leaders' grip over the candidate selection process—opening it up to voters instead. Democratic National Committee chair Larry O'Brien called the reforms "the greatest goddamn changes since the party system." George McGovern, who unexpectedly won the 1972 Democratic nomination, called the new primary system "the most open political process in our national history."

McGovern was right. The path to the nomination no longer had to pass through the party establishment. For the first time, the party gatekeepers could be circumvented—and beaten.

The Democrats, whose initial primaries were volatile and divisive, backtracked somewhat in the early 1980s, stipulating that a share of national delegates would be elected officials—governors, big-city mayors, senators, and congressional representatives—appointed by state parties rather than elected in primaries. These "superdelegates," representing between 15 and 20 percent of national delegates, would serve as a counterbalance to primary voters—and a mechanism for party leaders to fend off candidates they disapproved of. The Republicans, by contrast, were flying high under Ronald Reagan in the early 1980s. Seeing no need for superdelegates, the GOP opted, fatefully, to maintain a more democratic nomination system.

Some political scientists worried about the new system. Binding primaries were certainly more democratic. But might they be *too* democratic? By placing presidential nominations in the hands of voters, binding primaries weakened parties' gatekeeping function, potentially eliminating the peer review process and opening the door to outsiders. Just before the McGovern–Fraser Commission began its work, two prominent political scientists warned that primaries could "lead to the appearance of extremist candidates and demagogues" who, unrestrained by party allegiances, "have little to lose by stirring up mass hatreds or making absurd promises."

Initially, these fears seemed overblown. Outsiders did emerge: Civil rights leader Jesse Jackson ran for the Democratic Party nomination in 1984 and 1988, while Southern Baptist leader Pat Robertson (1988), television commentator Pat Buchanan (1992, 1996, 2000), and *Forbes* magazine publisher Steve Forbes (1996) ran for the Republican nomination. But they all lost.

Circumventing the party establishment was, it turned out, easier in theory than in practice. Capturing a majority of delegates required winning primaries all over the country, which, in turn, required money, favorable media coverage, and, crucially, people working on the ground in all states. Any candidate seeking to complete the grueling obstacle course of U.S. primaries needed allies among donors, newspaper editors, interest groups, activist groups, and state-level politicians such as governors, mayors, senators, and congressmen. In 1976, Arthur Hadley described this arduous process as the "invisible primary." He claimed that this phase, which occurred before the primary season even began, was "where the winning candidate is actually selected." Members of the party establishment—elected officials, activists, allied interest groups—were, thereby, not necessarily locked out of the game. Without them, Hadley argued, it was nearly impossible to win either party's nomination.

For a quarter of a century, Hadley was right.

The Great Republican Abdication

On June 15, 2015, real estate developer and reality-TV star Donald Trump descended an escalator to the lobby of his own building, Trump Tower, to make an announcement: He was running for president. At the time, he was just another long-shot candidate who thought his wealth and celebrity might give him a chance or, at the very least, allow him to bask in the spotlight for a few months. Like fellow businessman Henry Ford a century earlier, Trump held some extremist views—his most recent experience with politics had been as a "birther," questioning whether President Barack Obama was born in the United States. To the extent that leading media and political figures took him seriously, it was to denounce him.

But the primary system had opened up the presidential nomination process more than ever before in American history. And openness is always double-edged. In this new environment, a wider range of politicians, from George McGovern to Barack Obama, could now compete seriously for the presidency. But the window was now also open to true outsiders—individuals who had never held elective office. In the twenty-three years between 1945 and 1968, under the old convention system, only a

single outsider (Dwight Eisenhower) publicly sought the nomination of either party. By contrast, during the first two decades
of the primary system, 1972 to 1992, eight outsiders ran (five
Democrats and three Republicans), an average of 1.25 per election; and between 1996 and 2016, eighteen outsiders competed
in one of the two parties' primaries—an average of three per
election. Thirteen of these were Republicans.

The post-1972 primary system was especially vulnerable to
a particular kind of outsider: individuals with enough fame
or money to skip the "invisible primary." In other words, celebrities. Although conservative outsiders Pat Robertson, Pat
Buchanan, and Steve Forbes did not manage to overcome the
effects of the invisible primary during the 1980s and 1990s,
their relative success provided clues into how it might be done.
Forbes, an extraordinarily wealthy businessman, was able to
buy name recognition, while Robertson, a televangelist who
founded the Christian Broadcasting Network, and Buchanan,
a television commentator (and early Republican proponent
of white nationalism), were both colorful figures with special
media access. Although none of them won the nomination,
they used massive wealth and celebrity status to become contenders.

But in the end, celebrity outsiders had always fallen short.
And so on that early-summer afternoon in the gilded lobby of
Trump Tower, there seemed no reason to think things would
be different. To win the nomination, Trump would have to
compete in an intricate web of caucuses and primaries against
sixteen other candidates. Many of his rivals boasted the kind
of résumé that had been the hallmark of successful candidates
in the past. At the head of the pack was Florida governor Jeb
Bush, son and brother of former presidents. There were other

governors, as well, including Wisconsin's Scott Walker, Louisiana's Bobby Jindal, New Jersey's Chris Christie, and Ohio's John Kasich, and several rising Republican stars—younger, media-savvy politicians such as Senators Marco Rubio and Rand Paul, who hoped to replicate Barack Obama's fast track to the presidency. Texas, home to three of the last eight elected presidents, offered two more candidates: Senator Ted Cruz and former governor Rick Perry. Besides Trump, two other outsiders threw their hats into the ring: businesswoman Carly Fiorina and neurosurgeon Ben Carson.

Trump could not hope to win the support of the establishment. Not only did he lack any political experience, but he wasn't even a lifelong Republican. Whereas Bush, Rubio, Cruz, Christie, Walker, and Kasich all had deep Republican roots, Trump had switched his party registration several times and had even contributed to Hillary Clinton's campaign for the U.S. Senate.

Even after Trump began to surge in the polls, few people took his candidacy seriously. In August 2015, two months after Trump declared his candidacy, Las Vegas bookmakers gave him one-hundred-to-one odds of winning the White House. And in November 2015, as Trump sat high atop the Republican polls, Nate Silver, founder of the *FiveThirtyEight* blog, whose uncannily accurate predictions in the 2008 and 2012 elections had earned him fame and prestige, wrote an article titled "Dear Media: Stop Freaking Out About Donald Trump's Poll Numbers." The article predicted that Trump's weakness among party insiders would spell his demise. Despite Trump's seemingly large lead, Silver assured us, his chances of winning the nomination were "considerably less than 20 percent."

But the world had changed. Party gatekeepers were shells

of what they once were, for two main reasons. One was a dramatic increase in the availability of outside money, accelerated (though hardly caused) by the Supreme Court's 2010 Citizens United ruling. Now even marginal presidential candidates—Michele Bachmann, Herman Cain, Howard Dean, Bernie Sanders—could raise large sums of money, either by finding their own billionaire financier or through small donations via the Internet. The proliferation of well-funded primary candidates indicated a more open and fluid political environment.

The other major factor diminishing the power of traditional gatekeepers was the explosion of alternative media, particularly cable news and social media. Whereas the path to national name recognition once ran through relatively few mainstream channels, which favored establishment politicians over extremists, the new media environment made it easier for celebrities to achieve wide name recognition—and public support—practically overnight. This was particularly true on the Republican side, where the emergence of Fox News and influential radio talk-show personalities—what political commentator David Frum calls the "conservative entertainment complex"—radicalized conservative voters, to the benefit of ideologically extreme candidates. This gave rise to such phenomena as Herman Cain, the former Godfather Pizza CEO and radio talk-show host who rocketed to the top of the Republican polls in late 2011 before flaming out because of scandal.

The nomination process was now wide open. While the rules of the game hardly guaranteed the rise of a Trump-like figure, they could no longer prevent it, either. It was like a game of Russian roulette: The chances of an extremist outsider capturing the presidential nomination were higher than ever before in history.

Although many factors contributed to Donald Trump's stunning political success, his rise to the presidency is, in good measure, a story of ineffective gatekeeping. Party gatekeepers failed at three key junctures: the "invisible primary," the primaries themselves, and the general election.

Trump finished dead last in the invisible primary. When the actual primary season began on February 1, 2016, the day of the Iowa Caucus, he had no endorsements among Republican power brokers. Measured by the backing of governors, U.S. senators, and congressional representatives at the time of the Iowa Caucus, Jeb Bush won the invisible primary with 31 endorsements. Marco Rubio finished second with 27. Ted Cruz finished third with 18, followed by Rand Paul with 11. Chris Christie, John Kasich, Mike Huckabee, Scott Walker, Rick Perry, and Carly Fiorina all won more endorsements than Trump. By all standard wisdom, then, Trump's candidacy was a nonstarter. If history were any guide, his lead in the polls would inevitably fade.

Trump's performance in the first state contest, Iowa— 24 percent, good for second place—did little to alter these expectations. After all, outsiders Pat Robertson (25 percent of the vote in 1988), Pat Buchanan (23 percent in 1996), and Steve Forbes (31 percent in 2000) had all finished second in Iowa but faded away soon thereafter.

Then Trump did something no previous outsider had done: He easily won subsequent primaries in New Hampshire and South Carolina. Still, he was shunned by the party establishment. On the day of the South Carolina primary, Trump did not yet have a single endorsement from a sitting Republican

governor, senator, or congressperson. It was only after winning South Carolina that Trump gained his first supporters:
congressional backbenchers Duncan Hunter (California) and
Chris Collins (New York). Even as he proceeded to rout his
Republican rivals at the polling stations, Trump never gained a
substantial number of endorsements. When the primary season
ended, he had forty-six—less than a third of Marco Rubio's
total and barely as many as the long-ended Bush campaign.

By the time Trump rolled to victory in the March 1 Super
Tuesday primaries, it was clear that he had laid waste to the invisible primary, rendering it irrelevant. Undoubtedly, Trump's
celebrity status played a role. But equally important was the
changed media landscape. From early on in the campaign,
Trump had the sympathy or support of right-wing media personalities such as Sean Hannity, Ann Coulter, Mark Levin, and
Michael Savage, as well as the increasingly influential Breitbart
News. Although Trump initially had a contentious relationship
with Fox News, he reaped the benefits of its polarized media
landscape.

Trump also found new ways to use old media as a substitute
for party endorsements and traditional campaign spending. A
"candidate with qualities uniquely tailored to the digital age,"
Trump attracted free mainstream coverage by creating controversy. By one estimate, the Twitter accounts of MSNBC,
CNN, CBS, and NBC—four outlets that no one could accuse
of pro-Trump leanings—mentioned Trump twice as often as
his general election rival, Hillary Clinton. According to another
study, Trump enjoyed up to $2 billion in free media coverage
during the primary season. As the undisputed frontrunner in
free mainstream coverage and the favorite son of much of the
alternative right-wing media network, Trump did not need traditional Republican power brokers. The gatekeepers of the in-

visible primary were not merely invisible; by 2016, they had left the building entirely.

After Trump's Super Tuesday victories, panic set in among the Republican establishment. Prominent insiders and conservative opinion leaders began to make the case against Trump. In March 2016, former Republican presidential candidate Mitt Romney gave a high-profile speech at the Hinckley Institute of Politics in which he described Trump as a danger to both the Republican Party and the country. Echoing Ronald Reagan's 1964 "A Time for Choosing" speech, Romney declared that Trump was a "fraud" who had "neither the temperament nor the judgment to be president." Other party elders, including 2008 presidential candidate John McCain and Senator Lindsey Graham, warned against Trump. And leading conservative publications, including the *National Review* and the *Weekly Standard*, rejected Trump in blistering terms. But the #NeverTrump movement was always more talk than action. In reality, the primary system had left Republican leaders virtually weaponless to halt Trump's rise. The barrage of attacks had little impact and possibly even backfired where it counted: the voting booth.

Republican leaders' toothlessness was on display at the July 2016 Republican National Convention in Cleveland. In the lead-up to the convention, there was much talk of a deadlocked vote, of convincing committed delegates to cast their support to another candidate. In late June, a group called Delegates Unbound began to air national television advertisements telling Republican delegates that they were not, strictly speaking, legally bound to Trump and urging them to abandon him. Groups such as Free the Delegates, Courageous Conservatives, and Save Our Party led a campaign for the Republican National Committee's 112-member Rules Panel to modify the rules binding delegates to candidates, freeing delegates to vote as they had before the 1972 reforms. All these efforts came to naught; they, indeed, never had a chance.

The idea that the nomination could be wrested from Trump at the convention was pure wishful thinking. In the primary-based system we now have, votes confer a legitimacy that cannot easily be circumvented or ignored, and Donald Trump had the votes—nearly fourteen million of them. As Cindy Costa, a Republican National Committee member from South Carolina, put it, Trump "won it fair and square." To hand the nomination to anyone else would have created "magnificent chaos." Republican leaders were forced to face reality: They no longer held the keys to their party's presidential nomination.

As the battleground shifted to the general election, it became clear that this was no ordinary race. Quite simply, Donald Trump was no ordinary candidate. Not only was he uniquely inexperienced—no U.S. president who was not a successful general had ever been elected without having held an elective office or a cabinet post—but his demagoguery, extremist views on immigrants and Muslims, willingness to violate basic norms of civility, and praise for Vladimir Putin and other dictators generated unease in much of the media and the political establishment. Had Republicans nominated a would-be dictator? It was impossible to know for certain. Many Republicans latched on to the saying that whereas Trump's critics took him literally but not seriously, his supporters took him seriously but not literally. His campaign rhetoric, in this view, was "mere words."

There is always uncertainty over how a politician with no track record will behave in office, but as we noted earlier, anti-democratic leaders are often identifiable before they come to power. Trump, even before his inauguration, tested positive on all four measures on our litmus test for autocrats.

The first sign is a weak commitment to the democratic rules of the game. Trump met this measure when he questioned the legitimacy of the electoral process and made the unprecedented suggestion that he might not accept the results of the 2016 election. Levels of voter fraud in the United States are very low, and because elections are administered by state and local governments, it is effectively impossible to coordinate national-level voting fraud. Yet throughout the 2016 campaign, Trump insisted that millions of illegal immigrants and dead people on the voting rolls would be mobilized to vote for Clinton. For months, his campaign website declared "Help Me Stop Crooked Hillary from Rigging This Election!" In August, Trump told Sean Hannity, "We'd better be careful, because that election is going to be rigged. . . . I hope the Republicans are watching closely, or it's going to be taken away from us." In October, he tweeted, "Of course there is large scale voter fraud happening on and before election day." During the final presidential debate, Trump refused to say he would accept the results of the election if he were defeated.

According to historian Douglas Brinkley, no major presidential candidate had cast such doubt on the democratic system since 1860. Only in the run-up to the Civil War did we see major politicians "delegitimizing the federal government" in this way. As Brinkley put it, "That's a secessionist, revolutionary motif. That's someone trying to topple the apple cart entirely." And Trump's words mattered—a lot. A Politico/Morning Consult poll carried out in mid-October found that 41 percent of Americans, and 73 percent of Republicans, believed that the election could be stolen from Trump. In other words, three out of four Republicans were no longer certain that they were living under a democratic system with free elections.

The second category in our litmus test is the denial of the legitimacy of one's opponents. Authoritarian politicians cast their rivals as criminal, subversive, unpatriotic, or a threat to national security or the existing way of life. Trump met this criterion, as well. For one, he had been a "birther," challenging the legitimacy of Barack Obama's presidency by suggesting that he was born in Kenya and that he was a Muslim, which many of his supporters equated with being "un-American." During the 2016 campaign, Trump denied Hillary Clinton's legitimacy as a rival by branding her a "criminal" and declaring repeatedly that she "has to go to jail." At campaign rallies he applauded supporters who chanted "Lock her up!"

The third criterion is toleration or encouragement of violence. Partisan violence is very often a precursor of democratic breakdown. Prominent examples include the Blackshirts in Italy, the Brownshirts in Germany, the emergence of leftist guerrillas in Uruguay, and the rise of right- and left-wing paramilitary groups in early-1960s Brazil. In the last century, no major-party presidential candidate has ever endorsed violence (George Wallace did in 1968, but he was a third-party candidate). Trump broke this pattern. During the campaign, Trump not only tolerated violence among his supporters but at times appeared to revel in it. In a radical break with established norms of civility, Trump embraced—and even encouraged—supporters who physically assaulted protesters. He offered to pay the legal fees of a supporter who sucker-punched and threatened to kill a protester at a rally in Fayetteville, North Carolina. On other occasions, he responded to protesters at his rallies by inciting violence among his supporters. Here are a few examples, compiled by *Vox*.

"If you see somebody getting ready to throw a tomato, knock the crap out of them, would ya? Seriously. Just knock the hell out of them. I promise you I will pay the legal fees. I promise." (February 1, 2016, Iowa)

"I love the old days. You know what they used to do to guys like that when they were in a place like this? They'd be carried out on a stretcher, folks. It's true. . . . I'd like to punch him in the face, I'll tell you." (February 22, 2016, Nevada)

"In the good old days, they'd rip him out of that seat so fast. But today, everybody's politically correct. Our country's going to hell with being politically correct." (February 26, 2016, Oklahoma)

"Get out of here. Get out. Out! This is amazing. So much fun. I love it. I love it. We having a good time? USA, USA, USA! All right, get him out. Try not to hurt him. If you do, I'll defend you in court. Don't worry about it. . . . We had four guys, they jumped on him, they were swinging and swinging. The next day, we got killed in the press—that we were too rough. Give me a break. You know? Right? We don't want to be too politically correct anymore. Right, folks?" (March 4, 2016, Michigan)

"We had some people, some rough guys like we have right in here. And they started punching back. It was a beautiful thing. I mean, they started punching back. In the good old days, this doesn't happen, be-cause they used to treat them very, very rough. And when they protested once, you know, they would not do it so easily again. But today, they walk in and they put their hand up and put the wrong finger in the air at everybody, and they get away with murder, because we've become weak." (March 9, 2016, North Carolina)

In August 2016, Trump issued a veiled endorsement of violence against Hillary Clinton, telling supporters at a Wilmington, North Carolina, rally that a Clinton appointee to the Supreme Court could result in the abolition of the right to bear arms. He went on to say, "If she gets to pick her judges, nothing you can do, folks. . . . Although the Second Amendment people—maybe there is, I don't know."

The final warning sign is a readiness to curtail the civil liberties of rivals and critics. One thing that separates contemporary autocrats from democratic leaders is their intolerance of criticism, and their readiness to use their power to punish those—in the opposition, media, or civil society—who criticize them. Donald Trump displayed such a readiness in 2016. He said he planned to arrange for a special prosecutor to investigate Hillary Clinton after the election and declared that Clinton should be imprisoned. Trump also repeatedly threatened to punish unfriendly media. At a rally in Fort Worth, Texas, for example, he attacked *Washington Post* owner Jeff Bezos, declaring, "If I become president, oh, do they have problems. They are going to have such problems." Describing the media as "among the most dishonest groups of people I've ever met," Trump declared:

I'm going to open up our libel laws so when they write purposely negative and horrible and false ar-

ticles, we can sue them and win lots of money. . . .
So that when the *New York Times* writes a hit piece,
which is a total disgrace—or when the *Washington
Post* . . . writes a hit piece, we can sue them. . . .

With the exception of Richard Nixon, no major-party presidential candidate met even one of these four criteria over the
last century. As Table 2 shows, Donald Trump met them all.
No other major presidential candidate in modern U.S. history,
including Nixon, has demonstrated such a weak public commitment to constitutional rights and democratic norms. Trump
was precisely the kind of figure that had haunted Hamilton and
other founders when they created the American presidency.

Table 2: Donald Trump and the Four Key Indicators of Authoritarian Behavior

1. Rejection of (or weak commitment to) democratic rules of the game	Do they reject the Constitution or express a willingness to violate it?
	Do they suggest a need for antidemocratic measures, such as canceling elections, violating or suspending the Constitution, banning certain organizations, or restricting basic civil or political rights?
	Do they seek to use (or endorse the use of) extraconstitutional means to change the government, such as military coups, violent insurrections, or mass protests aimed at forcing a change in the government?
	Do they attempt to undermine the legitimacy of elections, for example, by refusing to accept credible electoral results?

2. Denial of the legitimacy of political opponents	Do they describe their rivals as subversive, or opposed to the existing constitutional order?
	Do they claim that their rivals constitute an existential threat, either to national security or to the prevailing way of life?
	Do they baselessly describe their partisan rivals as criminals, whose supposed violation of the law (or potential to do so) disqualifies them from full participation in the political arena?
	Do they baselessly suggest that their rivals are foreign agents, in that they are secretly working in alliance with (or the employ of) a foreign government—usually an enemy one?
3. Toleration or encouragement of violence	Do they have any ties to armed gangs, paramilitary forces, militias, guerrillas, or other organizations that engage in illicit violence?
	Have they or their partisan allies sponsored or encouraged mob attacks on opponents?
	Have they tacitly endorsed violence by their supporters by refusing to unambiguously condemn it and punish it?
	Have they praised (or refused to condemn) other significant acts of political violence, either in the past or elsewhere in the world?

4. Readiness to curtail civil liberties of opponents, including media	Have they supported laws or policies that restrict civil liberties, such as expanded libel or defamation laws or laws restricting protest, criticism of the government, or certain civic or political organizations?
	Have they threatened to take legal or other punitive action against critics in rival parties, civil society, or the media?
	Have they praised repressive measures taken by other governments, either in the past or elsewhere in the world?

This all should have set off alarm bells. The primary process had failed in its gatekeeping role and allowed a man unfit for office to run as a mainstream party candidate. But how could Republicans respond at this stage? Recall the lessons of democratic breakdowns in Europe in the 1930s and South America in the 1960s and 1970s: When gatekeeping institutions fail, mainstream politicians must do everything possible to keep dangerous figures away from the centers of power.

Collective abdication—the transfer of authority to a leader who threatens democracy—usually flows from one of two sources. The first is the misguided belief that an authoritarian can be controlled or tamed. The second is what sociologist Ivan Ermakoff calls "ideological collusion," in which the authoritarian's agenda overlaps sufficiently with that of mainstream politicians that abdication is desirable, or at least preferable to the alternatives. But when faced with a would-be authoritarian, establishment politicians must unambiguously reject him or her and do everything possible to defend democratic institutions—even if that means temporarily joining forces with bitter rivals.

For Republicans entering the general election of 2016, the implications were clear. If Trump threatened basic democratic principles, they had to stop him. To do anything else would put democracy at risk, and losing democracy is far worse than losing an election. This meant doing what was, to many, the unthinkable: backing Hillary Clinton for president. The United States has a two-party system; only two candidates stood a chance to win the 2016 election, and one of them was a demagogue. For Republicans, it tested their political courage. Would they accept short-term political sacrifice for the good of the country?

As we showed earlier, there is a precedent for such behavior. In 2016, Austrian conservatives backed Green Party candidate Alexander Van der Bellen to prevent the election of far-right radical Norbert Hofer. And in 2017, defeated French conservative candidate François Fillon called on his partisans to vote for center-left candidate Emmanuel Macron to keep far-right candidate Marine Le Pen out of power. In both these cases, right-wing politicians endorsed ideological rivals—angering much of the party base but redirecting substantial numbers of their voters to keep extremists out of power.

Some Republicans did endorse Hillary Clinton on the grounds that Donald Trump was dangerously unfit for office. Like their Austrian and French conservative counterparts, they deemed it vitally important to put their partisan interests aside out of a shared commitment to democracy. Here is what three of them said:

Republican 1: *"Our choice this election could not be more clear—Hillary Clinton is a strong and clear sup-*

porter of American democracy interests. . . . Donald Trump is a danger for our democracy."

Republican 2: *"It's time . . . to put country before party and vote for Secretary Clinton. Trump is too dangerous and too unfit to hold our nation's highest office."*

Republican 3: *"This is serious stuff, and I won't waste my vote on a protest candidate. Since the future of the country may depend on preventing Donald Trump from becoming president, I'm with her [Clinton] this November, and I urge Republicans to join me."*

Had these statements been made by House Speaker Paul Ryan, Senate Majority Leader Mitch McConnell, and former President George W. Bush, or perhaps a trio of such prominent senators as John McCain, Marco Rubio, and Ted Cruz, the course of the 2016 election would have changed dramatically. Alas, they were made by William Pierce, the former press secretary of retired Maine senator Olympia Snowe (Republican 1); Jack McGregor, a former state senator from Pennsylvania (Republican 2); and Rick Stoddard, a Republican banker in Denver (Republican 3).

Leading national Republican politicians such as Paul Ryan, Mitch McConnell, Marco Rubio, and Ted Cruz endorsed Donald Trump. The only Republican figures of any prominence who endorsed Hillary Clinton were retired politicians or former government officials—people who were not planning to compete in future elections, who, politically, had nothing to lose. On the eve of the election, the *Washington Post* published a list of seventy-eight Republicans who publicly endorsed Clinton. Only one of them, Congressman Richard Hanna of New

York, was an elected official. And he was retiring. No Republican governors were listed. No senators. And only one (retiring) member of Congress.

A handful of active Republican leaders, including Senators McCain, Mark Kirk, Susan Collins, Kelly Ayotte, Mike Lee, Lisa Murkowski, and Ben Sasse, Governors John Kasich and Charlie Baker, and former governors Jeb Bush and Mitt Romney, refused to endorse Trump. Former president George W. Bush remained silent. None of them, however, was willing to endorse Clinton.

In short, most Republican leaders ended up holding the party line. If they had broken decisively with Trump, telling Americans loudly and clearly that he posed a threat to our country's cherished institutions, and if, on those grounds, they had endorsed Hillary Clinton, Donald Trump might never have ascended to the presidency. In France, it is estimated that half of François Fillon's conservative Republican Party voters followed his surprising endorsement of Macron; about another third abstained, leaving around a sixth of Fillon's supporters who went for Le Pen, arguably making a key difference in that country's election. In the United States, we have no way of knowing how Republican voters would have split. Some, perhaps even most, of the base might still have voted for Trump. But enough would have been swayed by the image of both parties uniting to ensure Trump's defeat.

What happened, tragically, was very different. Despite their hemming and hawing, most Republican leaders closed ranks behind Trump, creating the image of a unified party. That, in turn, normalized the election. Rather than a moment of crisis, the election became a standard two-party race, with Republicans backing the Republican candidate and Democrats backing the Democratic candidate.

That shift proved highly consequential. Once the election became a normal race, it was essentially a toss-up, for two reasons. First, intensifying partisan polarization had hardened the electorate in recent years. Not only was the country increasingly sorted into Republicans and Democrats, with few truly independent or swing voters, but Republicans and Democrats had grown increasingly loyal to their party—and hostile to the other one. Voters became less movable, making the kind of landslide election that we saw in 1964 or 1972 far less likely. No matter who the candidates were in the 2000s, presidential elections were close.

Second, given the uneven state of the economy and President Obama's middling approval ratings, nearly all political science models predicted a tight election. Most of them forecast a narrow Clinton victory in the popular vote, but some predicted a narrow Trump win. In any case, the models converged in predicting a close race. Toss-up elections can go either way. They hinge on contingent events—on the accidents of history. In this context, "October surprises" can weigh heavily. So when a newly surfaced video paints one candidate in a negative light, or a letter from the FBI director casts doubt on the other candidate's trustworthiness, it can make all the difference.

Had Republican leaders publicly opposed Trump, the tightly contested, red-versus-blue dynamics of the previous four elections would have been disrupted. The Republican electorate would have split—some heeding the warnings of the party leadership and others sticking with Trump. Still, Trump's defeat would have required the defection of only a tiny fraction of Republican voters. Instead, the election was normalized. The race narrowed. And Trump won.

Subverting Democracy

Peru's Alberto Fujimori didn't plan to be dictator. He didn't even plan to be president. A little-known university rector of Japanese descent, Fujimori had hoped to run for a senate seat in 1990. When no party would nominate him, he created his own and nominated himself. Short of funds, he threw his hat into the presidential race to attract publicity for his senate campaign. But 1990 was a year of acute crisis. Peru's economy had collapsed into hyperinflation, and a Maoist guerrilla group called the Shining Path, whose brutal insurgency had killed tens of thousands of people since its launching in 1980, was closing in on Lima, the capital city. Peruvians were disgusted with the established parties. In protest, many of them turned to the political nobody whose campaign slogan was "A President Like You." Fujimori surged unexpectedly in the polls. He shocked Peru's political world by finishing second and qualifying for a runoff against Mario Vargas Llosa, the country's most prominent novelist. Peruvians admired Vargas Llosa, who would go on to win a Nobel Prize in literature. Virtually the entire establishment—politicians, media, business leaders—backed Vargas Llosa, but ordinary Peruvians viewed him as too cozy with the elites, who seemed deaf to their concerns. Fujimori, whose populist discourse tapped into this anger, struck many as the only real option for change. He won.

In his inaugural address, Fujimori warned that Peru faced "the most profound crisis in its republican history." The economy, he said, was "on the brink of collapse," and Peruvian society had been "broken apart by violence, corruption, terrorism, and drug trafficking." Fujimori pledged to "dig [Peru] out of the state that it's in and guide it to a better destiny." He was convinced that the country needed drastic economic reforms and that it would have to step up the fight against terrorism. But he had only a vague idea of how to accomplish these things.

He also faced daunting obstacles. As a political outsider, Fujimori had few friends among Peru's traditional power brokers. Opposition parties controlled congress, and their appointees sat on the supreme court. The traditional media, most of which had backed Vargas Llosa, distrusted him. Fujimori had been unsparing in his attacks on the political elite, describing it as a corrupt oligarchy that was ruining the country. Now he found that those he had attacked and defeated during the campaign still controlled many of the levers of power.

Fujimori got off to a rocky start. Congress failed to pass any legislation during his first months in office, and the courts did not seem up to the task of responding to the mounting terrorist threat. Fujimori not only lacked experience with the intricacies of legislative politics, he also lacked the patience for it. As one of his aides put it, Fujimori "couldn't stand the idea of inviting the President of the Senate to the presidential palace every time he wanted Congress to approve a law." He preferred, as he sometimes bragged, to govern Peru alone—from his laptop.

So instead of negotiating with the leaders of congress, Fujimori lashed out at them, calling them "unproductive charlatans." He attacked uncooperative judges as "jackals" and "scoundrels." More troubling still, he began to bypass congress, turning instead to executive decrees. Government officials began to complain that Peru's constitution was "rigid" and "confining," reinforcing fears that Fujimori's commitment to democratic institutions was weak. In a speech to business leaders, Fujimori asked, "Are we really a democracy? . . . I find it difficult to say yes. We are a country that in truth has always been governed by powerful minorities, oligopolies, cliques, lobbies. . . ."

Alarmed, Peru's establishment pushed back. When Fujimori sidestepped the courts to free thousands of prisoners convicted of petty crimes to make room for terrorists, the National Association of Judges accused him of "unacceptable antidemocratic authoritarianism." Indeed, the courts declared several of Fujimori's decrees unconstitutional. Soon, his critics were routinely denouncing him as "authoritarian," and the media began to depict him as a Japanese emperor. By early 1991, there was talk of impeachment. In March, the news magazine *Caretas* ran a cover with a picture of Fujimori in the crosshairs of a rifle, asking "Could Fujimori be deposed? Some are already studying the Constitution."

Feeling besieged, Fujimori doubled down. In a speech to business leaders, he declared, "I am not going to stop until I have broken all of the taboos that are left, one by one they are going to fall; we will be triply audacious in knocking down all the old walls that separate the country from progress." In November 1991 he sent a massive package of 126 decrees for congressional approval. The decrees were far-reaching, including some antiterrorism measures that threatened civil liberties.

Congress demurred. Not only did it repeal or water down several of the most important decrees, it passed legislation curbing Fujimori's power. The conflict escalated. Fujimori accused congress of being controlled by drug traffickers, and in response, the senate passed a motion to "vacate" the presidency because of Fujimori's "moral incapacity." Although the motion fell a few votes short in the Chamber of Deputies, the conflict had reached a point where one government official worried that "either the Congress would kill the President, or the President would kill the Congress."

The president killed congress. On April 5, 1992, Fujimori appeared on television and announced that he was dissolving congress and the constitution. Less than two years after his surprising election, the long-shot outsider had become a tyrant.

Although some elected demagogues take office with a blueprint for autocracy, many, such as Fujimori, do not. Democratic breakdown doesn't need a blueprint. Rather, as Peru's experience suggests, it can be the result of a sequence of unanticipated events—an escalating tit-for-tat between a demagogic norm-breaking leader and a threatened political establishment.

The process often begins with words. Demagogues attack their critics in harsh and provocative terms—as enemies, as subversives, and even as terrorists. When he first ran for president, Hugo Chávez described his opponents as "rancid pigs" and "squalid oligarchs." As president, he called his critics "enemies" and "traitors"; Fujimori linked his opponents to terrorism and drug trafficking; and Italian Prime Minister Silvio Berlusconi attacked judges who ruled against him as "communist." Journalists also become targets. Ecuadorian President Rafael Correa called the media a "grave political enemy" that "has to be defeated." Turkey's Recep Tayyip Erdoğan accused journalists of propagating "terrorism." These attacks can be consequential: If the public comes to share the view that opponents are linked to terrorism and the media are spreading lies, it becomes easier to justify taking actions against them.

The assault rarely ends there. Though observers often assure us that demagogues are "all talk" and that their words should not be taken too seriously, a look at demagogic leaders around the world suggests that many of them do eventually cross the line from words to action. This is because a demagogue's initial rise to power tends to polarize society, creating a climate of panic, hostility, and mutual distrust. The new leader's threatening words often have a boomerang effect. If the media feels threatened, it may abandon restraint and professional standards in a desperate effort to weaken the government. And the opposition may conclude that, for the good of the country, the government must be removed via extreme measures—impeachment, mass protest, even a coup.

When Juan Perón was first elected in Argentina in 1946, many of his opponents viewed him as a fascist. Members of the opposition Radical Civic Union, believing themselves to be in a "struggle against Nazism," boycotted Perón's inauguration. From day one of Perón's presidency, his rivals in congress adopted a strategy of "opposition, obstruction, and provocation," even calling on the supreme court to seize control of the government. Likewise, the Venezuelan opposition requested that the supreme court appoint a team of psychiatrists to determine whether Chávez could be removed from office on the grounds of "mental incapacity." Prominent newspapers and television networks endorsed extraconstitutional efforts to overthrow him. Would-be authoritarians, of course, interpret these attacks as a serious threat and, in turn, become more hostile.

They take this step for another reason, as well: Democracy is grinding work. Whereas family businesses and army squadrons may be ruled by fiat, democracies require negotiation, compromise, and concessions. Setbacks are inevitable, victories always partial. Presidential initiatives may die in congress or be blocked by the courts. All politicians are frustrated by these constraints, but democratic ones know they must accept them. They are able to weather the constant barrage of criticism. But for outsiders, particularly those of a demagogic bent, democratic politics is often intolerably frustrating. For them, checks and balances feel like a straitjacket. Like President Fujimori, who couldn't stomach the idea of having lunch with senate leaders every time he wanted to pass legislation, would-be authoritarians have little patience with the day-to-day politics of democracy. And like Fujimori, they want to break free.

How do elected authoritarians shatter the democratic institutions that are supposed to constrain them? Some do it in one fell swoop. But more often the assault on democracy begins slowly. For many citizens, it may, at first, be imperceptible. After all, elections continue to be held. Opposition politicians still sit in congress. Independent newspapers still circulate. The erosion of democracy takes place piecemeal, often in baby steps. Each individual step seems minor—none appears to truly threaten democracy. Indeed, government moves to subvert democracy frequently enjoy a veneer of legality: They are approved by parliament or ruled constitutional by the supreme court. Many of them are adopted under the guise of pursuing some legitimate—even laudable—public objective, such as combating corruption, "cleaning up" elections, improving the quality of democracy, or enhancing national security.

To better understand how elected autocrats subtly undermine institutions, it's helpful to imagine a soccer game. To
consolidate power, would-be authoritarians must capture the
referees, sideline at least some of the other side's star players,
and rewrite the rules of the game to lock in their advantage, in
effect tilting the playing field against their opponents.

It always helps to have the referees on your side. Modern states
possess various agencies with the authority to investigate and
punish wrongdoing by both public officials and private citizens.
These include the judicial system, law enforcement bodies,
and intelligence, tax, and regulatory agencies. In democracies,
such institutions are designed to serve as neutral arbiters. For
would-be authoritarians, therefore, judicial and law enforcement agencies pose both a challenge and an opportunity. If
they remain independent, they might expose and punish government abuse. It is a referee's job, after all, to prevent cheating.
But if these agencies are controlled by loyalists, they could serve
a would-be dictator's aims, shielding the government from investigation and criminal prosecutions that could lead to its removal from power. The president may break the law, threaten
citizens' rights, and even violate the constitution without having
to worry that such abuse will be investigated or censured. With
the courts packed and law enforcement authorities brought to
heel, governments can act with impunity.

Capturing the referees provides the government with more
than a shield. It also offers a powerful weapon, allowing the
government to selectively enforce the law, punishing opponents
while protecting allies. Tax authorities may be used to target
rival politicians, businesses, and media outlets. The police can
crack down on opposition protest while tolerating acts of vi-

olence by progovernment thugs. Intelligence agencies can be used to spy on critics and dig up material for blackmail.

Most often, the capture of the referees is done by quietly firing civil servants and other nonpartisan officials and replacing them with loyalists. In Hungary, for example, Prime Minister Viktor Orbán packed the nominally independent Prosecution Service, State Audit Office, Ombudsman's office, Central Statistical Office, and Constitutional Court with partisan allies after returning to power in 2010.

Institutions that cannot be easily purged may be hijacked, subtly, by other means. Few did this better than Alberto Fujimori's "intelligence advisor," Vladimiro Montesinos. Under Montesinos's direction, Peru's National Intelligence Service videotaped hundreds of opposition politicians, judges, congressmen, businessmen, journalists, and editors paying or receiving bribes, entering brothels, or engaging in other illicit activity—and then used the videotapes to blackmail them. He also maintained three supreme court justices, two members of the Constitutional Tribunal, and a "staggering" number of judges and public prosecutors on his payroll, delivering monthly cash payments to their homes. All this was done in secret; on the surface, Peru's justice system functioned like any other. But in the shadows, Montesinos was helping Fujimori consolidate power.

Judges who cannot be bought off may be targeted for impeachment. When Perón assumed the presidency in 1946, four of Argentina's five-member supreme court were conservative opponents, one of whom had called him a fascist. Concerned about the court's history of striking down pro-labor legislation, Perón's allies in congress impeached three of the justices on the grounds of malfeasance (a fourth resigned before he could be impeached). Perón then appointed four loyalists, and the court never opposed him again. Likewise, when Peru's Constitutional Tribunal threatened to block President Fujimori's bid for a third term in 1997, Fujimori's allies in congress impeached three of the body's seven justices—on the grounds that, in declaring Fujimori's effort to evade constitutional term limits "unconstitutional," they themselves had breached the constitution.

Governments that cannot remove independent judges may bypass them through court packing. In Hungary, for instance, the Orbán government expanded the size of the Constitutional Court from eight to fifteen, changed the nomination rules so that the ruling Fidesz party could single-handedly appoint the new justices, and then filled the new positions with Fidesz loyalists. In Poland, the governing Law and Justice Party had several of its initiatives blocked by the Constitutional Tribunal—the country's highest authority on constitutional matters—between 2005 and 2007. When the party returned to power in 2015, it took steps to avoid similar losses in the future. At the time, there were two openings in the fifteen-member Constitutional Tribunal and three justices who were approved by the outgoing parliament but had yet to be sworn in. In a dubiously constitutional move, the new Law and Justice government refused to swear in the three justices and instead imposed five new justices of its own. For good measure, it then passed a law requiring that all binding Constitutional Tribunal decisions have a two-thirds majority. This effectively gave government allies a veto power within the tribunal, limiting the body's ability to serve as an independent check on governmental power.

The most extreme way to capture the referees is to raze the courts altogether and create new ones. In 1999, the Chávez government called elections for a constituent assembly that, in violation of an earlier supreme court ruling, awarded itself the power to dissolve all other state institutions, including the court. Fearing for its survival, the supreme court acquiesced and ruled the move constitutional. Supreme court president Cecilia Sosa resigned, declaring that the court had "committed suicide to avoid being assassinated. But the result is the same. It is dead." Two months later, the supreme court was dissolved and replaced by a new Supreme Tribunal of Justice. Even that wasn't enough to ensure a pliant judiciary, however, so in 2004, the Chávez government expanded the size of the Supreme Tribunal from twenty to thirty-two and filled the new posts with "revolutionary" loyalists. That did the trick. Over the next nine years, not a single Supreme Tribunal ruling went against the government.

In each of these cases, the referees of the democratic game were brought over to the government's side, providing the incumbent with both a shield against constitutional challenges and a powerful—and "legal"—weapon with which to assault its opponents.

Once the referees are in tow, elected autocrats can turn to their opponents. Most contemporary autocracies do not wipe out all traces of dissent, as Mussolini did in fascist Italy or Fidel Castro did in communist Cuba. But many make an effort to ensure that key players—anyone capable of really hurting the government—are sidelined, hobbled, or bribed into throwing the game. Key players might include opposition politicians, business leaders who finance the opposition, major media outlets, and in some cases, religious or other cultural figures who enjoy a certain public moral standing.

The easiest way to deal with potential opponents is to buy them off. Most elected autocrats begin by offering leading political, business, or media figures public positions, favors, perks, or outright bribes in exchange for their support or, at least, their quiet neutrality. Cooperative media outlets may gain privileged access to the president, while friendly business executives may receive profitable concessions or government contracts. The Fujimori government was masterful at buying off its critics, particularly those in the media. By the late 1990s, every major television network, several daily newspapers, and popular tabloid papers were on the government's payroll. Vladimiro Montesinos paid the owners of Channel 4 about $12 million in exchange for signing a "contract" that gave Montesinos control over the channel's news programming. The principal stockholder of Channel 5 received $9 million from Montesinos, and Channel 9's principal stockholder was given $50,000 in exchange for firing two prominent investigative reporters. In a videotaped conversation in late 1999, Montesinos declared that the heads of the television networks were "all lined up now. . . . We made them sign papers and everything. . . . All of them, all lined up. Every day, I have a meeting at 12:30 . . . and we plan the evening news."

Media figures received Montesinos's largest bribes, but he also bought off politicians. In 1998, when opposition groups collected enough signatures to force a referendum on whether Fujimori could stand for reelection in 2000, the issue was thrown to congress, where, by law, it required the support of 40 percent of the legislature. In theory, the opposition had the forty-eight votes necessary to approve the referendum. But Montesinos bribed three legislators to skip the vote. One of them, Luis Chu, received a $130,000 payment on an apartment from an intelligence agency slush fund; another, Miguel Ciccia, received help in a legal case involving one of his businesses. The third, Susy Díaz, agreed to stay home for "personal reasons."

The vote fell just short, allowing Fujimori to run for, and win, an illegal third term in 2000. And when the electorate failed to deliver Fujimori a congressional majority, Montesinos bribed eighteen opposition legislators to switch sides.

Players who cannot be bought must be weakened by other means. Whereas old-school dictators often jailed, exiled, or even killed their rivals, contemporary autocrats tend to hide their repression behind a veneer of legality. This is why capturing the referees is so important. Under Perón, opposition leader Ricardo Balbín was imprisoned for "disrespecting" the president during an election campaign. Balbín appealed to the supreme court, but since Perón had packed the court, he stood no chance. In Malaysia, Prime Minister Mahathir Mohamad used a politically loyal police force and a packed judiciary to investigate, arrest, and imprison his leading rival, Anwar Ibrahim, on sodomy charges in the late 1990s. In Venezuela, opposition leader Leopoldo López was arrested and charged with "inciting violence" during a wave of antigovernment protest in 2014. Government officials provided no evidence of incitement, alleging at one point that it had been "subliminal."

Governments may also use their control of referees to "legally" sideline the opposition media, often through libel or defamation suits. Ecuadorian President Rafael Correa was masterful at this. In 2011, he won a massive $40 million libel suit against the owners and editor of a major newspaper, *El Universo*, for publishing an editorial that labeled him a "dictator." Correa called the case a "great step forward for the liberation of our Americas from one of the largest and most unpunished powers: the corrupt media." He later pardoned the owners, but the lawsuit had a powerful chilling effect on the press.

The Erdoğan and Putin governments also wielded the law

with devastating effectiveness. In Turkey, a major victim was the powerful Doğan Yayin media conglomerate, which controlled about 50 percent of the Turkish media market, including the country's most widely read newspaper, *Hurriyat*, and several television stations. Many Doğan group media outlets were secular and liberal, which put them at odds with the AKP government. In 2009, the government struck back, fining Doğan nearly $2.5 billion—an amount that nearly exceeded the company's total net worth—for tax evasion. Crippled, Doğan was forced to sell off much of its empire, including two large newspapers and a TV station. They were purchased by progovernment businessmen. In Russia, after Vladimir Gusinsky's independent NTV television network earned a reputation as a "pain in the neck," the Putin government unleashed the tax authorities on Gusinsky, arresting him for "financial misappropriation." Gusinsky was offered "a deal straight out of a bad Mafia movie: give up NTV in exchange for freedom." He took the deal, turned NTV over to the giant government-controlled energy company, Gazprom, and fled the country. In Venezuela, the Chávez government launched an investigation into financial irregularities committed by Globovisión television owner Guillermo Zuloaga, forcing him to flee the country to avoid arrest. Under intense financial pressure, Zuloaga eventually sold Globovisión to a government-friendly businessman.

As key media outlets are assaulted, others grow wary and begin to practice self-censorship. When the Chávez government stepped up its attacks in the mid-2000s, one of the country's largest television networks, Venevisión, decided to stop covering politics. Morning talk shows were replaced with astrology programs, and soap operas took precedence over evening news programs. Once considered a pro-opposition network, Venevisión barely covered the opposition during the 2006 election, giving President Chávez more than five times as much coverage as it did his rivals.

Elected autocrats also seek to weaken business leaders with the means to finance opposition. This was one of the keys to Putin's consolidation of power in Russia. In July 2000, less than three months into his presidency, Putin summoned twenty-one of Russia's wealthiest businessmen to the Kremlin, where he told them that they would be free to make money under his watch—but only if they stayed out of politics. Most of the so-called oligarchs heeded his warning. Billionaire Boris Berezovsky, the controlling shareholder of ORT television station, did not. When ORT coverage turned critical, the government revived a long-dormant fraud case and ordered Berezovsky's arrest. Berezovsky fled into exile, leaving his media assets in the hands of his junior partner, who "graciously put them at Putin's disposal." Another oligarch who ignored Putin's warning was Mikhail Khodorkovsky, head of the giant Yukos oil company. Russia's wealthiest man (worth $15 billion, according to *Forbes*), Khodorkovsky was believed to be untouchable. But he overplayed his hand. A liberal who disliked Putin, Khodorkovsky began to generously finance opposition parties, including the pro-Western Yabloko. At one point, as many as one hundred Duma (parliament) members were doing his bidding. There were rumors that he planned to seek the presidency. Threatened, Putin had Khodorkovsky arrested in 2003 for tax evasion, embezzlement, and fraud. He was imprisoned for nearly a decade. The message to the oligarchs was clear: Stay out of politics. Nearly all of them did. Starved of resources, opposition parties weakened, many to the point of extinction.

The Erdoğan government also pushed businessmen to the political margins. When the Young Party (GP), created and funded by wealthy tycoon Cem Uzan, emerged as a serious rival in 2004, financial authorities seized Uzan's business empire and charged Uzan with racketeering. Uzan fled to France, and the GP soon collapsed. A few years later, the Koc group, Turkey's largest industrial conglomerate, was accused of assisting the massive 2013 Gezi Park protests (a Koc-owned hotel near the park was used as a shelter and makeshift hospital amid police repression). That year, tax officials audited several Koc companies and canceled a massive defense ministry contract with a subsidiary. The Koc family learned its lesson. After 2013, it kept its distance from the opposition.

Finally, elected autocrats often try to silence cultural figures—artists, intellectuals, pop stars, athletes—whose popularity or moral standing makes them potential threats. When Argentine literary icon Jorge Luis Borges emerged as a high-profile critic of Perón (one fellow writer described Borges as a "sort of Anti-Perón"), government officials had him transferred from his municipal library post to what Borges described as an "inspectorship of poultry and rabbits." Borges resigned and was unable to find employment for months.

Usually, however, governments prefer to co-opt popular cultural figures or reach a mutual accommodation with them, allowing them to continue their work as long as they stay out of politics. Venezuela's Gustavo Dudamel, the internationally renowned conductor of the Bolivarian Symphony Orchestra and the Los Angeles Philharmonic, is an example. Dudamel was a prominent champion of El Sistema, Venezuela's world-famous music education program, which benefits hundreds of thousands of low-income Venezuelan youth. Due to El Sistema's dependence on government funding, its founders maintained strict political neutrality. Dudamel continued this practice, refusing to criticize the Chávez government even as it grew increasingly authoritarian. Dudamel conducted the Bolivarian

Symphony Orchestra at Chávez's funeral in 2012, and as late as 2015, when major opposition figures were in prison, he penned a *Los Angeles Times* op-ed defending his neutrality and declaring his "respect" for the Maduro government. In return, El Sistema received increased government funding, which allowed it to reach 700,000 children by 2015, up from 500,000 three years earlier. Things changed, however, in May 2017, with the killing by security forces of a young violinist—and El Sistema alumnus—during an antigovernment protest. Dudamel then broke his political silence, publishing a *New York Times* op-ed condemning government repression and Venezuela's slide into dictatorship. He paid a price: The following month, the government canceled his planned National Youth Orchestra tour to the United States.

The quiet silencing of influential voices—by co-optation or, if necessary, bullying—can have potent consequences for regime opposition. When powerful businesspeople are jailed or ruined economically, as in the case of Khodorkovsky in Russia, other businesspeople conclude that it is wisest to withdraw from politics entirely. And when opposition politicians are arrested or exiled, as in Venezuela, other politicians decide to give up and retire. Many dissenters decide to stay home rather than enter politics, and those who remain active grow demoralized. This is what the government aims for. Once key opposition, media, and business players are bought off or sidelined, the opposition deflates. The government "wins" without necessarily breaking the rules.

To entrench themselves in power, however, governments must do more—they must also change the rules of the game. Authoritarians seeking to consolidate their power often reform the constitution, the electoral system, and other institutions in ways that disadvantage or weaken the opposition, in effect tilting the playing field against their rivals. These reforms are often carried out under the guise of some public good, while in reality they are stacking the deck in favor of incumbents. And because they involve legal and even constitutional changes, they may allow autocrats to lock in these advantages for years and even decades.

Consider Malaysia, where the electoral system was historically tailored to suit the ruling UMNO, a predominantly Malay-based party. Although Malays constituted just over half the overall population, parliamentary districts were gerrymandered so that 70 percent of districts were Malay-majority, which allowed UMNO and its allies to win overwhelming parliamentary majorities. The situation changed, however, when the Malaysian Islamic Party (PAS) emerged as the country's leading opposition party in the late 1990s. The PAS was also an overwhelmingly Malay party. So in 2002, the UMNO-dominated electoral authorities reversed course and carried out a redistricting process that—in defiance of demographic trends—reduced the number of parliamentary seats in the rural areas that were considered PAS strongholds. The gerrymandering helped the UMNO-led coalition win a stunning 91 percent of parliamentary seats in the 2004 election.

The Orbán government in Hungary did something similar. After winning a two-thirds parliamentary majority in 2010, the ruling Fidesz party used its supermajority to rewrite the constitution and electoral laws to lock in its advantage. It adopted new majoritarian electoral rules that favored the largest party (Fidesz) and gerrymandered the country's electoral districts to maximize the number of seats it would win. Finally, it banned campaign advertising in private media, limiting television campaigning to the public broadcast station, which was run by Fidesz loyalists. The effect of these new institutional advantages was evident in the 2014 parliamentary election: Despite the fact that Fidesz's share of the vote fell markedly, from 53 percent in 2010 to 44.5 percent in 2014, the ruling party managed to preserve its two-thirds majority.

Perhaps the most striking example of rewriting the rules to lock in an authoritarian advantage comes from the United States. The end of post–Civil War Reconstruction in the 1870s led to the emergence of authoritarian single-party regimes in every post-Confederate state. Single-party rule was not some benign historical accident; rather, it was a product of brazenly antidemocratic constitutional engineering.

During the era of Reconstruction, the mass enfranchisement of African Americans posed a major threat to southern white political control and to the political dominance of the Democratic Party. Under the 1867 Reconstruction Act and the Fifteenth Amendment, which prohibited suffrage limitations on account of race, African Americans suddenly constituted a majority of the voting population in Mississippi, South Carolina, and Louisiana and a near-majority in Alabama, Florida, Georgia, and North Carolina. Federal troops oversaw the mass registration of black voters throughout the South. Nationwide, the percentage of black men who were eligible to vote increased from 0.5 percent in 1866 to 80.5 percent two years later. In many southern states, black registration rates exceeded 90 percent. And black citizens voted. In the 1880 presidential election, estimated black turnout was 65 percent or higher in North and South Carolina, Tennessee, Texas, and Virginia. Enfranchisement empowered African Americans: More than two thousand southern freedmen won elective office in the

1870s, including fourteen congressmen and two U.S. senators. At one point, more than 40 percent of legislators in Louisiana's and South Carolina's lower houses were black. And because African Americans voted overwhelmingly Republican, black enfranchisement invigorated Republican and other challengers to the once-dominant Democrats. The Democrats lost power in North Carolina, Tennessee, and Virginia in the 1880s and 1890s, and they nearly lost it in Alabama, Arkansas, Florida, Georgia, Mississippi, and Texas. If democratic elections continued, political scientist V. O. Key observed, it "would have been fatal to the status of black belt whites."

So they changed the rules—and did away with democracy. "Give us a [constitutional] convention, and I will fix it so that . . . the Negro shall never be heard from," former Georgia senator Robert Toombs declared as Reconstruction was coming to an end. Between 1885 and 1908, all eleven post-Confederate states reformed their constitutions and electoral laws to disenfranchise African Americans. To comply with the letter of the law as stipulated in the Fifteenth Amendment, no mention of race could be made in efforts to restrict voting rights, so states introduced purportedly "neutral" poll taxes, property requirements, literacy tests, and complex written ballots. "The overarching aim of all of these restrictions," historian Alex Keyssar observed, "was to keep poor and illiterate blacks . . . from the polls." And because African Americans were overwhelmingly Republican, their disenfranchisement could be expected to restore the Democrats' electoral dominance. The goal, as a state senator from North Carolina put it, was to write a "good square, honest law that will always give a good Democratic majority."

South Carolina, whose population was majority black, was a pioneer of vote restriction. The 1882 "Eight Box Law" created a complex ballot that made it nearly impossible for illiterates to exercise the franchise, and since most of the state's black residents were illiterate, black turnout plummeted. But that wasn't enough. In 1888, Governor John Richardson declared, "We now have the rule of a minority of 400,000 [whites] over a majority of 600,000 [blacks]. . . . The only thing that stands today between us and their rule is a flimsy statute—the Eight Box Law." Seven years later, the state introduced a poll tax and a literacy test. Black turnout, which had reached 96 percent in 1876, fell to just 11 percent in 1898. Black disenfranchisement "wrecked the Republican Party," locking it out of the statehouse for nearly a century.

In Tennessee, black suffrage made Republicans so competitive in 1888 that the pro-Democratic *Avalanche* predicted "a sweeping Republican victory" in the next election unless something were done. The following year, Democratic legislators introduced a poll tax, strict registration requirements, and the Dortch Law, which created a complex ballot that required literacy. As the legislature debated, the *Avalanche* proclaimed, "Give us the Dortch bill or we perish." Afterward, the headline of the *Memphis Daily Appeal* read: "Safe at Last—Goodbye Republicans, Goodbye." The Democrats swept to victory in 1890, while the Republicans "collapsed." The *Daily Appeal* editorialized that the Dortch Law's effects were "most admirable. The vote has been cut down woefully and wonderfully to be sure, but the ratio of Democratic majorities has been raised at least four-fold." By 1896, black turnout was close to zero.

In Alabama, where the Democrats nearly lost the governorship to a populist in 1892, they "turned to suffrage restrictions to escape their difficulties." After the state legislature approved a bill to suppress the black vote, Governor Thomas Jones reportedly said, "Let me sign that bill quickly, lest my hand or arm become paralyzed, because it forever wipes out the [populists] . . . and all the niggers." The story repeated itself in Arkansas, Florida, Georgia, Louisiana, Mississippi, North Carolina, Texas, and Virginia.

These "reform" measures effectively killed democracy in the American South. Even though African Americans constituted a majority or near-majority of the population in many states, and even though black suffrage was now enshrined in the Constitution, "legal" or neutral-sounding measures were used to "insure that the Southern electorate . . . would be almost all white." Black turnout in the South fell from 61 percent in 1880 to just 2 percent in 1912. The disenfranchisement of African Americans wiped out the Republican Party, locking in white supremacy and single-party rule for nearly a century. As one black southerner observed, "The whole South—every state in the South—had got into the hands of the very men that had held us as slaves."

By capturing the referees, buying off or enfeebling opponents, and rewriting the rules of the game, elected leaders can establish a decisive—and permanent—advantage over their opponents. Because these measures are carried out piecemeal and with the appearance of legality, the drift into authoritarianism doesn't always set off alarm bells. Citizens are often slow to realize that their democracy is being dismantled—even as it happens before their eyes.

One of the great ironies of how democracies die is that the very defense of democracy is often used as a pretext for its subversion. Would-be autocrats often use economic crises, natural disasters, and especially security threats—wars, armed insurgencies, or terrorist attacks—to justify antidemocratic measures. In 1969, after winning reelection to his second and final term in office, President Ferdinand Marcos of the Philippines began to consider how he might use an emergency to extend his rule. Marcos did not want to step aside when his second term expired in 1973, as the constitution dictated, so he drew up plans to declare martial law and rewrite the constitution. But he needed a reason. An opportunity arrived in July 1972, when a series of mysterious bombings rocked Manila. Following an apparent assassination attempt on Defense Secretary Juan Ponce Enrile, Marcos, blaming communist terrorists, enacted his plan. He announced martial law on national television, insisting somberly, "My countrymen . . . [this] is not a military takeover." He argued that "a democratic form of government is not a helpless government" and that the constitution—the one he was suspending—"wisely provided the means to protect it" when confronting a danger like insurrection. With this move, Marcos ensconced himself in power for the next fourteen years.

Crises are hard to predict, but their political consequences are not. They facilitate the concentration and, very often, abuse of power. Wars and terrorist attacks produce a "rally 'round the flag" effect in which public support for the government increases—often dramatically; in the aftermath of September 11, President Bush saw his approval rating soar from 53 percent to 90 percent—the highest figure ever recorded by Gallup. (The previous record high—89 percent—had been set by Bush's father, George H. W. Bush, in the wake of the 1991 Persian Gulf War.) Because few politicians are willing to stand up to a president with 90 percent support in the middle of a national security crisis, presidents are left virtually unchecked. The USA PATRIOT Act, signed into law by George W. Bush in October 2001, never would have passed had the September 11 attacks not occurred the previous month.

Citizens are also more likely to tolerate—and even support—authoritarian measures during security crises, especially when they fear for their own safety. In the aftermath of 9/11, 55 percent of surveyed Americans said they believed it was necessary to give up some civil liberties to curb terrorism, up from 29 percent in 1997. Likewise, Roosevelt's internment of Japanese Americans would have been unthinkable without the public fear generated by the Pearl Harbor attack. After Pearl Harbor, more than 60 percent of surveyed Americans supported expelling Japanese Americans from the country, and a year later, Japanese American internment still enjoyed considerable public support.

Most constitutions permit the expansion of executive power during crisis. As a result, even democratically elected presidents can easily concentrate power and threaten civil liberties during war. In the hands of a would-be authoritarian, this concentrated power is far more dangerous. For a demagogue who feels besieged by critics and shackled by democratic institutions, crises open a window of opportunity to silence critics and weaken rivals. Indeed, elected autocrats often *need* crises—external threats offer them a chance to break free, both swiftly and, very often, "legally."

The combination of a would-be authoritarian and a major crisis can, therefore, be deadly for democracy. Some leaders come into office facing crisis. For example, Fujimori took office amid hyperinflation and a mounting guerrilla insurgency, so when he justified his 1992 presidential coup as a necessary evil, most Peruvians agreed with him. Fujimori's approval rating shot up to 81 percent after the coup.

Other leaders invent crises. There was a backstory to Ferdinand Marcos's declaration of martial law in 1972: His "crisis" was largely fabricated. Acutely aware that he needed to justify his plan to skirt the constitution's two-term limit in the presidency, Marcos decided to manufacture a "communist menace." Facing only a few dozen actual insurgents, President Marcos fomented public hysteria to justify an emergency action. Marcos wanted to declare martial law as early as 1971, but selling his plan required an act of violence—a terrorist attack—that generated widespread fear. That would come the following year with the Manila bombings, which U.S. intelligence officials believed to be the work of government forces, and the assassination attempt on Defense Secretary Enrile—which Enrile later admitted was "a sham." In fact, he said he was "nowhere near the scene" of the reported attack.

Whether real or not, would-be authoritarians are primed to exploit crises to justify power grabs. Perhaps the best-known case is Adolf Hitler's response to the February 27, 1933, Reichstag fire, just a month after he was sworn in as chancellor. The question of whether a young Dutchman with communist sympathies started the fire in the Berlin parliament building or whether the Nazi leadership itself did remains a matter of debate among historians. Whatever the case, Hitler, Hermann Göring, and Joseph Goebbels arrived at the burning Reichstag and immediately used the event to justify emergency decrees that dismantled civil liberties. This, along with the Enabling Act one month later, destroyed all opposition, consolidating Nazi power until the end of the Second World War.

A security crisis also facilitated Vladimir Putin's authoritarian turn. In September 1999, shortly after Putin was named prime minister, a series of bombings in Moscow and other cities—presumably by Chechen terrorists—killed nearly three hundred people. Putin responded by launching a war in

Chechnya and a large-scale crackdown. As in the case of Nazi Germany, there is some debate over whether the bombings were committed by Chechen terrorists or by the Russian government's own intelligence service. What is clear, however, is that Putin's political popularity received a major boost with the bombings. The Russian public rallied behind Putin, tolerating, if not supporting, attacks on the opposition over the months and years that followed.

Most recently, the Erdoğan government in Turkey used security crises to justify his tightening grip on power. After the AKP lost its parliamentary majority in June 2015, a series of ISIS terrorist attacks enabled Erdoğan to use the rally-'round-the-flag effect to call snap elections and regain control of parliament just five months later. Even more consequential was the July 2016 coup attempt, which provided justification for a wide-ranging crackdown. Erdoğan responded to the coup by declaring a state of emergency and launching a massive wave of repression that included a purge of some 100,000 public officials, the closure of several newspapers, and more than 50,000 arrests—including hundreds of judges and prosecutors, 144 journalists, and even two members of the Constitutional Court. Erdoğan also used the coup attempt as a window of opportunity to make the case for sweeping new executive powers. The power grab culminated in the April 2017 passage of a constitutional amendment that demolished checks on presidential authority.

For demogagues hemmed in by constitutional constraints, a crisis represents an opportunity to begin to dismantle the inconvenient and sometimes threatening checks and balances that come with democratic politics. Crises allow autocrats to expand their room to maneuver and protect themselves from perceived enemies. But the question remains: Are democratic institutions so easily swept away?

The Guardrails of Democracy

For generations, Americans have retained great faith in their Constitution, as the centerpiece of a belief that the United States was a chosen nation, providentially guided, a beacon of hope and possibility to the world. Although this larger vision may be fading, trust in the Constitution remains high. A 1999 survey found that 85 percent of Americans believed the Constitution was the major reason "America had been successful during this past century." Indeed, our constitutional system of checks and balances was designed to prevent leaders from concentrating and abusing power, and for most of American history, it has succeeded. President Abraham Lincoln's concentration of power during the Civil War was reversed by the Supreme Court after the war ended. President Richard Nixon's illegal wiretapping, exposed after the 1972 Watergate break-in, triggered a high-profile congressional investigation and bipartisan pressure for a special prosecutor that eventually forced his resignation in the face of certain impeachment. In these and other instances, our political institutions served as crucial bulwarks against authoritarian tendencies.

But are constitutional safeguards, by themselves, enough to

secure a democracy? We believe the answer is no. Even well-designed constitutions sometimes fail. Germany's 1919 Weimar constitution was designed by some of the country's greatest legal minds. Its long-standing and highly regarded *Rechtsstaat* ("rule of law") was considered by many as sufficient to prevent government abuse. But both the constitution and the *Rechtsstaat* collapsed rapidly in the face of Adolf Hitler's usurpation of power in 1933.

Or consider the experience of postcolonial Latin America. Many of the region's newly independent republics modeled themselves directly on the United States, adopting U.S.-style presidentialism, bicameral legislatures, supreme courts, and in some cases, electoral colleges and federal systems. Some wrote constitutions that were near-replicas of the U.S. Constitution. Yet almost all the region's embryonic republics plunged into civil war and dictatorship. For example, Argentina's 1853 constitution closely resembled ours: Two-thirds of its text was taken directly from the U.S. Constitution. But these constitutional arrangements did little to prevent fraudulent elections in the late nineteenth century, military coups in 1930 and 1943, and Perón's populist autocracy.

Likewise, the Philippines' 1935 constitution has been described as a "faithful copy of the U.S. Constitution." Drafted under U.S. colonial tutelage and approved by the U.S. Congress, the charter "provided a textbook example of liberal democracy," with a separation of powers, a bill of rights, and a two-term limit in the presidency. But President Ferdinand Marcos, who was loath to step down when his second term ended, dispensed with it rather easily after declaring martial law in 1972.

If constitutional rules were enough, then figures such as Perón, Marcos, or Brazil's Getúlio Vargas—all of whom took office under U.S.-style constitutions that, on paper, contained an impressive array of checks and balances—would have been one- or two-term presidents rather than notorious autocrats.

Even well-designed constitutions cannot, by themselves, guarantee democracy. For one, constitutions are always incomplete. Like any set of rules, they have countless gaps and ambiguities. No operating manual, no matter how detailed, can anticipate all possible contingencies or prescribe how to behave under all possible circumstances.

Constitutional rules are also always subject to competing interpretations. What, exactly, does "advice and consent" entail when it comes to the U.S. Senate's role in appointing Supreme Court justices? What sort of threshold for impeachment does the phrase "crimes and misdemeanors" establish? Americans have debated these and other constitutional questions for centuries. If constitutional powers are open to multiple readings, they can be used in ways that their creators didn't anticipate.

Finally, the written words of a constitution may be followed to the letter in ways that undermine the spirit of the law. One of the most disruptive forms of labor protests is a "work to rule" campaign, in which workers do exactly what is asked of them in their contracts or job descriptions but nothing more. In other words, they follow the written rules to the letter. Almost invariably, the workplace ceases to function.

Because of the gaps and ambiguities inherent in all legal systems, we cannot rely on constitutions alone to safeguard democracy against would-be authoritarians. "God has never endowed any statesman or philosopher, or any body of them," wrote former U.S. president Benjamin Harrison, "with wisdom enough to frame a system of government that everybody could go off and leave."

That includes our own political system. The U.S. Constitution is, by most accounts, a brilliant document. But the original Constitution—only four pages long—can be interpreted in many different, and even contradictory, ways. We have, for example, few constitutional safeguards against filling nominally independent agencies (such as the FBI) with loyalists. According to constitutional scholars Aziz Huq and Tom Ginsburg, only the "thin tissue of convention" prevents American presidents from capturing the referees and deploying them against opponents. Likewise, the Constitution is virtually silent on the president's authority to act unilaterally, via decrees or executive orders, and it does not define the limits of executive power during crises. Thus, Huq and Ginsburg recently warned that "the constitutional and legal safeguards of [American] democracy . . . would prove to be fairly easy to manipulate in the face of a truly antidemocratic leader."

If the constitution written in Philadelphia in 1787 is not what secured American democracy for so long, then what did? Many factors mattered, including our nation's immense wealth, a large middle class, and a vibrant civil society. But we believe much of the answer also lies in the development of strong democratic norms. All successful democracies rely on informal rules that, though not found in the constitution or any laws, are widely known and respected. In the case of American democracy, this has been vital.

As in all facets of society, ranging from family life to the operation of businesses and universities, unwritten rules loom large in politics. To understand how they work, think of the example of a pickup basketball game. Street basketball is not governed by rules set up by the NBA, NCAA, or any other league. And there are no referees to enforce such rules. Only shared understandings about what is, and what is not, acceptable prevent such games from descending into chaos. The unwritten rules of a half-court game of pickup basketball are familiar to anyone who has played it. Here are some of the basics:

- Scoring is by ones, not by twos as in regular basketball, and the winning team must win by two points.
- The team that makes a basket keeps the ball ("make it, take it"). The scoring team takes the ball to the top of the key and, to ensure that the defending team is ready, "checks" it by passing it to the nearest opposing player.
- The player who starts with the ball cannot shoot; he or she must pass it in.
- Players call their own fouls but with restraint; only egregious fouls are legitimate ("no blood, no foul"). But when fouls are called, the calls must be respected.

Democracy, of course, is not street basketball. Democracies *do* have written rules (constitutions) and referees (the courts). But these work best, and survive longest, in countries where written constitutions are reinforced by their own unwritten rules of the game. These rules or norms serve as the soft guardrails of democracy, preventing day-to-day political competition from devolving into a no-holds-barred conflict.

Norms are more than personal dispositions. They do not simply rely on political leaders' good character, but rather are shared codes of conduct that become common knowledge within a particular community or society—accepted, respected, and enforced by its members. Because they are unwritten, they are often hard to see, especially when they're functioning well.

This can fool us into thinking they are unnecessary. But nothing could be further from the truth. Like oxygen or clean water, a norm's importance is quickly revealed by its absence. When norms are strong, violations trigger expressions of disapproval, ranging from head-shaking and ridicule to public criticism and outright ostracism. And politicians who violate them can expect to pay a price.

Unwritten rules are everywhere in American politics, ranging from the operations of the Senate and the Electoral College to the format of presidential press conferences. But two norms stand out as fundamental to a functioning democracy: mutual toleration and institutional forbearance.

Mutual toleration refers to the idea that as long as our rivals play by constitutional rules, we accept that they have an equal right to exist, compete for power, and govern. We may disagree with, and even strongly dislike, our rivals, but we nevertheless accept them as legitimate. This means recognizing that our political rivals are decent, patriotic, law-abiding citizens—that they love our country and respect the Constitution just as we do. It means that even if we believe our opponents' ideas to be foolish or wrong-headed, we do not view them as an existential threat. Nor do we treat them as treasonous, subversive, or otherwise beyond the pale. We may shed tears on election night when the other side wins, but we do not consider such an event apocalyptic. Put another way, mutual toleration is politicians' collective willingness to agree to disagree.

As commonsensical as this idea may sound, the belief that political opponents are not enemies is a remarkable and sophisticated invention. Throughout history, opposition to those in power had been considered treason, and indeed, the notion of legitimate opposition parties was still practically heretical at the time of America's founding. Both sides in America's early partisan battles—John Adams's Federalists and Thomas Jefferson's Republicans—regarded each other as a threat to the republic. The Federalists saw themselves as the embodiment of the Constitution; in their view, one could not oppose the Federalists without opposing the entire American project. So when Jefferson and Madison organized what would become the Republican Party, the Federalists regarded them as traitors, even suspecting them of harboring loyalties to Revolutionary France—with which the United States was nearly at war. The Jeffersonians, for their part, accused the Federalists of being Tories and of plotting a British-backed monarchic restoration. Each side hoped to vanquish the other, taking steps (such as the 1798 Alien and Sedition Acts) to legally punish mere political opposition. Partisan conflict was so ferocious that many feared the new republic would fail. It was only gradually, over the course of decades, that America's opposing parties came to the hard-fought recognition that they could be rivals rather than enemies, circulating in power rather than destroying each other. This recognition was a critical foundation for American democracy.

But mutual toleration is not inherent to all democracies. When Spain underwent its first genuine democratic transition in 1931, for example, hopes were high. The new left-leaning Republican government, led by Prime Minister Manuel Azaña, was committed to parliamentary democracy. But the government confronted a highly polarized society, ranging from anarchists and Marxists on the left to monarchists and fascists on the right. Opposing sides viewed each other not as partisan rivals but as mortal enemies. On the one hand, right-wing Catholics and monarchists, who watched in horror as the privileges of the social institutions they valued most—the Church, the army, and the monarchy—were dismantled, did not accept the new republic as legitimate. They viewed themselves, in the words of one historian, as engaged in a battle against "bolshevizing foreign agents." Unrest in the countryside and hundreds of acts of arson against churches, convents, and other Catholic institutions left conservatives feeling besieged, in the grips of a conspiratorial fury. Religious authorities darkly warned, "We have now entered the vortex . . . we have to be ready for everything."

On the other hand, many Socialists and other leftist Republicans viewed rightists such as José María Gil-Robles, the leader of the Catholic conservative Confederación Española de Derechas Autónomas (CEDA), as monarchist or fascist counterrevolutionaries. At best, many on the left regarded the well-organized CEDA as a mere front for the ultraconservative monarchists who were plotting the republic's violent overthrow. Although CEDA was apparently willing to play the democratic game by competing in elections, its leaders refused to unconditionally commit to the new regime. So they remained targets of extreme suspicion. In short, neither the Republicans on the left nor the Catholics and monarchists on the right fully accepted one another as legitimate opponents.

When norms of mutual toleration are weak, democracy is hard to sustain. If we view our rivals as a dangerous threat, we have much to fear if they are elected. We may decide to employ any means necessary to defeat them—and therein lies a justification for authoritarian measures. Politicians who are tagged as criminal or subversive may be jailed; governments deemed to pose a threat to the nation may be overthrown.

In the absence of strong norms of mutual toleration, the Spanish Republic quickly fell apart. The new republic descended into crisis after the right-wing CEDA won the 1933 elections and became the largest bloc in parliament. The governing center-left Republican coalition collapsed and was replaced by a minority centrist government that excluded the Socialists. Because many Socialists and left Republicans viewed the original (1931–33) center-left government as the embodiment of the republic, they regarded efforts to revoke or change its policies as fundamentally "disloyal" to the republic. And when CEDA—which had a fascist-leaning youth group among its rank and file—joined the government the following year, many Republicans viewed it as a profound threat. The Republican left party declared that

> the monstrous fact of turning over the government of the Republic to its enemy is a treason. [We] break all solidarity with the present institutions of the regime and affirm [our] decision to turn to all means in defense of the Republic.

Facing what they saw as a descent into fascism, leftists and anarchists rebelled in Catalonia and Asturias, calling a general strike and forming a parallel government. The rightist government brutally repressed the uprising. It then tried to associate the entire Republican opposition with it, even jailing former Prime Minister Azaña (who did not participate in the uprising). The country sank into increasingly violent conflict in which street battles, bombings, church burnings, political assassinations, and coup conspiracies replaced political competition. By 1936, Spain's nascent democracy had degenerated into a civil war.

In just about every case of democratic breakdown we have studied, would-be authoritarians—from Franco, Hitler, and Mussolini in interwar Europe to Marcos, Castro, and Pinochet during the Cold War to Putin, Chávez, and Erdoğan most recently—have justified their consolidation of power by labeling their opponents as an existential threat.

A second norm critical to democracy's survival is what we call institutional forbearance. *Forbearance* means "patient self-control; restraint and tolerance," or "the action of restraining from exercising a legal right." For our purposes, institutional forbearance can be thought of as avoiding actions that, while respecting the letter of the law, obviously violate its spirit. Where norms of forbearance are strong, politicians do not use their institutional prerogatives to the hilt, even if it is technically legal to do so, for such action could imperil the existing system.

Institutional forbearance has its origins in a tradition older than democracy itself. During the time when kings proclaimed divine-right rule—where religious sanction provided the basis of monarchic authority—no mortal constraint legally limited the power of kings. But many of Europe's predemocratic monarchs nevertheless acted with forbearance. To be "godly," after all, required wisdom and self-restraint. When a figure such as King Richard II, portrayed as a tyrant in one of Shakespeare's most famous historical plays, abuses his royal prerogatives in order to expropriate and plunder, his violations are not illegal; they merely violate custom. But the violations are highly consequential, for they unleash a bloody civil war. As Shakespeare's character Carlisle warns his compatriots in the play, abandoning forbearance meant "the Blood of English shall manure the ground. . . . And future ages groan for this foul act."

Just as divine-right monarchies required forbearance, so do democracies. Think of democracy as a game that we want to keep playing indefinitely. To ensure future rounds of the game, players must refrain from either incapacitating the other team or antagonizing them to such a degree, that they refuse to play again tomorrow. If one's rivals quit, there can be no future games. This means that although individuals play to win, they must do so with a degree of restraint. In a pickup basketball game, we play aggressively, but we know not to foul excessively—and to call a foul only when it is egregious. After all, you show up at the park to play a basketball game, not to fight. In politics, this often means eschewing dirty tricks or hardball tactics in the name of civility and fair play.

What does institutional forbearance look like in democracies? Consider the formation of governments in Britain. As constitutional scholar and author Keith Whittington reminds us, the selection of the British prime minister is "a matter of royal prerogative. Formally, the Crown could select anyone to occupy the role and form the government." In practice, the prime minister is a member of Parliament able to command a majority in the House of Commons—usually, the head of the largest parliamentary party. Today we take this system for granted, but for centuries the Crown adhered to it voluntarily. There is still no written constitutional rule.

Or take presidential term limits. For most of American history, the two-term limit was not a law but a norm of forbearance. Before ratification of the Twenty-Second Amendment in 1951, nothing in the Constitution dictated that presidents step down after two terms. But George Washington's retirement after two terms in 1797 set a powerful precedent. As Thomas Jefferson, the first sitting president to follow the norm, observed,

> If some termination of the services of the [President] be not fixed by the Constitution, or supplied by practice, his office, nominally for four years, will in fact become for life. . . . I should unwillingly be the person who, disregarding sound precedent set by an illustrious predecessor, should furnish the first example of prolongation beyond the second term in office.

Thus established, the informal two-term limit proved remarkably robust. Even ambitious and popular presidents such as Jefferson, Andrew Jackson, and Ulysses S. Grant refrained from challenging it. When friends of Grant encouraged him to seek a third term, it caused an uproar, and the House of Representatives passed a resolution declaring:

> The precedent established by Washington and other presidents . . . in retiring from . . . office after their second term has become . . . a part of our republican system. . . . [A]ny departure from this time-honored custom would be unwise, unpatriotic, and fraught with peril to our free institutions.

Likewise, the Democratic Party refused to nominate Grover Cleveland for a nonconsecutive third term in 1892, warning that such a candidacy would violate an "unwritten law." Only FDR's reelection in 1940 clearly violated the norm—a violation that triggered the passage of the Twenty-Second Amendment.

Norms of forbearance are especially important in presidential democracies. As Juan Linz argued, divided government can easily bring deadlock, dysfunction, and constitutional crisis. Unrestrained presidents can pack the Supreme Court or circumvent Congress by ruling via decree. And an unrestrained Congress can block the president's every move, threaten to throw the country into chaos by refusing to fund the government, or vote to remove the president on dubious grounds.

The opposite of forbearance is to exploit one's institutional prerogatives in an unrestrained way. Legal scholar Mark Tushnet calls this "constitutional hardball": playing by the rules but pushing against their bounds and "playing for keeps." It is a form of institutional combat aimed at permanently defeating one's partisan rivals—and not caring whether the democratic game continues.

Argentine presidents have long been masters of constitutional hardball. In the 1940s, President Juan Perón used his majority in congress to impeach three out of five supreme court justices, taking "maximum advantage" of a vaguely defined constitutional clause listing "malfeasance" as grounds for impeachment. Nearly half a century later, President Carlos Menem showed a similar flair for pushing the boundaries. Argentina's 1853 constitution was ambiguous in defining the president's authority to issue decrees. Historically, elected presidents had used this authority sparingly, issuing just twenty-five decrees between 1853 and 1989. Menem showed no such restraint, issuing 336 decrees in less than a single presidential term.

The judiciary may also be deployed for constitutional hardball. After opposition parties won control of the Venezuelan congress in a landslide election in December 2015, they hoped to use the legislature to check the power of autocratic president Nicolás Maduro. Thus, the new congress passed an amnesty law that would free 120 political prisoners, and it voted to block Maduro's declaration of a state of economic emergency (which granted him vast power to govern by decree). To fend off this challenge, Maduro turned to the supreme court, which was packed with loyalists. The *chavista* court effectively incapacitated the legislature by ruling nearly all of its bills—including the amnesty law, efforts to revise the national budget, and the rejection of the state of emergency—unconstitutional. According to the Colombian newspaper *El Tiempo*, the court ruled against congress twenty-four times in six months, striking down "all the laws it has approved."

Legislatures may also overindulge their constitutional prerogatives. Take the 2012 impeachment of President Fernando Lugo in Paraguay. Lugo, a leftist ex-priest, was elected in 2008, ending the Colorado Party's sixty-one-year run in power. An outsider with few friends in congress, Lugo faced impeachment attempts throughout his presidency. These efforts succeeded in 2012, after the president's popularity had eroded and his former Liberal allies had abandoned him. The trigger was a violent conflict between police and peasant squatters that killed seventeen people. Although similar violence had occurred under previous governments, the opposition used the incident to bring Lugo down. On June 21, just six days after the killings, the chamber of deputies voted to impeach Lugo on grounds of "poor performance of duties." A day later, following a rushed trial in which the president had only two hours to present his defense, Lugo was removed from office by the senate. According to one observer, the trial was an "obvious farce. . . . Lugo's impeachment barely even rose to the level of show trial." Strictly speaking, however, it was legal.

Something similar happened in Ecuador in the 1990s. President Abdalá Bucaram was a populist who rose to the presidency by attacking Ecuador's political establishment. Nicknamed *El Loco*, or "The Crazy One," Bucaram thrived on controversy, which tested the forbearance of his opponents. In his first months in office, he engaged in blatant nepotism, called former President Rodrigo Borja a "donkey," and distributed subsidized milk named after himself. Though scandalous, these were almost certainly not impeachable offenses. Nevertheless, efforts to impeach Bucaram began within weeks of his inauguration. When it became clear that the opposition lacked the two-thirds vote required for impeachment, it found a dubious but constitutional alternative: Ecuador's 1979 constitution allowed a simple legislative majority to remove the president on the grounds of "mental incapacity." On February 6, 1997, congress did just that. In a clear violation of the spirit of the constitution, it voted to remove Bucaram without even debating whether he was, in fact, mentally impaired.

The United States has also had its share of constitutional hardball. As we have noted, after the Fourteenth and Fifteenth Amendments formally established universal male suffrage, Democratic-controlled legislatures in the South came up with new means of denying African Americans the right to vote. Most of the new poll taxes and literacy tests were deemed to pass constitutional muster, but they were clearly designed to counter its spirit. As Alabama state legislator Anthony D. Sayre declared upon introducing such legislation, his bill would "eliminate the Negro from politics, and in a perfectly legal way."

Mutual toleration and institutional forbearance are closely related. Sometimes they reinforce each other. Politicians are more likely to be forbearing when they accept one another as legitimate rivals, and politicians who do not view their rivals as subversive will be less tempted to resort to norm breaking to keep them out of power. Acts of forbearance—for example, a Republican-controlled Senate approving a Democratic president's Supreme Court pick—will reinforce each party's belief that the other side is tolerable, promoting a virtuous circle.

But the opposite can also occur. The erosion of mutual toleration may motivate politicians to deploy their institutional powers as broadly as they can get away with. When parties view one another as mortal enemies, the stakes of political competition heighten dramatically. Losing ceases to be a routine and accepted part of the political process and instead becomes a full-blown catastrophe. When the perceived cost of losing is sufficiently high, politicians will be tempted to abandon forbearance. Acts of constitutional hardball may then in turn further undermine mutual toleration, reinforcing beliefs that our rivals pose a dangerous threat.

The result is politics without guardrails—what political theorist Eric Nelson describes as a "cycle of escalating constitutional brinksmanship." What does such politics look like? Nelson offers an example: the collapse of Charles I's monarchy in England during the 1640s. A religious conflict between the Crown, the Church of England, and the Puritans in Parliament led to mutual accusations of heresy and treason and a breakdown of the norms that had sustained the English monarchy. England's constitutional tradition endowed Parliament with the exclusive right to collect the taxes necessary to fund the government. But Parliament, which viewed Charles as dangerously close to the papacy, refused to fund the monarchy unless it met a set of far-reaching demands, including a virtual dismantling of the Church of England. Parliament maintained this position even after England was invaded by the Scots and desperately needed revenue for national defense. Charles responded to this norm violation with some of his own: He dissolved Parliament and ruled without it for eleven years.

As Nelson observes, "At no point . . . did Charles claim the right to make law without parliament." Rather, he "simply tried to make do without the passage of any new laws." Eventually, the need for revenue drove Charles to circumvent Parliament's monopoly on taxation, which left his outraged opposition even more unyielding when Parliament reopened in 1640. As Nelson concludes, "The spiral of legislative obstruction and royal overreaching continued until it could be resolved only by war." The civil war that ensued dismantled the English monarchy and cost Charles his life.

Some of history's most tragic democratic breakdowns were preceded by the degrading of basic norms. One example can be found in Chile. Prior to the 1973 coup, Chile had been Latin America's oldest and most successful democracy, sustained by vibrant democratic norms. Even though Chilean political parties ranged from a Marxist left to a reactionary right, a "culture of compromise" predominated throughout much of the twentieth century. As reporter Pamela Constable and Chilean political scientist Arturo Valenzuela put it:

> Chile's strong, law-abiding traditions kept competition confined within certain rules and rituals, softening class hostility and ideological conflict. There was no argument, it was said, that could not be settled over a bottle of Chilean cabernet.

Beginning in the 1960s, however, Chile's culture of compromise was strained by Cold War polarization. Some on the left, inspired by the Cuban Revolution, began to dismiss the country's tradition of political give and take as a bourgeois anachronism. Many on the right began to fear that if the leftist Popular Unity coalition gained power, it would turn Chile into another Cuba. By the 1970 presidential election, these tensions had reached extreme levels. Popular Unity candidate Salvador Allende faced what Radomiro Tomic, his Christian Democratic rival, described as a "gigantic campaign of hatred" in the media that "systematically foster[ed] fears" on the right.

Allende won, and although he was committed to democracy, the prospect of his presidency generated panic among conservatives. The extreme rightist Fatherland and Freedom Party demanded that Allende be kept out of office by any means necessary, and the right-wing National Party, funded by the CIA, engaged in hardball tactics before he was even sworn in. Chile's constitution stipulated that if no presidential candidate won at least 50 percent of the vote, the election would be decided by congress; Allende had won with only 36 percent. Although established norms dictated that congress elect the first-place candidate, no rule required such action. Abandoning forbearance, the National Party tried to persuade the centrist Christian Democrats to vote for its candidate, Jorge Alessandri, who had finished a close second. The Christian Democrats refused, but in exchange for their vote, they forced Allende to sign a constitutional Statute of Guarantees requiring the president to respect free elections and civil liberties such as press freedom. The demand was reasonable enough, but as Arturo Valenzuela observed, it "marked a breakdown in mutual understanding" between leaders "for whom a respect of the rules of the game had been implicit."

Allende's presidency witnessed the continued erosion of democratic norms. Lacking a legislative majority, his government was unable to fully implement its socialist program. So Allende exploited his presidential powers, threatening to pass laws via national referendum if congress blocked them and using "legal loopholes" to advance his program at the margins of the legislature. The opposition responded in kind. In a speech delivered at a social gathering during the second month of Allende's presidency, right-wing senator Raúl Morales mapped out what he called a strategy of "institutional checkmate." Although the opposition lacked the two-thirds vote in the senate necessary to impeach Allende, a senate majority could remove ministers via a vote of censure. On the books since 1833, the censure vote was designed for use only in exceptional circumstances and had been seldom used before 1970. Now, however, it would be a weapon. In January 1972, the senate impeached Interior Minister José Tohá, a close Allende ally. Allende responded by reappointing Tohá to the cabinet as defense minister.

Partisan hostility intensified over the course of Allende's presidency. His leftist allies took to describing opponents as fascists and "enemies of the people," while rightists described the government as totalitarian. The growing mutual intolerance undermined efforts by Allende and the Christian Democrats to negotiate any sort of modus vivendi: Whereas Allende's radical allies viewed such negotiations as "opening the door to fascism," right-wing groups criticized Christian Democrats for not resisting the communist threat. To pass legislation, the government needed Christian Democratic support, but by early 1973 the Christian Democrats had decided, in the words of party leader Patricio Aylwin, to "not let Allende score a single goal."

Polarization can destroy democratic norms. When socioeconomic, racial, or religious differences give rise to extreme partisanship, in which societies sort themselves into political camps whose worldviews are not just different but mutually exclusive, toleration becomes harder to sustain. Some polarization is healthy—even necessary—for democracy. And indeed, the historical experience of democracies in Western Europe shows us that norms can be sustained even where parties are separated by considerable ideological differences. But when societies grow so deeply divided that parties become wedded to incompatible worldviews, and especially when their members are so socially segregated that they rarely interact, stable partisan rivalries eventually give way to perceptions of mutual threat. As mutual toleration disappears, politicians grow tempted to abandon forbearance and try to win at all costs. This may encourage the rise of antisystem groups that reject democracy's rules altogether. When that happens, democracy is in trouble.

Politics without guardrails killed Chilean democracy. Both the government and the opposition viewed the March 1973 midterm legislative elections as an opportunity to win the fight for good. Whereas Allende sought the congressional majority he needed to legally impose his socialist program, the opposition sought the two-thirds majority necessary for Allende's "constitutional overthrow" via impeachment. But neither side achieved the majority it sought. Unable to permanently defeat each other and unwilling to compromise, Chilean parties threw their democracy into a death spiral. Hard-liners took over the Christian Democratic Party, vowing to employ any means necessary to block what ex-president Eduardo Frei described as Allende's "attempt to implement totalitarianism in Chile." And Allende's desperate efforts to reestablish a dialogue with the opposition were undercut by his own allies, who called on him to reject "all dialogues with reactionary . . . parties" and instead dissolve congress. Allende refused, but he sought to placate his allies by pushing harder against his opponents. When judicial authorities blocked the expropriation of forty firms seized by striking workers, Allende responded with a constitutionally dubious "decree of insistence," which in turn triggered opposition calls for his impeachment. One right-wing senator proclaimed on national television that Allende was now "an illegitimate head of state," and in August 1973, the Chamber of Deputies passed a resolution declaring that the government was unconstitutional.

Less than a month later, the military seized power. Chileans, who had long prided themselves on being South America's most stable democracy, succumbed to dictatorship. The generals would rule Chile for the next seventeen years.

The Unwritten Rules of American Politics

On March 4, 1933, as American families gathered around their radios during the darkest days of the Great Depression to listen to Franklin D. Roosevelt's first inaugural address, they heard his deliberate, thunderous voice declare, "I shall ask the Congress for the one remaining instrument to meet the crisis: broad executive power to wage a war against the emergency, as great as the power that would be given to me if we were in fact invaded by a foreign foe." Roosevelt was invoking the most open-ended enumerated power the Constitution offered him as president—war powers—to confront a *domestic* crisis.

Roosevelt concluded that even this wasn't enough. In November 1936, he was reelected with 61 percent of the vote—the largest popular presidential mandate in American history. But he found his ambitious policy agenda straitjacketed by an unexpected source: the conservative (and, in his view, backward-looking) Supreme Court—a body composed entirely of men who had completed their legal educations in the nineteenth century. Never had the Supreme Court been as active in blocking legislation as it was in 1935 and 1936. The Court found large portions of the New Deal program unconstitutional, often on questionable grounds. Roosevelt's agenda was hanging in the balance.

So in February 1937, two weeks into his second term, Roosevelt unveiled a proposal to expand the size of the Supreme Court. The "court-packing scheme," as his opponents called it, took advantage of a gap in the Constitution: Article III does not specify the number of Supreme Court justices. Roosevelt's proposal would have allowed him to add a new justice to the Court for every member over seventy years of age, with a maximum court size of fifteen. Since six justices were seventy or older, Roosevelt would be able to name six judges immediately. The president's motivation was, perhaps, understandable—he sought a more secure legal basis to achieve the goals of the New Deal. Had it passed, however, it would have set a dangerous precedent. The Court would have become hyperpoliticized, its membership, size, and selection rules open to constant manipulation, not unlike Argentina under Perón or Venezuela under Chávez. Had Roosevelt passed his judicial act, a key norm—that presidents should not undermine another coequal branch—would have been demolished.

But the norm held. Roosevelt's court-packing plan faced greater opposition than any other initiative undertaken during his presidency. It was opposed not only by Republicans but by the press, prominent lawyers and judges, and a surprisingly large number of fellow Democrats. Within months, the proposal was dead—killed by a Congress dominated by Roosevelt's own party. Even amid a crisis as profound as the Great Depression, the system of checks and balances had worked.

The American republic was not born with strong democratic norms. In fact, its early years were a textbook case of politics

without guardrails. As we have seen, norms of mutual toleration were at best embryonic in the 1780s and 1790s: Far from
accepting one another as legitimate rivals, Federalists and Republicans initially suspected each other of treason.

This climate of partisan hostility and distrust encouraged
what we would today call constitutional hardball. In 1798, the
Federalists passed the Sedition Act, which, though purportedly
criminalizing false statements against the government, was so
vague that it virtually criminalized criticism of the government.
The act was used to target Republican Party newspapers and
activists. In the 1800 election, which pitted President Adams,
a Federalist, against Jefferson, the leader of the Republican opposition, each side aimed for a permanent victory—to put the
other party out of business forever. Federalist leader Alexander
Hamilton talked of finding a "legal and constitutional step" to
block Jefferson's ascent to the presidency, while Jefferson described the election as a last opportunity to save America from
monarchy. Jefferson's victory did not put an end to the intense
partisan acrimony. The lame-duck Federalist Congress reduced
the size of the Supreme Court from six to five to limit Jefferson's
influence over the Court. With its new majority, the Republican
Congress repealed the move, and a few years later, it expanded
the Court to seven to give Jefferson another appointment.

It took several decades for this hard-edged quest for permanent victory to subside. The demands of everyday politics
and the rise of a new generation of career politicians helped
lower the stakes of competition. The post-Revolutionary generation grew accustomed to the idea that one sometimes wins
and sometimes loses in politics—and that rivals need not be
enemies. Typical of this new view was Martin Van Buren, a
founder of the modern Democratic Party and later U.S. president. According to Richard Hofstadter, Van Buren

typified the spirit of the amiable county courthouse lawyer translated to politics, the lawyer who may enjoy over a period of many years a series of animated courtroom duels with an antagonist, but who sustains outside the courtroom the mutual respect, often the genial friendship, of the co-professional.

Although Van Buren had "many opponents" during his career, a biographer writes, he had "few enemies." Whereas the founders had only grudgingly accepted partisan opposition, Van Buren's generation took it for granted. The politics of total opposition had become the politics of mutual toleration.

America's nascent norms soon unraveled, however, over an issue the founders had tried to suppress: slavery. During the 1850s, an increasingly open conflict over slavery's future polarized the country, investing politics with what one historian has called a new "emotional intensity." To white southern planters and their Democratic allies, abolitionism—a cause associated with the new Republican Party—posed an existential threat. South Carolina senator John C. Calhoun, one of slavery's most influential defenders, described a postemancipation South in near-apocalyptic terms, in which former slaves would be

raised above the whites . . . in the political and social scale. We would, in a word, change conditions with them—a degradation greater than has ever yet fallen to the lot of a free and enlightened people, and one from which we could not escape . . . but by fleeing the homes of ourselves and ancestors, and by abandoning our country to our former slaves, to become the permanent abode of disorder, anarchy, poverty, misery and wretchedness.

Polarization over slavery shattered America's still-fragile norm of mutual toleration. Democratic representative Henry Shaw assailed Republicans as "traitors to the Constitution and the Union," while Georgia senator Robert Toombs vowed to "never permit this federal government to pass into the traitorous hands of the Black Republican Party." Antislavery politicians, for their part, accused proslavery politicians of "treason" and "sedition."

The erosion of basic norms expanded the zone of acceptable political action. Several years before shots were fired at Fort Sumter, partisan violence pervaded Congress. Yale historian Joanne Freeman estimates that there were 125 incidents of violence—including stabbings, canings, and the pulling of pistols—on the floor of the U.S. House and Senate between 1830 and 1860. Before long, Americans would be killing each other in the hundreds of thousands.

The Civil War broke America's democracy. One-third of American states did not participate in the 1864 election; twenty-two of fifty Senate seats and more than a quarter of House seats were left vacant. President Lincoln famously suspended habeas corpus and issued constitutionally dubious executive orders, though, of course, one notable executive order freed the slaves. And following the Union victory, much of the former Confederacy was placed under military rule.

The trauma of the Civil War left Americans with searing questions about what went wrong. The sheer destruction—including more than 600,000 dead—shattered many northern intellectuals' belief in the superiority of their form of democracy. Was the U.S. Constitution not the providentially inspired document it had been thought to be? This wave of self-examination gave rise to a new interest in unwritten rules. In 1885, the then–political science professor Woodrow Wilson, the son of a southern Confederate family, published a book about Congress that explored the disparity between the promise of constitutional arrangements and the way institutions really worked. In addition to good laws, America needed effective norms.

Rebuilding democratic norms after a civil war is never easy, and America was no exception. The wounds of war healed slowly; Democrats and Republicans only grudgingly accepted one another as legitimate rivals. At an 1876 campaign event for Republican candidate Rutherford B. Hayes, politician Robert Ingersoll spoke out against Democrats in ghastly terms:

> Every man that tried to destroy this nation was a Democrat. Every enemy this great Republic has had for twenty years has been a Democrat. . . . Every man that denied to the Union prisoners even the worm-eaten crust of famine, and when some poor, emaciated Union patriot, driven to insanity by famine, saw in an insane dream the face of his mother, and she beckoned him and he followed, hoping to press her lips once again against his fevered face, and when he stepped one step beyond the dead line, the wretch that put the bullet through his loving, throbbing heart was—and is—a Democrat.

This kind of rhetoric, known as "waving the bloody shirt," persisted for years.

With enduring partisan animosity came constitutional hardball. In 1866, the Republican Congress reduced the size of the Supreme Court from ten to seven to prevent President Andrew Johnson, a Democrat whom Republicans viewed as subverting Reconstruction, from making any appointments, and a year later, it passed the Tenure of Office Act, which prohibited

Johnson from removing Lincoln's cabinet members without Senate approval. Viewing the law as a violation of his constitutional authority, Johnson ignored it—a "high misdemeanor" for which he was impeached in 1868.

Gradually, though, as the Civil War generation passed from the scene, Democrats and Republicans learned to live with one another. They heeded the words of former House Speaker James Blaine, who in 1880 advised fellow Republicans to "fold up the bloody shirt" and shift the debate to economic issues.

It was not just time, however, that healed partisan wounds. Mutual toleration was established only after the issue of racial equality was removed from the political agenda. Two events were critical in this regard. The first was the infamous Compromise of 1877, which ended the 1876 presidential election dispute and elevated Republican Rutherford B. Hayes to the presidency in exchange for a promise to remove federal troops from the South. The pact effectively ended Reconstruction, which, by stripping away hard-fought federal protections for African Americans, allowed southern Democrats to undo basic democratic rights and consolidate single-party rule. The second event was the failure of Henry Cabot Lodge's 1890 Federal Elections Bill, which would have allowed federal oversight of congressional elections to ensure the realization of black suffrage. The bill's failure ended federal efforts to protect African American voting rights in the South, thereby ensuring their demise.

It is difficult to overstate the tragic significance of these events. Because civil and voting rights were regarded by many southern Democrats as a fundamental threat, the parties' agreement to abandon those issues provided a basis for restoring mutual toleration. The disenfranchisement of African Americans preserved white supremacy and Democratic Party dominance in the South, which helped maintain the Democrats' national viability. With racial equality off the agenda, southern Democrats' fears subsided. Only then did partisan hostility begin to soften. Paradoxically, then, the norms that would later serve as a foundation for American democracy emerged out of a profoundly undemocratic arrangement: racial exclusion and the consolidation of single-party rule in the South.

After Democrats and Republicans accepted each other as legitimate rivals, polarization gradually declined, giving rise to the kind of politics that would characterize American democracy for the decades that followed. Bipartisan cooperation enabled a series of important reforms, including the Sixteenth Amendment (1913), which permitted the federal income tax, the Seventeenth Amendment (1913), which established the direct election of U.S. senators, and the Nineteenth Amendment (1919), which granted women the right to vote.

Mutual toleration, in turn, encouraged forbearance. By the late nineteenth century, informal conventions or work-arounds had already begun to permeate all branches of government, enabling our system of checks and balances to function reasonably well. The importance of these norms was not lost on outside observers. In his two-volume masterpiece, *The American Commonwealth* (1888), British scholar James Bryce wrote that it was not the U.S. Constitution itself that made the American political system work but rather what he called "usages": our unwritten rules.

By the turn of the twentieth century, then, norms of mutual toleration and institutional forbearance were well-established. Indeed, they became the foundation of our much-admired system of checks and balances. For our constitutional system to function as we expect it to, the executive branch, Congress, and the judiciary must strike a delicate balance. On the one hand, Congress and the courts must oversee and, when necessary, check the power of the president. They must be democracy's watchdogs. On the other, Congress and the courts must allow the government to operate. This is where forbearance comes in. For a presidential democracy to succeed, institutions that are muscular enough to check the president must routinely underuse that power.

In the absence of these norms, this balance becomes harder to sustain. When partisan hatred trumps politicians' commitment to the spirit of the Constitution, a system of checks and balances risks being subverted in two ways. Under divided government, where legislative or judicial institutions are in the hands of the opposition, the risk is constitutional hardball, in which the opposition deploys its institutional prerogatives as far as it can extend them—defunding the government, blocking all presidential judicial appointments, and perhaps even voting to remove the president. In this scenario, legislative and judicial watchdogs become partisan attack dogs.

Under unified government, where legislative and judicial institutions are in the hands of the president's party, the risk is not confrontation but abdication. If partisan animosity prevails over mutual toleration, those in control of congress may prioritize defense of the president over the performance of their constitutional duties. In an effort to stave off opposition victory, they may abandon their oversight role, enabling the president to get away with abusive, illegal, and even authoritarian acts. Such a transformation from watchdog into lapdog—think of Perón's acquiescent congress in Argentina or the *chavista* supreme court in Venezuela—can be an important enabler of authoritarian rule.

The American system of checks and balances, therefore, requires that public officials use their institutional prerogatives judiciously. U.S. presidents, congressional leaders, and Supreme Court justices enjoy a range of powers that, if deployed without restraint, could undermine the system. Consider six of these powers. Three are available to the president: executive orders, the presidential pardon, and court packing. Another three lie with the Congress: the filibuster, the Senate's power of advice and consent, and impeachment. Whether these prerogatives are formally stipulated in the Constitution or merely permitted under the Constitution, their weaponization could easily result in deadlock, dysfunction, and even democratic breakdown. For most of the twentieth century, however, American politicians used them all with remarkable forbearance.

We begin with presidential power. The American presidency is a potent—and potentially dominant—institution, due, in part, to gaps in the Constitution. Article II of the Constitution, which lays out the formal powers of the presidency, does not clearly define its limits. It is virtually silent on the president's authority to act unilaterally, via executive orders or decrees. Presidential power has, moreover, swelled over the last century. Driven by the imperatives of war and depression, the executive branch has built up vast legal, administrative, budgetary, intelligence, and war-making capacities, transforming itself into what historian Arthur M. Schlesinger Jr. famously called the "Imperial Presidency." Postwar American presidents controlled the largest military force in the world. And the challenges of governing a global superpower and complex industrial economy and society generated ever-growing demands for more concentrated executive action. By the early twenty-first century, administrative resources at the executive's disposal were so vast that legal scholar Bruce Ackerman described the presidency as a "constitutional battering ram."

The immense powers of the executive branch create a temptation for presidents to rule unilaterally—at the margins of Congress and the judiciary. Presidents who find their agenda stalled can circumvent the legislature by issuing executive orders, proclamations, directives, executive agreements, or presidential memoranda, which can assume the weight of law without the endorsement of Congress. The Constitution does not prohibit such action.

Likewise, presidents can circumvent the judiciary, either by refusing to abide by court rulings, as Lincoln did when the Supreme Court rejected his suspension of the writ of habeas corpus, or by using the prerogative of the presidential pardon. Alexander Hamilton argued in Federalist 74 that because the power of pardon was so far-reaching, it would "naturally inspire scrupulousness and caution." But in the hands of a president without scruples or caution, the pardon can be used to thoroughly shield the government from judicial checks. The president can even pardon himself. Such action, though constitutional, would undermine the independence of the judiciary.

Given the vast potential for unilateral action, nearly all of which is either prescribed or permitted by the Constitution, the importance of executive forbearance is hard to overstate. George Washington was an important precedent-setting figure in this regard. Washington knew his presidency would help establish the future scope of executive authority; as he put it, "I walk on untrodden ground. There is scarcely any part of my conduct which may not hereafter be drawn into precedent." As the occupant of an office many feared would become a new form of monarchy, Washington worked hard to establish norms and practices that would complement—and strengthen—constitutional rules. He energetically defended his designated areas of authority but was careful not to encroach on areas within the domain of Congress. He limited his use of the veto to bills he regarded as constitutionally dubious, issuing only two vetoes in eight years and writing that he "signed many bills with which my Judgement is at variance," out of "motives of respect to the legislature." Washington was also reluctant to issue decrees that could be seen as encroaching on congressional jurisdiction. In eight years, he issued only eight executive orders.

Throughout his life, Washington had learned that he "gained power from his readiness to give it up." Thanks to his enormous prestige, this forbearance infused many of the American republic's other nascent political institutions. As historian Gordon Wood put it, "If any single person was responsible for establishing the young Republic on a firm footing, it was Washington."

Norms of presidential restraint took hold. Although occasionally tested, especially during wartime, they were robust enough to constrain even our most ambitious presidents. Consider Theodore Roosevelt, who ascended to the office in 1901 after President William McKinley's assassination. Roosevelt subscribed to what he called the stewardship theory of the presidency, which asserted that all executive actions were allowed unless expressly prohibited by law. This expansive view of presidential power, Roosevelt's fondness for populist-style appeals to "the people," and his "boundless energy and ambition" alarmed contemporary observers, including leaders of his own Republican Party. President McKinley's powerful advisor, Mark Hanna, had warned against selecting Roosevelt as his vice president, reportedly saying, "Don't you realize that there's only one life between that madman and the White House?" As president, however, Roosevelt acted with surprising restraint.

He took great care, for example, to avoid appearing to bully Congress by speaking directly to the people or attacking individual members of Congress as they debated crucial votes. In the end, Roosevelt operated well within the bounds of our constitutional checks and balances.

Even as the executive's legal, administrative, military, and intelligence capabilities soared during the twentieth century, presidents abided by established norms of self-limitation in their interactions with Congress and the courts. Outside of wartime, they were judicious in their use of executive orders. They never used pardons for self-protection or narrow political gain, and most sought the advice of the Justice Department before issuing them. And, crucially, twentieth-century presidents rarely defied other branches of government, as Lincoln and Andrew Johnson had done during the nineteenth century. President Harry Truman complied with the Supreme Court's blocking of his 1952 executive order to nationalize the steel industry in the face of a strike that he viewed as a national emergency. Eisenhower enforced the Supreme Court's *Brown v. Board of Education* decision despite his own displeasure with it. Even Nixon acceded to congressional demands that he turn over his secret tapes after the Supreme Court ruled in Congress's favor.

So although the office of the American presidency strengthened during the twentieth century, American presidents demonstrated considerable restraint in their exercise of that power. Even in the absence of constitutional barriers, unilateral executive action remained largely a wartime exception, rather than the rule.

A similar story can be told about presidential court packing. Court packing may take one of two forms: impeaching unfriendly Supreme Court justices and replacing them with partisan allies, or altering the size of the Court and filling the new seats with loyalists. Both of these maneuvers are, strictly speaking, legal; the Constitution permits impeachment and does not specify the size of the Supreme Court. Presidents may purge and pack the Court without violating the letter of the law. They have not done so, however, for well over a century.

The only instance of Supreme Court impeachment in American history occurred in 1804, when the Republican-dominated House of Representatives voted to impeach Justice Samuel Chase, an "ardent Federalist" who had campaigned against Jefferson and criticized him during his presidency. Viewing Chase's behavior as sedition, Jefferson pushed for his impeachment. Although Republicans tried to wrap the move in legality, the impeachment was, by all accounts, a "political persecution from beginning to end." The Senate acquitted Chase, setting a powerful precedent against impeachment.

The Supreme Court's size was a more frequent target of partisan machinations during America's first century. Beginning with the Federalists' move to shrink the Court to deny President-elect Jefferson an appointment, the U.S. Supreme Court changed size seven times between 1800 and 1869—each time for political reasons. By the late nineteenth century, however, court packing was widely viewed as unacceptable. In an 1893 book on the American political system, future president Woodrow Wilson wrote that "such outrages" were "a violation of the spirit of the Constitution." Former President Benjamin Harrison wrote around the same time that although expanding the Court "is very tempting to partisans," it would be "destructive, fatally so to our constitutional union." By the 1920s, British journalist H. W. Horwill concluded that there existed an informal norm "strong enough to prohibit the most powerful

President and Congress, whatever the provocation, from taking a course which would make the Supreme Court the plaything of party politics."

President Franklin Roosevelt, of course, violated this particular norm with his 1937 court-packing effort. As constitutional scholars Lee Epstein and Jeffrey Segal wrote, Roosevelt's norm-violating proposal was "extraordinary in its hubris." Equally extraordinary, however, was the resistance it generated. At the time, Roosevelt was extremely popular—he had just been re-elected in a historic landslide, and his Democratic allies enjoyed solid majorities in both houses of Congress. Few American presidents have ever enjoyed such political strength. Yet court packing triggered across-the-board opposition. Media criticism was fierce—the *San Francisco Chronicle* described the plan as an "open declaration of war on the Supreme Court." And congressional opposition was immediate, not only from Republicans but also from many Democrats. Missouri senator James A. Reed called Roosevelt's proposal "a step toward making himself dictator in fact." Edward Cox, a Democratic congressman from Georgia, warned that it would "change the meaning of our basic laws and our whole system of government" and thus represented "the most terrible threat to constitutional government that has ever arisen in the entire history of the country." Even loyal New Dealers turned against Roosevelt. Wyoming senator Joseph O'Mahoney was such a close ally that he had been seated next to Eleanor Roosevelt at a pre-inaugural dinner at the White House only two weeks earlier. Yet O'Mahoney opposed the Court plan, writing to a friend, "The whole mess smells of Machiavelli and Machiavelli stinks!"

It is worth noting that the Supreme Court itself played a major role in defeating Roosevelt's plan. In a move that has been described as a "masterly retreat" to preserve the Supreme Court's integrity, the previously anti–New Deal Court quickly reversed itself on a series of decisions. In spring 1937, the Court ruled in quick succession in favor of several pieces of New Deal legislation, including the National Labor Relations Act and Roosevelt's Social Security legislation. With the New Deal program on more secure constitutional ground, liberal Democrats in Congress could more easily oppose the president's Court plan. In July 1937, it died in the Senate. The president, at the peak of his popularity and power, strained against the limits of his constitutional authority and was blocked. Never again would an American president try to pack the Supreme Court.

Norms of forbearance also operate in Congress. Take the U.S. Senate. As a body whose original purpose was to protect minorities from the power of majorities (which, the founders believed, would be represented by the House), the Senate was designed, from its inception, to allow deliberation. It developed a range of tools—many of them unwritten—that enabled legislative minorities, and even individual senators, to slow down or block projects put forth by the majority. Prior to 1917, the Senate lacked any rules limiting discussion, which meant that any senator could prevent a vote on (or "filibuster") any legislation indefinitely by simply prolonging debate.

These informal prerogatives are essential checks and balances, serving as both a source of protection for minority parties and a constraint on potentially overreaching presidents. Without forbearance, however, they could easily lead to gridlock and conflict. As political scientist Donald Matthews wrote:

> [Each senator] has vast power over the chamber's
> rules. A single senator, for example, can slow the Sen-
> ate almost to a halt by systematically objecting to all
> unanimous consent requests. A few, by exercising
> their right to filibuster, can block the passage of all
> bills.

For most of American history, such dysfunction did not occur,
in part because prevailing norms discouraged senators from
overusing their political authority. As Matthews observed, although tools such as the filibuster "exist as a potential threat,
the amazing thing is that they are rarely used. The spirit of
reciprocity results in much, if not most, of the senators' actual
power not being exercised."

Matthews's seminal study of the U.S. Senate during the
late 1950s highlights how informal norms, or what he called
"folkways," helped the institution function. Two of these folkways are closely associated with forbearance: courtesy and reciprocity. Courtesy meant, first and foremost, avoiding personal
or embarrassing attacks on fellow senators. The cardinal rule,
Matthews observed, was for senators to not let "political disagreements influence personal feelings." This was difficult, for,
as one senator put it, "it is hard not to call a man a liar when you
know he is one." But senators viewed courtesy as critical to their
success, since, as one senator put it, "your enemies on one issue
may be your friends on the next." In the words of another senator, political self-preservation "dictates at least a semblance of
friendship. And then before you know it, you really are friends."

Norms of reciprocity entailed restraint in the use of one's
power so as not to overly antagonize other senators and endan-
ger future cooperation. In his study, Matthews concludes, "If
a senator does push his formal power to the limit, he has bro-

ken the implicit bargain and can expect, not cooperation from his colleagues, but only retaliation in kind," making legislative work much more difficult. As one senator described the norm, "It's not a matter of friendship; it's just a matter of, 'I won't be an S.O.B. if you won't be one.'"

No institutional tool illustrates the importance of these norms more clearly than the filibuster. Prior to 1917, again, any senator could obstruct legislation by using a filibuster to delay a vote indefinitely. Yet this rarely happened. Though available to any senator, at any time, most senators treated the filibuster as a "procedural weapon of last resort." According to one count, only twenty-three manifest filibusters occurred during the entire nineteenth century. A modest increase in filibuster use in the early twentieth century gave rise to the 1917 cloture rule, by which two-thirds (now three-fifths) of the Senate could vote to end debate. But even then, only thirty filibusters occurred between 1880 and 1917, according to political scientists Sarah Binder and Steven Smith. Filibuster use remained low through the late 1960s—in fact, between 1917 and 1959, the Senate saw an average of only one per congressional term.

Another congressional prerogative central to the system of checks and balances is the Senate's power of "advice and consent" over presidential appointments to the Supreme Court and other key positions. Though stipulated in the Constitution, the actual scope of the Senate's advice and consent role is open to interpretation and debate. In theory, the Senate could block presidents from appointing any of their preferred cabinet members or justices—an act that, though nominally constitutional, would hobble the government. This has not happened, in part, because of an established Senate norm of deferring to presidents to fill their cabinets and open Supreme Court seats. Only nine presidential cabinet nominations were blocked between 1800 and 2005; when the Senate blocked Calvin Coolidge's attorney general pick in 1925, Coolidge angrily accused the Senate of violating an "unbroken practice of three generations permitting the president to choose his own cabinet."

The Senate has always reserved the right to reject individual Supreme Court nominees. Even President Washington had a nomination blocked in 1795. But the Senate has historically been judicious in the use of this right. Between 1880 and 1980, more than 90 percent of Supreme Court nominees were approved, and only three presidents—Grover Cleveland, Herbert Hoover, and Richard Nixon—had nominees rejected. Highly qualified nominees were invariably approved even when senators disagreed with them ideologically. The ultraconservative Antonin Scalia, a Reagan appointee, was approved in 1986 by a vote of 98 to 0, despite the fact that the Democrats had more than enough votes (47) to filibuster.

Whether or not individual nominees are approved, the Senate has long accepted the president's ultimate authority to appoint justices. In the 150-year span between 1866 and 2016, the Senate never once prevented the president from filling a Supreme Court seat. On seventy-four occasions during this period, presidents attempted to fill Court vacancies prior to the election of their successor. And on all seventy-four occasions— though not always on the first try—they were allowed to do so.

Finally, one of the most potentially explosive prerogatives granted to Congress by the Constitution is the power to remove a sitting president via impeachment. This, British scholar James Bryce noted more than a century ago, is "the heaviest piece of artillery in the congressional arsenal." But, Bryce continued, "because it is so heavy, it is unfit for ordinary use." If deployed casually, constitutional scholar Keith Whittington warns, impeachment can become a "partisan tool for undermining electoral officials and overturning electoral results."

This is precisely what happened, as we have already noted, in Paraguay in 2012 with the two-day "quickie" impeachment of Fernando Lugo, and in Ecuador in 1997 with the removal of Abdalá Bucaram on bogus grounds of "mental incapacity." In these cases, impeachment was weaponized—the leaders of congress used it to remove a president they didn't like.

In theory, American presidents could suffer Lugo's or Bucaram's fate. The legal barriers to impeachment in the United States are actually quite low. Constitutionally, it only takes a simple majority in the House of Representatives. Although the conviction and removal of a president requires a two-thirds vote in the Senate, impeachment without conviction is still a traumatic event that can weaken presidents to the point of political impotence—as occurred with Andrew Johnson after 1868.

Unlike in Paraguay or Ecuador, however, impeachment in the United States has long been governed by norms of forbearance. Constitutional scholar Mark Tushnet describes the norm: "The House of Representatives should not aggressively carry out an impeachment unless . . . there is a reasonable probability that the impeachment will result in the target's removal from office." Since removal requires a two-thirds vote in the Senate, this means that impeachment should have at least some bipartisan support. After Johnson's impeachment in 1868, there were no serious congressional efforts to impeach the president until the Nixon scandal more than a century later.

America's system of checks and balances worked in the twentieth century because it was embedded in robust norms of mutual toleration and forbearance. This is not to say that America ever experienced an unadulterated golden age, where some variant of the gentlemanly Queensberry boxing rules of good sportsmanship governed the country's politics. At various points, democratic norms have been challenged and even violated. Three such incidents are worth noting.

One we have already explored: Roosevelt's unprecedented concentration of executive power during the Great Depression and World War II. Beyond the court-packing attempt, Roosevelt's reliance on unilateral action posed a serious challenge to traditional checks and balances. His use of executive orders—more than 3,000 during his presidency, averaging more than 300 a year—was unmatched at the time or since. His decision to seek a third (and later a fourth) term in office shattered a nearly 150-year-old norm restricting the president to two terms.

Roosevelt's presidency never slid into autocracy, however. There are many reasons for this, but one of them is that many of Roosevelt's executive excesses triggered bipartisan resistance. The court-packing scheme was rejected by both parties, and although Roosevelt destroyed the unwritten rule limiting presidents to two terms in office, support for the old norm was so strong that in 1947, less than two years after his death, a bipartisan coalition in Congress passed the Twenty-Second Amendment, which enshrined it in the Constitution. The guardrails were tested during the Roosevelt era, but they held.

McCarthyism posed the second significant challenge to America's institutions, threatening norms of mutual toleration in the early 1950s. The rise of communism scared many Americans, particularly after the Soviet Union emerged as a nuclear superpower in the late 1940s. Anticommunist hysteria could be harnessed for partisan ends: Politicians could red-bait, or seek votes by casting their opponents as communists or communist sympathizers.

Between 1946 and 1954, anticommunism found its way into partisan politics. The advent of the Cold War had created a frenzy over national security, and the Republican Party, which had been out of national power for nearly twenty years, was searching desperately for a new electoral appeal.

Wisconsin senator Joseph McCarthy found such an appeal. First elected to the Senate in 1947, McCarthy took the national stage on February 9, 1950, with an infamous speech in front of the Ohio County Republican Women's Club in Wheeling, West Virginia. McCarthy ranted against communism and the presence of "traitors" within, and then stumbled onto a line that instantly became iconic: "I have here in my hand a list of 205 names that were made known to the Secretary of State and who nevertheless are still working and shaping the policy of the State Department." The reaction was immediate. The press went wild. McCarthy, a demagogue who loved the attention, began repeating the speech, realizing he had hit upon a political gold mine. Democrats were outraged. Moderate Republicans were alarmed, but conservative Republicans saw the potential political benefits and supported McCarthy. Republican senator Robert Taft passed on the message, "Keep talking." Three days later, McCarthy sent a wire to President Truman that said, "Pick up your phone and ask [Secretary of State Dean] Acheson how many Communists he failed to discharge. . . . Failure on your part will label the Democratic Party of being the bedfellow of international Communism."

Red-baiting became a common tactic among Republican candidates in the early 1950s. Richard Nixon deployed it in his 1950 Senate campaign, vilifying his Democratic rival, Helen

Gahagan Douglas, as the "Pink Lady," who "follows the Communist line." In Florida, Republican George Smathers unleashed a vicious campaign to defeat incumbent Claude Pepper, labeling his Democratic rival "Red Pepper."

By the time of the 1952 presidential race, it was clear that McCarthy's virulent anticommunism was a useful club with which to beat Democrats. McCarthy was called in to speak in races across the country. Even moderate Republican presidential candidate Dwight Eisenhower, though ambivalent about McCarthy, relied on the political energy he generated. McCarthy repeatedly impugned Democratic candidate Adlai Stevenson as a traitor, intentionally confusing his name with that of accused Soviet spy Alger Hiss. Eisenhower initially resisted joint appearances with McCarthy, but at the insistence of the Republican National Committee, the two men campaigned together in Wisconsin a month before the election.

The McCarthyite assault on mutual toleration peaked in 1952. With Eisenhower installed in the White House, Republican leaders found McCarthy's tactics less useful. And McCarthy's attacks on the Eisenhower administration and, especially, on the U.S. Army, left him disgraced. The turning point came in the live-televised 1954 Army–McCarthy hearings in which McCarthy was humbled by Army chief counsel Joseph Welch, who responded to McCarthy's baseless accusations by saying, "Have you no sense of decency, sir? At long last, have you left no sense of decency?" McCarthy's popularity declined, and six months later the Senate voted to censure him, effectively ending his career.

McCarthy's fall discredited the practice of red-baiting, giving rise to a new pejorative label: "McCarthyism." After 1954, few Republicans so overtly employed the tactic, and those who did were criticized. Even Nixon, always pragmatic, began to reconsider his use of McCarthyite rhetoric. According to a biographer, even the vice president "was at pains to acknowledge the loyalty of the Democratic Party" during his 1956 reelection campaign. Although groups such as the extremist John Birch Society "kept the McCarthyist spirit alive," they operated at the Republican Party's fringes. But norms of mutual toleration remained intact within the dominant factions of both parties until late in the twentieth century.

The third notable test of America's democratic institutions was the authoritarian behavior of the Nixon administration. Despite his public gestures toward it in the 1950s, Nixon never fully embraced norms of mutual toleration. He viewed public opponents and the press as enemies, and he and his staff justified illicit activities with the claim that their domestic opponents— often depicted as anarchists and communists—posed a threat to the nation or the constitutional order. In ordering H. R. Haldeman to organize a break-in at the Brookings Institution in 1971 (an act that was never carried out), Nixon told his aide, "We're up against an enemy, a conspiracy. We're using any means. . . . Is that clear?" Likewise, Watergate conspirator G. Gordon Liddy justified the 1972 break-in of the Democratic National Committee headquarters by claiming that the White House was "at war, internally as well as externally."

The Nixon administration's path away from democratic norms began with widespread wiretapping and other surveillance of journalists, opposition activists, the Democratic National Committee, and prominent Democrats such as Senator Edward Kennedy. In November 1970, Nixon sent a memo to Haldeman ordering him to compile a list of the administration's opponents to develop an "intelligence program . . . to take them on." Hundreds of names, including "dozens of Democrats," made the list. The administration also deployed the Internal Revenue Service as a political weapon, auditing such key opponents as National Democratic Committee Chair Larry O'Brien. Most prominent, however, was Nixon's campaign to sabotage his Democratic rivals in the 1972 election, which culminated in the botched Watergate break-in.

As is well known, Nixon's criminal assault on democratic institutions was contained. In February 1973, the Senate established a bipartisan Select Committee on Presidential Campaign Activities, chaired by Democratic senator Sam Ervin of North Carolina. The Ervin committee was bipartisan: Its vice chair, Tennessee Republican Howard Baker, described its mission as a "bipartisan search for the unvarnished truth." As the committee began its work, nearly a dozen Republican senators joined Democrats in calling for an independent special prosecutor. Archibald Cox was named in May. By mid-1973, investigations were closing in on Nixon. Senate hearings revealed the existence of secret White House tapes that could implicate the president. Cox requested that Nixon release the tapes—a demand that was echoed by leaders of both parties. Nixon played hardball, refusing to turn over the tapes and eventually firing Cox, but to no avail.

The move triggered widespread calls for Nixon's resignation, and the House Judiciary Committee, chaired by New Jersey representative Peter Rodino, took initial steps toward impeachment proceedings. On July 24, 1974, the Supreme Court ruled that Nixon must turn over the tapes. By then, Rodino had sufficient Republican support on the Judiciary Committee to move ahead with impeachment. Although Nixon held out hope that he could muster up the 34 Republican votes needed to avoid a Senate conviction, Senate Republicans sent Barry Goldwater to inform him of the inevitability of impeachment. When Nixon asked Goldwater how many votes he had, Goldwater reportedly replied, "Ten at most, maybe less." Two days later, Nixon resigned. Due in part to bipartisan cooperation, Congress and the courts had checked the abuse of presidential power.

America's democratic institutions were challenged on several occasions during the twentieth century, but each of these challenges was effectively contained. The guardrails held, as politicians from both parties—and often, society as a whole—pushed back against violations that might have threatened democracy. As a result, episodes of intolerance and partisan warfare never escalated into the kind of "death spiral" that destroyed democracies in Europe in the 1930s and Latin America in the 1960s and 1970s.

We must conclude with a troubling caveat, however. The norms sustaining our political system rested, to a considerable degree, on racial exclusion. The stability of the period between the end of Reconstruction and the 1980s was rooted in an original sin: the Compromise of 1877 and its aftermath, which permitted the de-democratization of the South and the consolidation of Jim Crow. Racial exclusion contributed directly to the partisan civility and cooperation that came to characterize twentieth-century American politics. The "solid South" emerged as a powerful conservative force within the Democratic Party, simultaneously vetoing civil rights and serving as a bridge to Republicans. Southern Democrats' ideological proximity to conservative Republicans reduced polarization and facilitated bipartisanship. But it did so at the great cost of keeping civil rights—and America's full democratization—off the political agenda.

America's democratic norms, then, were born in a context of exclusion. As long as the political community was restricted largely to whites, Democrats and Republicans had much in common. Neither party was likely to view the other as an existential threat. The process of racial inclusion that began after World War II and culminated in the 1964 Civil Rights Act and 1965 Voting Rights Act would, at long last, fully democratize the United States. But it would also polarize it, posing the greatest challenge to established forms of mutual toleration and forbearance since Reconstruction.

7

The Unraveling

On the afternoon of Saturday, February 13, 2016, a San Antonio newspaper reported that Supreme Court Justice Antonin Scalia had died in his sleep while on a hunting trip in Texas. Social media erupted. Within minutes, a former Republican staffer and founder of the conservative legal publication *The Federalist* tweeted, "If Scalia has actually passed away, the Senate must refuse to confirm any justices in 2016 and leave the nomination to the next president." Shortly afterward, the communications director for Republican senator Mike Lee tweeted, "What is less than zero? The chances of Obama successfully appointing a Supreme Court Justice to replace Scalia." By early evening, Senate Majority Leader Mitch McConnell issued a statement sending his condolences to the Scalia family but also declaring, "This vacancy should not be filled until we have a new president."

On March 16, 2016, President Barack Obama nominated appellate judge Merrick Garland to fill Scalia's seat. No one doubted that Garland was a qualified candidate, and by all accounts he was an ideological moderate. But for the first time in American history, the U.S. Senate refused to even consider an elected president's nominee for the Supreme Court. As we have seen, the Senate had always used forbearance in exercising its advice and consent in the selection of Supreme Court justices: Since 1866, every time a president had moved to fill a Supreme Court vacancy prior to the election of his successor, he had been allowed to do so.

But the world had changed by 2016. Now, in a radical departure from historical precedent Senate Republicans denied the president's authority to nominate a new justice. It was an extraordinary instance of norm breaking. Within a year, a Republican was in the White House and Senate Republicans got their wish: a conservative justice nominee, Neil Gorsuch, whom they quickly approved. The GOP had trampled on a basic democratic norm—in effect, stealing a Supreme Court seat—and gotten away with it.

The traditions underpinning America's democratic institutions are unraveling, opening up a disconcerting gap between how our political system works and long-standing expectations about how it *ought* to work. As our soft guardrails have weakened, we have grown increasingly vulnerable to antidemocratic leaders.

Donald Trump, a serial norm breaker, is widely (and correctly) criticized for assaulting America's democratic norms. But the problem did not begin with Trump. The process of norm erosion started decades ago—long before Trump descended an escalator to announce his presidential candidacy.

In a 1978 congressional race in northwestern Georgia, a young Newt Gingrich made his third bid for office in a district outside Atlanta. After two previous failed runs as a self-identified liberal Republican, he finally won—this time as a conservative, capturing a district that hadn't been in Republican hands in 130 years. Gingrich's bespectacled academic look (he had been a history professor at a local university), his chirpy speech, and his thick mop of hair and bushy sideburns belied a ruthlessness that would help transform American politics.

In June of his 1978 campaign, Gingrich had met with a group of College Republicans at an Atlanta Airport Holiday Inn, wooing them with a blunter, more cutthroat vision of politics than they were accustomed to. He found a hungry audience. Gingrich warned the young Republicans to stop using "Boy Scout words, which would be great around the campfire, but are lousy in politics." He continued:

> You're *fighting a war. It is a war for power.* . . . This party does not need another generation of cautious, prudent, careful, bland, irrelevant quasi-leaders. . . . What we really need are people who are willing to stand up in a slug-fest. . . . What's the primary purpose of a political leader? . . . To build a majority.

When Gingrich arrived in Washington in 1979, his vision of politics as warfare was at odds with that of the Republican leadership. House Minority Leader Bob Michel, an amiable figure who carpooled home to Illinois for congressional recesses with his Democratic colleague Dan Rostenkowski, was committed to abiding by established norms of civility and bipartisan cooperation. Gingrich rejected this approach as too "soft." Winning a Republican majority, Gingrich believed, would require playing a harder form of politics.

Backed by a small but growing group of loyalists, Gingrich

launched an insurgency aimed at instilling a more combative approach in the party. Taking advantage of a new media technology, C-SPAN, Gingrich "used adjectives like rocks," deliberately employing over-the-top rhetoric. He described Congress as "corrupt" and "sick." He questioned his Democratic rivals' patriotism. He even compared them to Mussolini and accused them of trying to "destroy our country." According to former Georgia state Democratic Party leader Steve Anthony, "the things that came out of Gingrich's mouth . . . we had never [heard] that before from either side. Gingrich went so far over the top that the shock factor rendered the opposition frozen for a few years."

Through a new political action committee, GOPAC, Gingrich and his allies worked to spread these tactics across the party. GOPAC produced more than two thousand training audiotapes, distributed each month to get the recruits of Gingrich's "Republican Revolution" on the same rhetorical page. Gingrich's former press secretary Tony Blankley compared this tactic of audiotape distribution to one used by the Ayatollah Khomeini on his route to power in Iran. In the early 1990s, Gingrich and his team distributed memos to Republican candidates instructing them to use certain negative words to describe Democrats, including *pathetic, sick, bizarre, betray, antiflag, antifamily*, and *traitors*. It was the beginning of a seismic shift in American politics.

Even as Gingrich ascended the Republican leadership structure—becoming minority whip in 1989 and Speaker of the House in 1995—he refused to abandon his hard-line rhetoric. And rather than repelling the party, he pulled it to him. By the time he became Speaker, Gingrich was a role model to a new generation of Republican legislators, many of them elected in the 1994 landslide that gave the GOP its first House majority in forty years. The Senate was likewise transformed by the arrival of "Gingrich Senators," whose ideology, aversion to compromise, and willingness to obstruct legislation helped speed the end of the body's traditional "folkways."

Though few realized it at the time, Gingrich and his allies were on the cusp of a new wave of polarization rooted in growing public discontent, particularly among the Republican base. Gingrich didn't create this polarization, but he was one of the first Republicans to exploit the shift in popular sentiment. And his leadership helped to establish "politics as warfare" as the GOP's dominant strategy. According to Democratic congressman Barney Frank, Gingrich

> transformed American politics from one in which people presume the good will of their opponents, even as they disagreed, into one in which people treated the people with whom they disagreed as bad and immoral. He was a kind of McCarthyite who succeeded.

The Republicans' new hardball approach was manifest during the presidency of Bill Clinton. In April 1993, four months into Clinton's first term, Senate Minority Leader Robert Dole claimed that Clinton's modest popular victory meant the traditional honeymoon period in which deference was given to a new president was not warranted, and so orchestrated a filibuster to block the president's $16 billion job initiative. Filibuster use, which had already risen markedly in the 1980s and early 1990s, reached what one former senator described as "epidemic" levels during the first two years of the Clinton presidency. Before the 1970s, the annual number of cloture motions filed to end Senate debate—a good indicator of a filibuster attempt—never exceeded seven; by 1993–94, the number had reached eighty. Senate Republicans also pushed aggressively for investigations into a series of dubious scandals, most notably a Clinton 1980s land deal in Arkansas (the so-called Whitewater investigation). These efforts culminated in the 1994 appointment of Kenneth Starr as independent counsel. A shadow would linger over the entire Clinton presidency.

But the era of politics as warfare moved into full gear after the Republicans' landslide 1994 election. With Gingrich now Speaker of the House, the GOP adopted a "no compromise" approach—a signal of ideological purity to the party base—that brazenly rejected forbearance in pursuit of victory by "any means necessary." House Republicans refused to compromise, for example, in budget negotiations, leading to a five-day government shutdown in 1995 and a twenty-one-day shutdown in 1996. This was a dangerous turn. Without forebearance, checks and balances give way to deadlock and dysfunction.

The apogee of 1990s constitutional hardball was the December 1998 House vote to impeach President Clinton. Only the second presidential impeachment in U.S. history, the move ran afoul of long-established norms. The investigation, beginning with the dead-end Whitewater inquiry and ultimately centering on President Clinton's testimony about an extramarital affair, never revealed anything approaching conventional standards for what constitute high crimes and misdemeanors. In the words of constitutional scholar Keith Whittington, the Republicans impeached Clinton "on a technicality." The Republican House members also moved ahead with impeachment without bipartisan support, which meant that President Clinton would almost certainly not be convicted by the Senate (he was acquitted there in February 1999). In an act without precedent in U.S. history, House Republicans had politicized the impeachment process, downgrading it, in the words of congressional experts Thomas Mann and Norman Ornstein, to "just another weapon in the partisan wars."

While Newt Gingrich may have led the initial assault on mutual toleration and forbearance, the descent into politics as warfare only accelerated after he left Congress in 1999. Although Gingrich was succeeded as Speaker by Dennis Hastert, the real power fell into the hands of House Majority Leader Tom DeLay. Nicknamed "the Hammer," DeLay shared Gingrich's partisan ruthlessness. He demonstrated this, in part, through the K Street Project, which packed lobbying firms with Republican operatives and instituted a pay-to-play system that rewarded lobbyists with legislation based on their support for GOP officeholders. Republican congressman Chris Shays described DeLay's philosophy in blunt terms: "If it wasn't illegal, do it." The result was further norm erosion. "Time and time again," one reporter observed, DeLay "has burst through the invisible fence that keeps other partisans in check." DeLay brought routine norm breaking into the twenty-first century.

On the evening of December 14, 2000, after Al Gore conceded the presidency to George W. Bush following a bitter postelection fight, Bush spoke to the country from the Texas House of Representatives. Having been introduced by the state's Democratic House Speaker, Bush declared that he had chosen to speak from the Texas House

> because it has been a home to bipartisan cooperation. Here in a place where Democrats have the majority, Republicans and Democrats have worked together to do what is right for the people we represent. The spirit

of cooperation I have seen in this hall is what we need
in Washington.

No such spirit materialized. Bush had promised to be a "uniter,
not a divider," but partisan warfare only intensified during his
eight years in office. Just prior to Bush's inauguration, DeLay
gave the president-elect a reality check, reportedly telling him:
"We don't work with Democrats. There'll be none of that
uniter-divider stuff."

President Bush governed hard to the right, abandoning all
pretense of bipartisanship on the counsel of his political advisor
Karl Rove, who had concluded that the electorate was so polarized that Republicans could win by mobilizing their own base
rather than seeking independent voters. And with the exception
of the aftermath of the September 11 attacks and subsequent
military actions in Afghanistan and Iraq, congressional Democrats eschewed bipartisan cooperation in favor of obstruction.
Harry Reid and other Senate leaders used Senate rules to slow
down or block Republican legislation and broke with precedent
by routinely filibustering Bush proposals they opposed.

Senate Democrats also began to stray from the norm of
forbearance in the area of advice and consent, obstructing an
unprecedented number of President Bush's judicial nominees,
either by rejecting them outright or by allowing them to lan-
guish by not holding hearings. The norm of deference to the
president on appointments was dissolving. Indeed, the *New
York Times* quoted one Democratic strategist as saying that the
Senate needed to "change the ground rules . . . there [is] no ob-
ligation to confirm someone just because they are scholarly or
erudite." After the Republicans won back the Senate in 2002,
the Democrats turned to filibusters to block the confirmation

of several appeals court nominations. Republicans reacted with outrage. Conservative columnist Charles Krauthammer wrote that "one of the great traditions, customs, and unwritten rules of the Senate is that you do not filibuster judicial nominees." During the 110th Congress, the last of Bush's presidency, the number of filibusters reached an all-time high of 139—nearly double that of even the Clinton years.

If Democrats eschewed forbearance to obstruct the president, Republicans did so in order to protect him. In the House, the informal practice of "regular order," which assured the minority party opportunities to speak and to amend legislation, was largely abandoned. The share of bills introduced under "closed rules" prohibiting amendments skyrocketed. As congressional observers Thomas Mann and Norman Ornstein put it, "long-standing norms of conduct in the House . . . were shredded for the larger goal of implementing the president's program." The GOP effectively abandoned oversight of a Republican president, weakening Congress's ability to check the executive. Whereas the House had conducted 140 hours of sworn testimony investigating whether President Clinton had abused the White House Christmas card list in an effort to drum up new donors, it never once subpoenaed the White House during the first six years of George Bush's presidency. Congress resisted oversight of the Iraq War, launching only superficial investigations into serious abuse cases, including the torture at the Abu Ghraib prison. The congressional watchdog became a lapdog, abdicating its institutional responsibilities.

Norm breaking was also evident at the state level. Among the most notorious cases was the 2003 Texas redistricting plan. Under the Constitution, state legislatures may modify congressional districts to maintain districts of equal population.

However, there exists a long-standing and widely shared norm that redistricting should occur once a decade, immediately after publication of the census. This is with good reason: Because people move continuously, redistricting that occurs later in a decade will be based on less accurate population figures. Though there is no legal impediment to mid-decade redistricting, it has always been rare.

In 2003, Texas Republicans, led by House Majority Leader Tom DeLay, carried out a radical out-of-cycle redistricting plan that, as they themselves admitted, aimed only at partisan advantage. Although the Texas electorate was increasingly Republican, seventeen of the state's thirty-two representatives were Democrats, and many of them were entrenched incumbents. This mattered to national GOP leaders because Republicans held a narrow (229–204) majority in the House of Representatives. The Democrats only needed to win thirteen Republican seats in 2004 to recapture the House, so a swing of even a handful of seats would be decisive.

Under DeLay's guidance, Texas Republicans drew up a redistricting plan designed to gerrymander African American and Latino voters into a small number of Democratic districts while adding Republican voters to the districts of white incumbent Democrats, thereby ensuring their defeat. The new map left six Democratic congressmen especially vulnerable. The plan was pure hardball. As one analyst posited, it "was as partisan as the Republicans thought the law would allow."

It would take another audacious move to pass the Texas bill. The Texas House requires a quorum—the presence of two-thirds of its members—to vote on a bill. And Democrats had the votes to deny a quorum. So when the redistricting was brought to the floor in May 2003, the Democrats responded with an unusual maneuver of their own: Forty-seven state legislators boarded buses and drove to Ardmore, Oklahoma. They remained there for four days, until the House dropped the bill.

In response, Governor Rick Perry called a special session of the House in June, and because the Democrats were too exhausted to organize another walkout, the redistricting bill passed. The bill then moved to the state Senate, where the Democrats, following the precedent of their House colleagues, tried to thwart the bill in absentia by boarding a plane and flying to Albuquerque, New Mexico. They remained there for more than a month, until Senator John Whitmire (soon to be known as "Quitmire") gave in and returned to Austin. When the bill finally passed, DeLay flew in from Washington to oversee the reconciliation process, which produced an even more radical redistricting plan. An aide to Republican congressman Joe Barton admitted in an e-mail that it was "the most aggressive map I have ever seen. This . . . should assure that Republicans keep the House no matter the national mood." Indeed, the redistricting plan worked nearly to perfection. Six Texas congressional seats changed hands from Democrats to Republicans in 2004, helping to preserve Republican control of the House.

In addition to the decline in forbearance, the Bush presidency also saw some early challenges to the norm of mutual toleration. To his great credit, President Bush did not question the patriotism of his Democratic rivals, even when anti-Muslim hysteria in the aftermath of the September 11 attacks created an opportunity to do so. But Fox News commentators and influential radio talk-show hosts used the moment to imply that Democrats lacked patriotism. Commentators began at times to link Democrats to Al Qaeda—as Rush Limbaugh did in 2006, when he accused Senator Patrick Leahy of "taking up arms for

Al Qaeda" after Leahy probed Supreme Court nominee Samuel Alito on the Bush administration's use of torture.

Among the most brazen agents of partisan intolerance in the early 2000s was Ann Coulter. Coulter wrote a series of bestselling books attacking liberals and Democrats in a McCarthyite voice. The books' titles speak for themselves: *Slander* (2002); *Treason* (2003); *Godless* (2006); *Guilty* (2009); *Demonic* (2011); *Adios, America!* (2015). *Treason*, published around the time of the U.S. invasion of Iraq, defends Joseph McCarthy and embraces his tactics. The book claims that anti-Americanism is "intrinsic to [liberals'] entire worldview" and accuses liberals of having committed "fifty years of treason" during the Cold War. While doing publicity for *Treason*, Coulter declared, "There are millions of suspects here. . . . I am indicting the entire Democratic Party." The book spent thirteen weeks on the *New York Times* bestseller list.

The 2008 presidential election was a watershed moment in partisan intolerance. Through the right-wing media ecosystem—including Fox News, America's most-watched cable news channel—Democratic presidential candidate Barack Obama was cast as Marxist, anti-American, and secretly Muslim. The campaign even featured a sustained effort to link Obama to "terrorists" like Bill Ayers, a Chicago-area professor who had been active in the Weather Underground in the early 1970s (Ayers had hosted a gathering for Obama in 1995 as he prepared his Illinois state Senate bid). The Fox News program *Hannity & Colmes* discussed the Ayers story in at least sixty-one different episodes during the 2008 campaign.

But what was especially troubling about the 2008 campaign is that the right-wing media's rhetoric of intolerance was picked up by leading Republican politicians. Tom DeLay, for example, declared that "unless Obama proves me wrong, he's a Marx-ist," while Steve King, a Republican congressman from Iowa, called Obama "anti-American" and warned that he would lead America into "totalitarian dictatorship." Although Republican presidential candidate John McCain did not employ such rhet-oric, he nevertheless selected a running mate, Sarah Palin, who did. Palin embraced the Bill Ayers story, declaring that Obama had been "palling around with terrorists." On the campaign trail, Palin told supporters that Obama "launched his political career in the living room of a domestic terrorist!," continuing: "This is not a man who sees America the way you and I see America. . . . I'm afraid this is someone who sees America as imperfect enough to work with a former domestic terrorist who had targeted his own country." Her racially coded speeches elic-ited cries of "Treason!," "Terrorist!," and even "Kill him!" from crowds.

Barack Obama's 2008 presidential victory revived hopes for a return to a more civilized brand of politics. On election night, as he gathered his family onstage in Chicago, the president-elect spoke generously, congratulating McCain on a heroic ca-reer of contributions to America. Earlier, in Phoenix, Arizona, McCain had delivered a gracious concession speech in which he described Obama as a good man who loved his country, and wished him "Godspeed." It was a textbook case of postelection reconciliation. But something was not right in Phoenix. When McCain mentioned Obama, the crowd booed loudly, forcing the Arizona senator to calm them down. Many looked over at Sarah Palin, who stood off to the side in grim silence. Although the stage belonged to McCain that evening, his tradition-bound plea for Republicans to "bridge our differences" with the new president seemed to sit uneasily with those who had gathered to hear him.

Rather than ushering in a new era of tolerance and cooperation, the Obama presidency was marked by rising extremism and partisan warfare. Challenges to President Obama's legitimacy, which had begun with fringe conservative authors, talk-radio personalities, TV talking heads, and bloggers, was soon embodied in a mass political movement: the Tea Party, which started to organize just weeks after President Obama's inauguration. Although the Tea Party framed its mission in terms of such traditional conservative ideas as limited government, low taxes, and resistance to health care reform, its opposition to Obama was far more pernicious. The difference? The Tea Party questioned President Obama's very right to be president.

Two threads that broke with established norms consistently ran through Tea Party discourse. One was that President Obama posed a threat to our democracy. Just days after Obama's election, Georgia congressman Paul Broun warned of a coming dictatorship comparable to Nazi Germany or the Soviet Union. He later tweeted, "Mr. President, you don't believe in the Constitution. You believe in socialism." Iowa Tea Partier Joni Ernst, who would soon be elected to the U.S. Senate, claimed that President Obama "has become a dictator."

The second thread was that Barack Obama was not a "real American." During the 2008 campaign, Sarah Palin had used the expression "real Americans" to describe her (overwhelmingly white Christian) supporters. This was central to the Tea Party's campaign against President Obama, as followers stressed repeatedly that he did not love America or share American values. According to Tea Party activist and radio host Laurie Roth:

This was not a shift to the Left like Jimmy Carter or Bill Clinton. This is a worldview clash. We are seeing a worldview clash in our White House. A man who is a closet secular-type Muslim, but he's still a Muslim. He's no Christian. We're seeing a man who's a Socialist Communist in the White House, pretending to be an American.

Mass e-mails sent rumors and innuendo through Tea Party circles, including one with a photograph showing President Obama carrying a book, *The Post-American World*, by CNN host Fareed Zakaria. The e-mail read: *"THIS WILL CURDLE YOUR BLOOD!!! The name of the book Obama is reading is called The Post-American World and it was written by a fellow Muslim."*

The rhetoric wasn't limited to Tea Party activists. Republican politicians also questioned President Obama's "Americanness." Former Colorado congressman Tom Tancredo declared, "I do not believe Barack Obama loves the same America that I do, the one the founders put together." Newt Gingrich, who attempted a political comeback and sought the GOP presidential nomination in 2012, called Obama "the first anti-American president." And at a private fund-raising dinner for Wisconsin governor Scott Walker in February 2015, former New York City mayor Rudy Giuliani openly questioned the sitting president's patriotism, declaring: "I do not believe, and I know this is a horrible thing to say, but I do not believe that the president loves America."

If the Tea Party hammered home the accusation that President Obama did not love America, the "birther movement" went even further, questioning whether he was born in the United States—and thus challenging his constitutional right to hold the presidency. The idea that Obama was not even from America first circulated in the blogosphere during his 2004 Senate campaign and resurfaced in 2008. Republican politicians discovered that questioning President Obama's citizenship was an easy way to elicit crowd enthusiasm at public appearances. So they began to do it. Colorado representative Mike Coffman told supporters, "I do not know if Barack Obama was born in the United States of America. . . . But I do know this, that in his heart, he's not an American. He's just not an American." At least eighteen Republican senators and House members were called "birther enablers" because of their refusal to reject the myth. U.S. Senators Roy Blunt, James Inhofe, Richard Shelby, and David Vitter, former vice presidential candidate Sarah Palin, and 2012 presidential candidate Mike Huckabee all made statements endorsing or encouraging the birther campaign.

The most notorious birther of all was Donald Trump. In the spring of 2011, as he pondered a 2012 presidential bid, Trump told the *Today* show that he had "doubts" about whether President Obama was a natural-born U.S. citizen. "I have people who actually have been studying it," Trump claimed, "and they cannot believe what they are finding." Trump became America's most prominent birther, appearing repeatedly on television news programs to call on the president to release his birth certificate. And when Obama's certificate was made public in 2011, Trump suggested it was a forgery. Although Trump opted not to run against Obama in 2012, his high-profile questioning of President Obama's nationality gained him media attention and endeared him to the Republicans' Tea Party base. Intolerance was politically useful.

Such attacks have a long and dishonorable pedigree in American history. Henry Ford, Father Coughlin, and the John

Birch Society all adopted similar language. But the challenges to Obama's legitimacy were different in two important ways. First, they were not confined to the fringes, but rather accepted widely by Republican voters. According to a 2011 Fox News poll, 37 percent of Republicans believed that President Obama was not born in the United States, and 63 percent said they had some doubts about his origins. Forty-three percent of Republicans reported believing he was a Muslim in a CNN/ORC poll, and a *Newsweek* poll found that a majority of Republicans believed President Obama favored the interests of Muslims over those of other religions.

Second, unlike past episodes of extremism, this wave reached into the upper ranks of the Republican Party. With the exception of the McCarthy period, the two major parties had typically kept such intolerance of each other at the margins for more than a century. Neither Father Coughlin nor the John Birch Society had the ear of top party leaders. Now, open attacks on President Obama's legitimacy (and later, Hillary Clinton's) were carried out by leading national politicians. In 2010, Sarah Palin advised the Republicans to "absorb as much of the Tea Party movement as possible." They did. Republican senators, governors, and even presidential candidates mirrored the language of the fringe, and they were joined by Republican donors who viewed the Tea Party movement as an opportunity to push the GOP into a harder line against the Obama administration. Well-funded organizations such as Freedom Works and Americans for Prosperity and political action committees such as the Tea Party Express and Tea Party Patriots sponsored dozens of Republican candidates. In 2010, more than one hundred Tea Party–backed candidates ran for Congress, and more than forty were elected. By 2011, the House Tea Party Caucus had sixty members, and in 2012, Tea Party–friendly candidates emerged as contenders for the Republican presidential nomination. In 2016, the Republican presidential nomination went to a birther, at a national party convention in which Republican leaders called their Democratic rival a criminal and led chants of "Lock her up."

For the first time in many decades, top Republican figures—including one who would soon be president—had overtly abandoned norms of mutual toleration, goaded by a fringe that was no longer fringe. By the end of the Obama presidency, many Republicans embraced the view that their Democratic rivals were anti-American or posed a threat to the American way of life. This was dangerous territory. Such extremism encourages politicians to abandon forbearance. If Barack Obama is a "threat to the rule of law," as Senator Ted Cruz claimed, then it made sense to block his judicial appointments by any means necessary.

Rising partisan intolerance thus led to an erosion of institutional forbearance during the Obama years. Immediately after President Obama's election, a group of young House members, led by Kevin McCarthy, Eric Cantor, and Paul Ryan, held a series of meetings to develop a strategy to confront the new administration. The self-styled "Young Guns" decided to make the GOP the "Party of No." The United States was mired in the deepest economic crisis since the Great Depression, yet Republican legislators planned to *not* cooperate with the new administration. Senate Minority Leader Mitch McConnell echoed this sentiment when he declared that the "single most important thing we want to achieve [in the Senate] is for President Obama to be a one-term president." So McConnell, too, embraced obstructionism. The very first bill in front of the Senate in January 2009 was the innocuous Public Land Management Act—a bipartisan conservation measure to secure two million acres of wilderness in nine states. As if to send a message, the Republicans filibustered it.

This behavior became standard practice. Senate obstructionism spiked after 2008. Senate "holds," traditionally used to delay a floor debate for up to a week to allow senators extra time to prepare, became "indefinite or permanent vetoes." A stunning 385 filibusters were initiated between 2007 and 2012—equal to the total number of filibusters in the seven decades between World War I and the end of the Reagan administration. And Senate Republicans continued using the judicial confirmation process as a partisan tool: The confirmation rate of presidential circuit court appointments, which had been over 90 percent in the 1980s, fell to barely 50 percent under President Obama.

The Democrats responded with norm breaking of their own. In November 2013, Senate Democrats voted to eliminate the filibuster for most presidential nominations, including federal judicial (but not Supreme Court) nominees, a move so extreme it was widely referred to as the "nuclear option." Republican senators criticized the Democrats' "raw exercise of political power," but President Obama defended it, claiming that the filibuster had been transformed into a "reckless and relentless tool" of obstruction and adding that "today's pattern of obstruction . . . just isn't normal; it's not what our founders envisioned."

President Obama also responded with norm breaking—in the form of unilateral executive actions. In October 2011, the president presented what would become his mantra for achieving policy goals: "We can't wait for an increasingly dysfunctional Congress to do its job," he told an audience in Nevada. "Whenever they won't act, I will." Obama began to use executive authority in a way he might not have expected to before coming into office. In 2010, in the face of Congress's failure to pass a new energy bill, he issued an "executive memorandum" instructing government agencies to raise fuel efficiency standards for all cars. In 2012, in response to Congress's inability to pass immigration reform, he announced an executive action to cease deportation of illegal immigrants who came to the United States before the age of sixteen and were either in school or were high school graduates or military veterans. In 2015, President Obama responded to Congress's refusal to pass legislation to combat climate change by issuing an executive order to all federal agencies to reduce greenhouse gas emissions and use more renewable energy. Unable to get Senate consent for a nuclear treaty with Iran, the Obama administration negotiated an "executive agreement," which, because it was not formally a treaty, did not require Senate approval. The president's actions were not out of constitutional bounds, but by acting unilaterally to achieve goals that had been blocked by Congress, President Obama violated the norm of forbearance.

President Obama's efforts to circumvent Congress triggered further escalation. In March 2015, the Republican Senate leadership publicly encouraged U.S. states to defy the president's authority. In an op-ed in the *Lexington Herald Leader*, Mitch McConnell urged states to ignore Obama's regulatory order limiting greenhouse gas emissions. It was a stunning undermining of federal authority. The following year, Arizona state legislators debated and nearly passed a bill prohibiting the state government from using any of its personnel or resources to enforce executive orders that had not been voted on by Congress. As the *New York Times* editorialized, "This sounds like John Calhoun's Secessionist screed from 1828, the South Carolina Exposition and Protest."

Three dramatic events during Obama's presidency revealed

how severely norms of forbearance had eroded. The first was the 2011 crisis over the federal debt limit. Because a failure to raise the debt ceiling could cause the U.S. government to default, destroying America's credit rating and potentially throwing the economy into a tailspin, Congress could, in theory, use the debt limit as a "hostage," refusing to raise it unless the president met certain demands. This extraordinary brinksmanship was never seriously contemplated—before 2011. Raising the debt limit was a long-standing bipartisan practice; between 1960 and 2011 it had been done 78 times, 49 under Republican presidents and 29 under Democrats. Although the process was often contentious, leaders of both parties knew it was just political posturing.

This changed after the Republicans, pushed by a new class of Tea Party–backed representatives, gained control of Congress in 2011. Not only were they willing to use the debt limit as a hostage, many of them were willing to kill it—to "bring the whole system crashing down"—if their demands for dramatic spending cuts were not met. Likewise, Tea Party–backed Senators Pat Toomey of Pennsylvania and Mike Lee of Utah openly called for a default if President Obama did not accede to their demands. As Congressman Jason Chaffetz put it afterward, "We weren't kidding. . . . We would have taken it down." Although a last-minute deal prevented a default, considerable damage had already been done. Markets responded badly, and Standard & Poor's downgraded America's credit rating for the first time in history.

March 2015 brought another unprecedented event, when Arkansas senator Tom Cotton and forty-six other Republican senators wrote an open letter to Iran's leaders insisting that President Obama had no authority to negotiate a deal over Iran's nuclear program. Opposed to the Iran deal and angered by

Obama's decision to use an "executive agreement" rather than a treaty, Senate Republicans intervened in diplomatic negotiations, long the domain of the executive branch. Florida senator Bill Nelson, a moderate Democrat, described the letter as "jaw-dropping. . . . I couldn't help but reflect, would I have signed such a letter under President George W. Bush? I would never even have contemplated that." Cotton and his allies had brazenly sought to undermine the authority of a sitting president.

A third norm-breaking moment was the Senate's refusal to take up President Obama's 2016 nomination of Merrick Garland to the Supreme Court. It bears repeating that not once since Reconstruction had a president been denied the opportunity to fill a Supreme Court vacancy when he nominated someone before the election of his successor. But the threat of obstruction did not end there. In the run-up to the 2016 election, when it was widely believed that Hillary Clinton would win, several Republican senators, including Ted Cruz, John McCain, and Richard Burr, vowed to block all of Clinton's Supreme Court nominations for the next four years, effectively reducing the Court's size to eight. Burr, a senator from North Carolina, told a private meeting of Republican volunteers that "if Hillary Clinton becomes president, I am going to do everything I can do to make sure four years from now, we still got an opening on the Supreme Court." Although the Constitution does not specify the size of the Supreme Court, the nine-member Court had long ago become an established tradition. Republicans and Democrats had both defended the Court's autonomy against President Roosevelt's overreach in 1937. This was now unimaginable. Although Ted Cruz claimed there was a long "historical precedent" for changing the size of the Supreme Court, that precedent died shortly after the Civil War. Cruz's initiative would have broken a 147-year-old norm.

With tactics like these, the Republicans had begun to be-have like an antisystem political party. By the end of the Obama presidency, democracy's soft guardrails were becoming danger-ously unmoored.

If, twenty-five years ago, someone had described to you a coun-try in which candidates threatened to lock up their rivals, polit-ical opponents accused the government of stealing the election or establishing a dictatorship, and parties used their legislative majorities to impeach presidents and steal supreme court seats, you might have thought of Ecuador or Romania. You probably would not have thought of the United States.

Behind the unraveling of basic norms of mutual tolerance and forbearance lies a syndrome of intense partisan polariza-tion. Although it began with the radicalization of the Repub-lican Party, the consequences of this polarization have been felt through the entire American political system. Government shutdowns, legislative hostage-taking, mid-decade redistrict-ing, and the refusal to even consider Supreme Court nomina-tions are not aberrant moments. Over the last quarter century, Democrats and Republicans have become much more than just two competing parties, sorted into liberal and conservative camps. Their voters are now deeply divided by race, religious belief, geography, and even "way of life."

Consider this extraordinary finding: In 1960, political sci-entists asked Americans how they would feel if their child mar-ried someone who identified with another political party. Four percent of Democrats and five percent of Republicans reported they would be "displeased." In 2010, by contrast, 33 percent of Democrats and 49 percent of Republicans reported feel-ing "somewhat or very unhappy" at the prospect of interparty marriage. Being a Democrat or a Republican has become not just a partisan affiliation but an identity. A 2016 survey conducted by the Pew Foundation found that 49 percent of Republicans and 55 percent of Democrats say the other party makes them "afraid." Among politically engaged Americans, the numbers are even higher—70 percent of Democrats and 62 percent of Republicans say they live in fear of the other party.

These surveys point to the rise of a dangerous phenomenon in American politics: intense partisan animosity. The roots of this phenomenon lie in a long-term partisan realignment that began to take form in the 1960s. For most of the twentieth century, American parties were ideological "big tents," each encompassing diverse constituencies and a wide range of political views. The Democrats represented the New Deal coalition of liberals, organized labor, second- and third-generation Catholic immigrants, and African Americans, but they also represented conservative whites in the South. For its part, the GOP ranged from liberals in the Northeast to conservatives in the Midwest and West. Evangelical Christians belonged to both parties, with slightly more of them supporting the Democrats—so neither party could be charged with being "Godless."

Because the two parties were so internally heterogeneous, polarization between them was far lower than it is today. Congressional Republicans and Democrats divided on such issues as taxes and spending, government regulation, and unions, but the parties overlapped on the potentially explosive issue of race. Although both parties contained factions supporting civil rights, southern Democrats' opposition and strategic control of Congress's committee system kept the issue off the agenda. This internal heterogeneity defused conflict. Rather than viewing one another as enemies, Republicans and Democrats frequently found common ground. Whereas liberal Democrats and Republicans often voted in Congress together to push the cause of civil rights, southern Democrats and right-wing northern Republicans maintained a "conservative coalition" in Congress that thwarted it.

The civil rights movement, culminating in the 1964 Civil Rights Act and 1965 Voting Rights Act, put an end to this partisan arrangement. Not only did it democratize the South, at long last, by enfranchising blacks and ending single-party rule, but it accelerated a long-run party system realignment whose consequences are still unfolding today. It was the Civil Rights Act, which Democratic president Lyndon Johnson embraced and 1964 Republican presidential candidate Barry Goldwater opposed, that would define the Democrats as the party of civil rights and Republicans as the party of racial status quo. In the decades that followed, southern white migration to the Republican Party quickened. The racial appeals of Nixon's "Southern Strategy" and, later on, Ronald Reagan's coded messages about race communicated to voters that the GOP was the home for white racial conservatives. By century's end, what had long been a solidly Democratic region had become solidly Republican. At the same time, southern blacks—able to vote for the first time in nearly a century—flocked to the Democrats, as did many northern liberal Republicans who supported civil rights. As the South went Republican, the Northeast went reliably blue.

The post-1965 realignment also began a process of sorting out voters ideologically. For the first time in nearly a century, partisanship and ideology converged, with the GOP becoming primarily conservative and the Democrats becoming predominantly liberal. By the 2000s, the Democratic and Republican parties were no longer ideological "big tents." With the disappearance of conservative Democrats and liberal Republicans, areas of overlap between the parties gradually disappeared.

Now that most senators and representatives had more in common with their partisan allies than with members of the opposing party, they cooperated less frequently and voted consistently with their own party. As both voters and their elected representatives clustered into increasingly homogeneous "camps," the ideological differences between the parties grew more marked.

But the sorting of the American electorate into liberal Democrats and conservative Republicans cannot alone explain the depth of partisan hostility that has emerged in America. Nor does it explain why this polarization has been so asymmetric, moving the Republican Party more sharply to the right than it has moved the Democrats to the left. Ideologically sorted parties don't necessarily generate the "fear and loathing" that erodes norms of mutual toleration, leading politicians to begin to question the legitimacy of their rivals. Voters are ideologically sorted in Britain, Germany, and Sweden, but in none of these countries do we see the kind of partisan hatred we now see in America.

Realignment has gone well beyond liberal versus conservative. The social, ethnic, and cultural bases of partisanship have also changed dramatically, giving rise to parties that represent not just different policy approaches but different communities, cultures, and values. We have already mentioned one major driver of this: the civil rights movement. But America's ethnic diversification was not limited to black enfranchisement. Beginning in the 1960s, the United States experienced a massive wave of immigration, first from Latin America and later from Asia, which has dramatically altered the country's demographic map. In 1950, nonwhites constituted barely 10 percent of the U.S. population. By 2014, they constituted 38 percent, and the U.S. Census Bureau projects that a majority of the population will be nonwhite by 2044.

Together with black enfranchisement, immigration has transformed American political parties. These new voters have disproportionately supported the Democratic Party. The non-white share of the Democratic vote rose from 7 percent in the 1950s to 44 percent in 2012. Republican voters, by contrast, were still nearly 90 percent white into the 2000s. So as the Democrats have increasingly become a party of ethnic minorities, the Republican Party has remained almost entirely a party of whites.

The Republican Party has also become the party of evangelical Christians. Evangelicals entered politics en masse in the late 1970s, motivated, in large part, by the Supreme Court's 1973 *Roe v. Wade* decision legalizing abortion. Beginning with Ronald Reagan in 1980, the GOP embraced the Christian Right and adopted increasingly pro-evangelical positions, including opposition to abortion, support for school prayer, and, later, opposition to gay marriage. White evangelicals—who had leaned Democratic in the 1960s—began to vote Republican. In 2016, 76 percent of white evangelicals identified as Republican. Democratic voters, in turn, grew increasingly secular. The percentage of white Democrats who attended church regularly fell from nearly 50 percent in the 1960s to below 30 percent in the 2000s.

This is an extraordinary change. As the political scientist Alan Abramowitz points out, in the 1950s, married white Christians were the overwhelming majority—nearly 80 percent—of American voters, divided more or less equally between the two parties. By the 2000s, married white Christians constituted barely 40 percent of the electorate, and they were now concentrated in the Republican Party. In other words, the two parties are now divided over race and religion—two deeply polarizing issues that tend to generate greater intolerance and hostility than traditional policy issues such as taxes and government spending.

By the 2000s, then, Democratic and Republican voters, and the politicians representing them, were more divided than at any point in the previous century. But why was most of the norm breaking being done by the Republican Party?

For one, the changing media landscape had a stronger impact on the Republican Party. Republican voters rely more heavily on partisan media outlets than do Democrats. In 2010, 69 percent of Republican voters were Fox News viewers. And popular radio talk-show hosts such as Rush Limbaugh, Sean Hannity, Michael Savage, Mark Levin, and Laura Ingraham, all of whom have helped to legitimate the use of uncivil discourse, have few counterparts among liberals.

The rise of right-wing media also affected Republican officeholders. During the Obama administration, Fox News commentators and right-wing radio personalities almost uniformly adopted a "no compromise" position, viciously attacking any Republican politician who broke with the party line. When California Republican representative Darrell Issa declared that the GOP could accomplish more of its agenda if it were willing to work, on occasion, with President Obama, Rush Limbaugh forced him to publicly repudiate his claim and pledge loyalty to the obstructionist agenda. As former Republican Senate Majority Leader Trent Lott put it, "If you stray the slightest from the far right, you get hit by the conservative media."

Hard-line positions were reinforced by well-funded conservative interest groups. In the late 1990s, organizations such as Grover Norquist's Americans for Tax Reform and the Club for

Growth became leading voices in the GOP, pulling Republican politicians toward more ideologically inflexible positions. Norquist demanded that GOP congressmen sign "no tax" pledges, essentially forcing them into an obstructionist stance. Thanks, in part, to the loosening of campaign finance laws in 2010, outside groups such as Americans for Prosperity and the American Energy Alliance—many of them part of the Koch billionaire family network—gained outsize influence in the Republican Party during the Obama years. In 2012 alone, the Koch family was responsible for some $400 million in election spending. Along with the Tea Party, the Koch network and other similar organizations helped elect a new generation of Republicans for whom *compromise* was a dirty word. A party with a core that was hollowed out by donors and pressure groups was also more vulnerable to extremist forces.

But it is not only media and outside interests that have pushed the Republican Party toward extremism. Social and cultural changes have also played a major role. Unlike the Democratic Party, which has grown increasingly diverse in recent decades, the GOP has remained culturally homogeneous. This is significant because the party's core white Protestant voters are not just any constituency—for nearly two centuries, they comprised the majority of the U.S. electorate and were politically, economically, and culturally dominant in American society. Now, again, white Protestants are a minority of the electorate—and declining. And they have hunkered down in the Republican Party.

In his 1964 essay "The Paranoid Style in American Politics," historian Richard Hofstadter described the phenomenon of "status anxiety," which, he believed, is most likely to emerge when groups' social status, identity, and sense of belonging are perceived to be under existential threat. This leads to a style of politics that is "overheated, oversuspicious, overaggressive, grandiose, and apocalyptic." Half a century after its publication, Hofstadter's essay may be more relevant than ever. The struggle against declining majority status is, in good part, what fuels the intense animosity that has come to define the American Right. Survey evidence suggests that many Tea Party Republicans share the perception that the country they grew up in is "slipping away, threatened by the rapidly changing face of what they believe is the 'real' America." To quote the title of sociologist Arlie Hochschild's recent book, they perceive themselves to be "strangers in their own land."

This perception may explain the rise of a discourse that distinguishes "real Americans" from those associated with liberals and the Democratic Party. If the definition of "real Americans" is restricted to those who are native-born, English-speaking, white, and Christian, then it is easy to see how "real Americans" may view themselves as declining. As Ann Coulter chillingly put it, "The American electorate isn't moving to the left—it's shrinking." The perception among many Tea Party Republicans that their America is disappearing helps us understand the appeal of such slogans as "Take Our Country Back" or "Make America Great Again." The danger of such appeals is that casting Democrats as *not* real Americans is a frontal assault on mutual toleration.

Republican politicians from Newt Gingrich to Donald Trump learned that in a polarized society, treating rivals as enemies can be useful—and that the pursuit of politics as warfare can be appealing to those who fear they have much to lose. But war always has its price. The mounting assault on norms of mutual toleration and forbearance—mostly, though not entirely, by Republicans—has eroded the soft guardrails that long protected us from the kind of partisan fight to the death that has destroyed democracies in other parts of the world. When Donald Trump took office in January 2017, the guardrails were still there, but they were weaker than they had been in a century—and things were about to get worse.

Trump Against the Guardrails

Donald Trump's first year in office followed a familiar script. Like Alberto Fujimori, Hugo Chávez, and Recep Tayyip Erdoğan, America's new president began his tenure by launching blistering rhetorical attacks on his opponents. He called the media the "enemy of the American people," questioned judges' legitimacy, and threatened to cut federal funding to major cities. Predictably, these attacks triggered dismay, shock, and anger across the political spectrum. Journalists found themselves at the front lines, exposing—but also provoking—the president's norm-breaking behavior. A study by the Shorenstein Center on Media, Politics, and Public Policy found that the major news outlets were "unsparing" in their coverage of the Trump administration's first hundred days. Of news reports with a clear tone, the study found, 80 percent were negative—much higher than under Clinton (60 percent), George W. Bush (57 percent), and Obama (41 percent).

Soon, Trump administration officials were feeling besieged. Not a single week went by in which press coverage wasn't at least 70 percent negative. And amid swirling rumors about the

Trump campaign's ties to Russia, a high-profile special counsel, Robert Mueller, was appointed to oversee investigations into the case. Just a few months into his presidency, President Trump faced talk of impeachment. But he retained the support of his base, and like other elected demagogues, he doubled down. He claimed his administration was beset by powerful establishment forces, telling graduates of the U.S. Coast Guard Academy that "no politician in history, and I say this with great surety, has been treated worse or more unfairly." The question, then, was how Trump would respond. Would an outsider president who considered himself to be under unwarranted assault lash out, as happened in Peru and Turkey?

President Trump exhibited clear authoritarian instincts during his first year in office. In Chapter 4, we presented three strategies by which elected authoritarians seek to consolidate power: capturing the referees, sidelining the key players, and rewriting the rules to tilt the playing field against opponents. Trump attempted *all three* of these strategies.

President Trump demonstrated striking hostility toward the referees—law enforcement, intelligence, ethics agencies, and the courts. Soon after his inauguration, he sought to ensure that the heads of U.S. intelligence agencies, including the FBI, the CIA, and the National Security Agency, would be personally loyal to him, apparently in the hope of using these agencies as a shield against investigations into his campaign's Russia ties. During his first week in office, President Trump summoned FBI Director James Comey to a one-on-one dinner in the White House in which, according to Comey, the president asked for a pledge of loyalty. He later reportedly pressured Comey to drop

investigations into his recently departed national security direc-
tor, Michael Flynn, pressed Director of National Intelligence
Daniel Coats and CIA Director Mike Pompeo to intervene in
Comey's investigation, and personally appealed to Coats and
NSA head Michael Rogers to release statements denying the
existence of any collusion with Russia (both refused).

President Trump also tried to punish or purge agencies
that acted with independence. Most prominently, he dismissed
Comey after it became clear that Comey could not be pressured into protecting the administration and was expanding
its Russia investigation. Only once in the FBI's eighty-two-year
history had a president fired the bureau's director before his ten-
year term was up—and in that case, the move was in response
to clear ethical violations and enjoyed bipartisan support.

The Comey firing was not President Trump's only as-
sault on referees who refused to come to his personal defense.
Trump had attempted to establish a personal relationship with
Manhattan-based U.S. Attorney Preet Bharara, whose investigations into money laundering reportedly threatened to reach
Trump's inner circle; when Bharara, a respected anticorruption
figure, continued the investigation, the president removed him.
After Attorney General Jeff Sessions recused himself from the
Russia investigation and his deputy, Rod Rosenstein, appointed
the respected former FBI Director Robert Mueller as special
counsel to oversee the investigation, Trump publicly shamed
Sessions, reportedly seeking his resignation. White House lawyers even launched an effort to dig up dirt on Mueller, seeking
conflicts of interest that could be used to discredit or dismiss
him. By late 2017, many of Trump's allies were openly calling
on him to fire Mueller, and there was widespread concern that
he would soon do so.

President Trump's efforts to derail independent investigations evoked the kind of assaults on the referees routinely seen in less democratic countries—for example, the dismissal of Venezuelan Prosecutor General Luisa Ortega, a *chavista* appointee who asserted her independence and began to investigate corruption and abuse in the Maduro government. Although Ortega's term did not expire until 2021 and she could be legally removed only by the legislature (which was in opposition hands), the government's dubiously elected Constituent Assembly sacked her in August 2017.

President Trump also attacked judges who ruled against him. After Judge James Robart of the Ninth Circuit of the U.S. Court of Appeals blocked the administration's initial travel ban, Trump spoke of "the opinion of this so-called judge, which essentially takes law-enforcement away from our country." Two months later, when the same court temporarily blocked the withholding of federal funds from sanctuary cities, the White House denounced the judgment as an attack on the rule of law by an "unelected judge." Trump himself responded by threatening to break up the Ninth Circuit.

The president took an indirect swipe at the judiciary in August 2017 when he pardoned the controversial former Arizona sheriff Joe Arpaio, who was convicted of violating a federal court order to stop racial profiling. Arpaio was a political ally and a hero to many of Trump's anti-immigrant supporters. As we noted earlier, the chief executive's constitutional power to pardon is without limit, but presidents have historically exercised it with great restraint, seeking advice from the Justice Department and never issuing pardons for self-protection or political gain. President Trump boldly violated these norms. Not only did he not consult the Justice Department, but the pardon was clearly political—it was popular with his base. The move reinforced fears that the president would eventually pardon himself and his inner circle—something that was reportedly explored by his lawyers. Such a move would constitute an unprecedented attack on judicial independence. As constitutional scholar Martin Redish put it, "If the president can immunize his agents in this manner, the courts will effectively lose any meaningful authority to protect constitutional rights against invasion by the executive branch."

The Trump administration also trampled, inevitably, on the Office of Government Ethics (OGE), an independent watchdog agency that, though lacking legal teeth, had been respected by previous administrations. Faced with the numerous conflicts of interest created by Trump's business dealings, OGE director Walter Shaub repeatedly criticized the president-elect during the transition. The administration responded by launching attacks on the OGE. House Oversight Chair Jason Chaffetz, a Trump ally, even hinted at an investigation of Shaub. In May, administration officials tried to force the OGE to halt investigations into the White House's appointment of ex-lobbyists. Alternately harassed and ignored by the White House, Shaub resigned, leaving behind what journalist Ryan Lizza called a "broken" OGE.

President Trump's behavior toward the courts, law enforcement and intelligence bodies, and other independent agencies was drawn from an authoritarian playbook. He openly spoke of using the Justice Department and the FBI to go after Democrats, including Hillary Clinton. And in late 2017, the Justice Department considered nominating a special counsel to investigate Clinton. Despite its purges and threats, however, the administration could not capture the referees. Trump did not replace Comey with a loyalist, largely because such a move was vetoed by key Senate Republicans. Likewise, Senate Republicans resisted Trump's efforts to replace Attorney General Sessions. But the president had other battles to wage.

The Trump administration also mounted efforts to sideline key players in the political system. President Trump's rhetorical attacks on critics in the media are an example. His repeated accusations that outlets such as the *New York Times* and CNN were dispensing "fake news" and conspiring against him look familiar to any student of authoritarianism. In a February 2017 tweet, he called the media the "enemy of the American people," a term that, critics noted, mimicked one used by Stalin and Mao. Trump's rhetoric was often threatening. A few days after his "enemy of the people" tweet, Trump told the Conservative Political Action Committee:

> I love the First Amendment; nobody loves it better than me. Nobody. . . . But as you saw throughout the entire campaign, and even now, the fake news doesn't tell the truth. . . . I say it doesn't represent the people. It never will represent the people, and we're going to do something about it.

Do what, exactly? The following month, President Trump returned to his campaign pledge to "open up the libel laws," tweeting that the *New York Times* had "disgraced the media world. Gotten me wrong for two solid years. Change libel laws?" When asked by a reporter whether the administration was really considering such changes, White House Chief of Staff Reince Priebus said, "I think that's something we've looked at." Ecuadorian President Rafael Correa used this approach. His multimillion-dollar defamation suits and jailing of journalists on charges of defamation had a powerfully chilling effect on the media. Although Trump dropped the libel issue, he continued his threats. In July, he retweeted an altered video clip made from old WWE footage of him tackling and then punching someone with a CNN logo superimposed on his face.

President Trump also considered using government regulatory agencies against unfriendly media companies. During the 2016 campaign, he had threatened Jeff Bezos, the owner of the *Washington Post* and Amazon, with antitrust action, tweeting: "If I become president, oh do they have problems." He also threatened to block the pending merger of Time Warner (CNN's parent company) and AT&T, and during the first months of his presidency, there were reports that White House advisors considered using the administration's antitrust authority as a source of leverage against CNN. And finally, in October 2017, Trump attacked NBC and other networks by threatening to "challenge their license."

There was one area in which the Trump administration went beyond threats to try to use the machinery of government to punish critics. During his first week in office, President Trump signed an executive order authorizing federal agencies to withhold funding from "sanctuary cities" that refused to cooperate with the administration's crackdown on undocumented immigrants. "If we have to," he declared in February 2017, "we'll defund." The plan was reminiscent of the Chávez government's repeated moves to strip opposition-run city governments of their control over local hospitals, police forces, ports, and other infrastructure. Unlike the Venezuelan president, however, President Trump was blocked by the courts.

Although President Trump has waged a war of words against the media and other critics, those words have not (yet) led to action. No journalists have been arrested, and no media outlets have altered their coverage due to pressure from the government. Trump's efforts to tilt the playing field to his advantage have been more worrying. In May 2017, he called for changes in what he called "archaic" Senate rules, including the elimination of the filibuster, which would have strengthened the Republican majority at the expense of the Democratic minority. Senate Republicans did eliminate the filibuster for Supreme Court nominations, clearing the way for Neil Gorsuch's ascent to the Court, but they rejected the idea of doing away with it entirely.

Perhaps the most antidemocratic initiative yet undertaken by the Trump administration is the creation of the Presidential Advisory Commission on Election Integrity, chaired by Vice President Mike Pence but run by Vice Chair Kris Kobach. To understand its potential impact, recall that the Civil Rights and Voting Rights Acts prompted a massive shift in party identification: The Democratic Party became the primary representative of minority and first- and second-generation immigrant voters, while GOP voters remained overwhelmingly white. Because the minority share of the electorate is growing, these changes favor the Democrats, a perception that was reinforced by Barack Obama's 2008 victory, in which minority turnout rates were unusually high.

Perceiving a threat, some Republican leaders came up with a response that evoked memories of the Jim Crow South: make it harder for low-income minority citizens to vote. Because poor minority voters were overwhelmingly Democratic, measures that dampened turnout among such voters would likely tilt the playing field in favor of Republicans. This would be done via strict voter identification laws—requiring, for example, that voters present a valid driver's license or other government-issued photo ID upon arrival at the polling station.

The push for voter ID laws was based on a false claim: that voter fraud is widespread in the United States. All reputable studies have concluded that levels of such fraud in this country are low. Yet Republicans began to push for measures to combat this nonexistent problem. The first two states to adopt voter ID laws were Georgia and Indiana, both in 2005. Georgia congressman John Lewis, a longtime civil rights leader, described his state's law as a "modern day poll tax." An estimated 300,000 Georgia voters lacked the required forms of ID, and African Americans were five times more likely than whites to lack them. Indiana's voter ID law, which Judge Terence Evans of the Seventh Circuit Court of Appeals called "a not-too-thinly veiled attempt to discourage election day turnout by certain folks believed to skew Democratic," was taken to the Supreme Court, where it was upheld in 2008. After that, voter ID laws proliferated. Bills were introduced in thirty-seven states between 2010 and 2012, and by 2016 fifteen states had adopted such laws, although only ten had them in effect for the election.

The laws were passed exclusively in states where Republicans controlled both legislative chambers, and in all but Arkansas, the governor was also a Republican. There is little doubt that minority voters were a primary target. Voter ID laws are almost certain to have a disproportionate impact on low-income minority voters: According to one study, 37 percent of African Americans and 27 percent of Latinos reported not possessing a valid driver's license, compared to 16 percent of whites. A study by the Brennan Center for Justice estimated that 11 percent of American citizens (twenty-one million eligible voters) did not possess government-issued photo IDs, and that among African American citizens, the figure rose to 25 percent.

Of the eleven states with the highest black turnout in 2008, seven adopted stricter voter ID laws, and of the twelve states that experienced the highest rates of Hispanic population growth between 2000 and 2010, nine passed laws making it harder to vote. Scholars have just begun to evaluate the impact of voter ID laws, and most studies have found only a modest effect on turnout. But a modest effect can be decisive in close elections, especially if the laws are widely adopted.

That is precisely what the Presidential Advisory Commission on Election Integrity hopes to make happen. The Commission's de facto head, Kris Kobach, has been described as America's "premier advocate of vote suppression." As Kansas's secretary of state, Kobach helped push through one of the nation's strictest voter ID laws. For Kobach, Donald Trump was a useful ally. During the 2016 campaign, Trump had complained that the election was "rigged," and afterward, he made the extraordinary claim that he had "won the popular vote if you deduct the millions of people who voted illegally." He repeated this point in a meeting with congressional leaders, saying that there had been between three and five million illegal votes. The claim was baseless: A national vote-monitoring project led by the media organization ProPublica found no evidence of fraud. *Washington Post* reporter Philip Bump scoured Nexis for documented cases of fraud in 2016 and found a total of four.

But President Trump's apparent obsession with having "won" the popular vote converged with Kobach's voter suppression goals. Kobach endorsed Trump's claims, declaring that he was "absolutely correct" in asserting that the number of illegal votes exceeded Clinton's margin of victory. (Kobach later said that "we will probably never know" who won the popular vote.) Kobach gained Trump's ear, helped convince him to create the Commission, and was appointed to run it.

The Commission's early activities suggested that its objective was voter suppression. First, it is collecting stories of fraud from across the country, which could provide political ammunition for state-level voter-restriction initiatives or, perhaps, for efforts to repeal the 1993 "Motor Voter" law. In effect, the Commission is poised to serve as a high-profile national mouthpiece for Republican efforts to pass tougher voter ID laws. Second, the Commission aims to encourage or facilitate state-level voter roll purges, which, existing research suggests, would invariably remove many legitimate voters. The Commission has already sought to cross-check local voter records to uncover cases of double registration, in which people are registered in more than one state. There are also reports that the Commission plans to use a Homeland Security database of green card and visa holders to scour the voter rolls for noncitizens. The risk, as one study shows, is that the number of mistakes—because of the existence of many people with the same name and birthdate—will vastly exceed the number of illegal registrations that are uncovered.

Efforts to discourage voting are fundamentally antidemocratic, and they have a particularly deplorable history in the United States. Although contemporary voter-restriction efforts are nowhere near as far-reaching as those undertaken by southern Democrats in the late nineteenth century, they are nevertheless significant. Because strict voter ID laws disproportionately affect low-income minority voters, who are overwhelmingly Democratic, they skew elections in favor of the GOP.

Trump's Commission on Election Integrity did not carry out any concrete reforms in 2017, and its clumsy request for voter information was widely rebuffed by the states. But if the Commission proceeds with its project unchecked, it has the potential to inflict real damage on our country's electoral process.

In many ways, President Trump followed the electoral authoritarian script during his first year. He made efforts to capture the referees, sideline the key players who might halt him, and tilt the playing field. But the president has talked more than he has acted, and his most notorious threats have not been realized. Troubling antidemocratic initiatives, including packing the FBI with loyalists and blocking the Mueller investigation, were derailed by Republican opposition and his own bumbling. One important initiative, the Advisory Commission on Election Integrity, is just getting off the ground, so its impact is harder to evaluate. Overall, then, President Trump repeatedly scraped up against the guardrails, like a reckless driver, but he did not break through them. Despite clear causes for concern, little actual backsliding occurred in 2017. We did not cross the line into authoritarianism.

It is still early, however. The backsliding of democracy is often gradual, its effects unfolding slowly over time. Comparing Trump's first year in office to those of other would-be authoritarians, the picture is mixed. Table 3 offers an illustrative list of nine countries in which potentially authoritarian leaders came to power via elections. In some countries, including Ecuador and Russia, backsliding was evident during the first year. By contrast, in Peru under Fujimori and Turkey under Erdoğan, there was no initial backsliding. Fujimori engaged in heated rhetorical battles during his first year as president but did not assault democratic institutions until nearly two years in. Breakdown took even longer in Turkey.

Table 3: The Authoritarian Report Card After One Year

Country	Leader	Start Date	Capturing Referees	Sidelining Players	Changing Rules	Eventual Fate of Regime
Argentina	Juan Perón	June 1946	YES	NO	NO	Authoritarian
Ecuador	Rafael Correa	January 2007	YES	YES	YES	Mildly authoritarian
Hungary	Viktor Orbán	May 2010	LIMITED	NO	NO	Mildly authoritarian
Italy	Silvio Berlusconi	June 2001	NO	NO	NO	Democratic
Peru	Alberto Fujimori	July 1990	NO	NO	NO	Authoritarian
Peru	Ollanta Humala	July 2011	NO	NO	NO	Democratic
Poland	Jaroslaw Kaczyński	November 2015	YES	NO	NO	Mildly authoritarian
Russia	Vladimir Putin	May 2000	NO	YES	NO	Highly authoritarian
Turkey	Recep Erdoğan	March 2003	NO	NO	NO	Authoritarian
Venezuela	Hugo Chávez	February 1999	YES	YES	YES	Authoritarian

Democracy's fate during the remainder of Trump's presidency will depend on several factors. The first is the behavior of Republican leaders. Democratic institutions depend crucially on the willingness of governing parties to defend them—even against their own leaders. The failure of Roosevelt's court-packing scheme and the fall of Nixon were made possible, in part, when key members of the president's own party—Democrats in Roosevelt's case and Republicans in the case of Nixon—decided to stand up and oppose him. More recently, in

Poland, the Law and Justice Party government's efforts to dismantle checks and balances suffered a setback when President Andrzej Duda, a Law and Justice Party member, vetoed two bills that would have enabled the government to thoroughly purge and pack the supreme court. In Hungary, by contrast, Prime Minister Viktor Orbán faced little resistance from the governing Fidesz party as he made his authoritarian push.

The relationship between Donald Trump and his party is equally important, especially given the Republicans' control over both houses of Congress. Republican leaders could choose to remain loyal. Active loyalists do not merely support the president but publicly defend even his most controversial moves. Passive loyalists retreat from public view when scandals erupt but still vote with the president. Critical loyalists try, in a sense, to have it both ways: They may publicly distance themselves from the president's worst behavior, but they do not take any action (for example, voting in Congress) that will weaken, much less bring down, the president. In the face of presidential abuse, any of these responses will enable authoritarianism.

A second approach is containment. Republicans who adopt this strategy may back the president on many issues, from judicial appointments to tax and health care reform, but draw a line at behavior they consider dangerous. This can be a difficult stance to maintain. As members of the same party, they stand to benefit if the president succeeds—yet they realize that the president could inflict real damage on our institutions in the long term. They work with the president wherever possible while at the same time taking steps to ensure that he does not abuse power, allowing the president to remain in office but, they would hope, constraining him.

Finally, in principle, congressional leaders could seek the president's removal. This would be politically costly for them.

Not only does bringing down one's own president risk accusations of treason from fellow partisans (imagine, for example, the responses of Sean Hannity and Rush Limbaugh), but it also risks derailing the party's legislative agenda. It would hurt the party's short-term electoral prospects, as it did after Nixon's resignation. But if the threat coming from the presidency is severe enough (or if the president's behavior starts to hurt their own poll numbers), party leaders may deem it necessary to bring down one of their own.

During President Trump's first year in office, Republicans responded to presidential abuse with a mix of loyalty and containment. At first, loyalty predominated. But after the president fired James Comey in May 2017, some GOP senators moved toward containment, making it clear that they would not approve a Trump loyalist to succeed him. Republican senators also worked to ensure that an independent investigation into Russia's involvement in the 2016 election would go forward. A few of them pushed quietly for the Justice Department to name a special counsel, and many of them embraced Robert Mueller's appointment. When reports emerged that the White House was exploring ways of removing Mueller, and when some Trump loyalists called for Mueller's removal, important Republican senators, including Susan Collins, Bob Corker, Lindsey Graham, and John McCain, came out in opposition. And when President Trump leaned toward sacking Attorney General Jeff Sessions, who, having recused himself, could not fire Mueller, GOP senators jumped to Sessions's defense. Senate Judiciary Committee Chair Chuck Grassley said he would not schedule hearings for a replacement if Sessions was fired.

Although Senators Graham, McCain, and Corker hardly joined the opposition (each voted with Trump at least 85 percent of the time), they took important steps to contain the president. No Republican leaders sought the president's removal in 2017, but as journalist Abigail Tracy put it, some of them appeared to have "found their own red line."

Another factor affecting the fate of our democracy is public opinion. If would-be authoritarians can't turn to the military or organize large-scale violence, they must find other means of persuading allies to go along and critics to back off or give up. Public support is a useful tool in this regard. When an elected leader enjoys, say, a 70 percent approval rating, critics jump on the bandwagon, media coverage softens, judges grow more reluctant to rule against the government, and even rival politicians, worried that strident opposition will leave them isolated, tend to keep their heads down. By contrast, when the government's approval rating is low, media and opposition grow more brazen, judges become emboldened to stand up to the president, and allies begin to dissent. Fujimori, Chávez, and Erdoğan all enjoyed massive popularity when they launched their assault on democratic institutions.

To understand how public support could affect the Trump presidency, ask yourself: What if America were like West Virginia? West Virginia is the most pro-Trump state in the union. According to a Gallup poll, President Trump's approval rating there averaged 60 percent in the first half of 2017, compared to 40 percent in favor of him nationwide. In the face of the president's popularity, opposition to him withered in West Virginia—even among Democrats. Democratic senator Joe Manchin voted with President Trump 54 percent of the time through August 2017, more than any other Democrat in the Senate. *The Hill* listed Manchin among Trump's "10 Biggest Allies in Congress." The state's Democratic governor, Jim Justice, went further: He switched parties. Embracing President Trump at a rally, Justice not only praised him as a "good man" with "real ideas" but dismissed the Russia investigation, declaring: "Have we not heard enough about the Russians?" If Democrats across the country behaved as they did in West Virginia, President Trump would face little resistance—even on the issue of foreign interference in our election.

The higher President Trump's approval rating, the more dangerous he is. His popularity will depend on the state of the economy, as well as on contingent events. Events that put the government's incompetence on display, such as the Bush administration's inept response to Hurricane Katrina in 2005, can erode public support. But other developments, such as security threats, can boost it.

That brings us to a final factor shaping President Trump's ability to damage our democracy: crisis. Major security crises—wars or large-scale terrorist attacks—are political game changers. Almost invariably, they increase support for the government. Citizens become more likely to tolerate, and even endorse, authoritarian measures when they fear for their security. And it's not only average citizens who respond this way. Judges are notoriously reluctant to block presidential power grabs in the midst of crises, when national security is perceived to be at risk. According to political scientist William Howell, institutional constraints on President Bush disappeared in the wake of the 9/11 attacks, allowing Bush to "do whatever he liked to define and respond to the crisis."

Security crises are, therefore, moments of danger for democracy. Leaders who can "do whatever they like" can inflict great harm upon democratic institutions. As we have seen, that is precisely what leaders such as Fujimori, Putin, and Erdoğan did. For a would-be authoritarian who feels unfairly besieged by opponents and shackled by democratic institutions, crisis opens up a window of opportunity.

In the United States, too, security crises have permitted executive power grabs, from Lincoln's suspension of habeas corpus to Roosevelt's internment of Japanese Americans to Bush's USA PATRIOT Act. But there was an important difference. Lincoln, Roosevelt, and Bush were committed democrats, and at the end of the day, each of them exercised considerable forbearance in wielding the vast authority generated by crisis.

Donald Trump, by contrast, has rarely exhibited forbearance in any context. The chances of a conflict occurring on his watch are also considerable. They would be for any president—the United States fought land wars or suffered major terrorist attacks under six of its last twelve elected presidents. But given President Trump's foreign policy ineptitude, the risks are especially high. We fear that if Trump were to confront a war or terrorist attack, he would exploit this crisis fully—using it to attack political opponents and restrict freedoms Americans take for granted. In our view, this scenario represents the greatest danger facing American democracy today.

Even if President Trump does not directly dismantle democratic institutions, his norm breaking is almost certain to corrode them. President Trump has, as David Brooks has written, "smashed through the behavior standards that once governed public life." His party rewarded him for it by nominating him for president. In office, his continued norm violation has expanded the zone of acceptable presidential behavior, giving tactics that were once considered aberrant and inadmissible, such as lying, cheating, and bullying, a prominent place in politicians' tool kits.

Presidential norm breaking is not inherently bad. Many violations are innocuous. In January 1977, Jimmy Carter surprised the police, the press, and the 250,000 Americans gathered to watch his inauguration when he and his wife *walked* the mile and a half from the Capitol to the White House. The *New York Daily News* described the Carters' decision to abandon the "closed and armored limousine" as an "unprecedented departure from custom." Ever since, it has become what the *New York Times* called "an informal custom" for the president-elect to at least step out of his protected limousine during the inaugural parade to show that he is "the people's president."

Norm breaking can also be democratizing: In the 1840 presidential election, William Henry Harrison broke tradition by going out and campaigning among voters. The previous norm had been for candidates to avoid campaigning, preserving a Cincinnatus-like fiction that they harbored no personal ambition for power—but limiting voters' ability to get to know them.

Or take another example: In 1901, a routine White House press release was issued on behalf of new president Theodore Roosevelt headlined, "Booker T. Washington of Tuskegee, Alabama, dined with the President last evening." While prominent black political leaders had visited the White House before, a dinner with a leading African American political figure was, as one historian has described it, a violation of "the prevailing social etiquette of white domination." The response was immediate and vicious. One newspaper described it as "the most damnable outrage which has ever been perpetrated by any citizen of the United States." Senator William Jennings Bryan commented, "It is hoped that both of them [Roosevelt and Washington] will upon reflection, realize the wisdom of abandoning their purpose to wipe out race lines." In the face of the uproar, the White House's press operation first denied the event happened, later said it had "merely" been a lunch, and then defended it by saying that at least no women had been present.

Because societal values change over time, a degree of presidential norm breaking is inevitable—even desirable. But Donald Trump's norm violations in his first year of office differed fundamentally from those of his predecessors. For one, he was a serial norm breaker. Never has a president flouted so many unwritten rules so quickly. Many of the transgressions were trivial—President Trump broke a 150-year White House tradition by not having a pet. Others were more ominous. Trump's first inaugural address, for example, was darker than such addresses typically are (he spoke, for example, of "American carnage"), leading former President George W. Bush to observe: "That was some weird shit."

But where President Trump really stands out from his predecessors is in his willingness to challenge unwritten rules of greater consequence, including norms that are essential to the health of democracy. Among these are long-standing norms of separating private and public affairs, such as those governing nepotism. Existing legislation, which prohibits presidents from appointing family members to the cabinet or agency positions, does not include White House staff positions. So Trump's appointment of his daughter, Ivanka, and son-in-law, Jared Kushner, to high-level advisory posts was technically legal—but it flouted the spirit of the law.

There were also norms regulating presidential conflicts of interest. Because presidents must not use public office for private enrichment, those who own businesses must separate themselves from these enterprises before they take office. Yet the laws governing such separation are surprisingly lax. Government officials are not technically required to divest themselves of their holdings, but only to recuse themselves from decisions that affect their interests. It has become standard practice for government officials to simply divest themselves, however, to avoid even the appearance of a wrongdoing. President Trump exercised no such forbearance, despite his unprecedented conflicts of interest. He granted his sons control over his business holdings, in a move deemed vastly insufficient by government ethics officials. The Office of Government Ethics reported receiving 39,105 public complaints involving Trump administration conflicts of interest between October 1, 2016, and March 31, 2017, a massive increase over the same period in 2008–2009 (when President Obama took office), when just 733 complaints were recorded.

President Trump also violated core democratic norms when he openly challenged the legitimacy of elections. Although his claim of "millions" of illegal voters was rejected by fact checkers, repudiated by politicians from both parties, and dismissed as baseless by social scientists, the new president repeated it in public and in private. No major politician in more than a century had questioned the integrity of the American electoral process—not even Al Gore, who lost one of the closest elections in history at the hands of the Supreme Court.

False charges of fraud can undermine public confidence in elections—and when citizens do not trust the electoral process, they often lose faith in democracy itself. In Mexico, after the losing presidential candidate, Andrés Manuel López Obrador, insisted that the 2006 election was stolen from him, confidence in Mexico's electoral system declined. A poll taken prior to the 2012 presidential election found that 71 percent of Mexicans believed that fraud could be in play. In the United States, the figures were even more dramatic. In a survey carried out prior to the 2016 election, 84 percent of Republican voters said they believed a "meaningful amount" of fraud occurred in American elections, and nearly 60 percent of Republican voters said they believed illegal immigrants would "vote in meaningful amounts" in November. These doubts persisted after the election. According to a July 2017 Morning Consult/Politico poll, 47 percent of Republicans believed that Trump won the popular vote, compared to 40 percent who believed Hillary Clinton won. In other words, about half of self-identified Republicans said they believe that American elections are massively rigged. Such beliefs may be consequential. A survey conducted in June 2017 asked, "If Donald Trump were to say that the 2020 presidential election should be postponed until the country can make sure that only eligible American citizens can vote, would you support or oppose postponing the election?" Fifty-two percent of Republicans said they would support postponement.

President Trump also abandoned basic rules of political civility. He broke with norms of postelection reconciliation by continuing to attack Hillary Clinton. He also violated the unwritten rule that sitting presidents should not attack their predecessor. At 6:35 A.M. on March 4, 2017, President Trump tweeted, "Terrible! Just found out that Obama had my 'wires tapped' in Trump Tower just before the victory. Nothing found. This is McCarthyism!" He followed up half an hour later with: "How low has President Obama gone to tapp [*sic*] my phones during the very sacred election process. This is Nixon/Watergate. Bad (or sick) guy!"

Perhaps President Trump's most notorious norm-breaking behavior has been lying. The idea that presidents should tell the truth in public is uncontroversial in American politics. As Republican consultant Whit Ayers likes to tell his clients,

candidates seeking credibility must "never deny the undeniable" and "never lie." Given this norm, politicians typically
avoid lying by changing the topic of debate, reframing difficult
questions, or only partly answering them. President Trump's
routine, brazen fabrications are unprecedented. His tendencies
were manifest during the 2016 campaign. *PolitiFact* classified
69 percent of his public statements as "mostly false" (21 percent), "false" (33 percent), or "pants on fire" (15 percent). Only
17 percent were coded as "true" or "mostly true."

Trump continued to lie as president. Tracing all the president's public statements since taking office, the *New York Times*
showed that even using a conservative metric—demonstrably
false statements, as opposed to merely dubious ones—President
Trump "achieved something remarkable": He made at least
one false or misleading public statement every single day of his
first forty days in office. No lie is too obvious. President Trump
claimed the largest Electoral College victory since Ronald Reagan (in fact, George H. W. Bush, Clinton, and Obama all won
by larger margins than he did); he claimed to have signed more
bills in his first six months than any other president (he was
well behind several presidents, including George H. W. Bush
and Clinton). In July 2017, he bragged that the head of the Boy
Scouts told him he had "made the greatest speech ever made to
them," only to have the claim disputed immediately by the Boy
Scouts organization itself.

President Trump himself did not pay much of a price for
his lies. In a political and media environment in which engaged
citizens increasingly filter events through their own partisan
lenses, his supporters did not come to view him as dishonest
during the first year of his presidency. For our political system, however, the consequences of his dishonesty are devastating. Citizens have a basic right to information in a democracy.

Without credible information about what our elected leaders do, we cannot effectively exercise our right to vote. When the president of the United States lies to the public, our access to credible information is jeopardized, and trust in government is eroded (how could it *not* be?). When citizens do not believe their elected leaders, the foundations of representative democracy weaken. The value of elections is diminished when citizens have no faith in the leaders they elect.

Exacerbating this loss of faith is President Trump's abandonment of basic norms of respect for the media. An independent press is a bulwark of democratic institutions; no democracy can live without it. Every American president since Washington has done battle with the media. Many of them privately despised it. But with few exceptions, U.S. presidents have recognized the media's centrality as a democratic institution and respected its place in the political system. Even presidents who scorned the media in private treated it with a certain minimum of respect and civility in public. This basic norm gave rise to a host of unwritten rules governing the president's relationship with the press. Some of these norms—such as waving to the press corps before boarding Air Force One—were superficial, but others, such as holding press conferences accessible to all members of the White House press corps, were more significant.

President Trump's public insults of media outlets and even individual journalists were without precedent in modern U.S. history. He described the media as "among the most dishonest human beings on Earth," and repeatedly accused such critical news outlets as the *New York Times*, the *Washington Post*, and CNN of lying or delivering "fake news." Trump was not above personal attacks. In June 2017, he went after television host Mika Brzezinski and her cohost Joe Scarborough in a uniquely vitriolic tweetstorm:

> I heard poorly rated @Morning_Joe speaks badly of me (don't watch anymore). Then how come low I.Q. Crazy Mika, along with Psycho Joe, came . . .
>
> . . . to Mar-a-Lago 3 nights in a row around New Year's Eve, and insisted on joining me. She was bleeding badly from a face-lift. I said no!

Even Richard Nixon, who privately viewed the media as "the enemy," never made such public attacks. To find comparable behavior in this hemisphere one must look at Hugo Chávez and Nicolás Maduro in Venezuela or Rafael Correa in Ecuador.

The Trump administration also broke established norms by selectively excluding reporters from press events. On February 24, 2017, Press Secretary Sean Spicer barred reporters from the *New York Times*, CNN, *Politico*, *BuzzFeed*, and the *Los Angeles Times* from attending an untelevised press "gaggle," while handpicking journalists from smaller but sympathetic outlets such as the *Washington Times* and One America News Network to round out the pool. The only modern precedent for such a move was Nixon's decision to bar the *Washington Post* from the White House after it broke the Watergate scandal.

In 1993, New York's Democratic senator Daniel Patrick Moynihan, a former social scientist, made an incisive observation: Humans have a limited ability to cope with people behaving in ways that depart from shared standards. When unwritten rules are violated over and over, Moynihan observed, societies have a tendency to "define deviancy down"—to shift the standard. What was once seen as abnormal becomes normal.

Moynihan applied this insight, controversially, to America's growing social tolerance for single-parent families, high murder rates, and mental illness. Today it can be applied to American democracy. Although political deviance—the violation of unwritten rules of civility, of respect for the press, of *not lying*—did not originate with Donald Trump, his presidency is accelerating it. Under President Trump, America has been defining political deviancy down. The president's routine use of personal insult, bullying, lying, and cheating has, inevitably, helped to normalize such practices. Trump's tweets may trigger outrage from the media, Democrats, and some Republicans, but the effectiveness of their responses is limited by the sheer quantity of violations. As Moynihan observed, in the face of widespread deviance, we become overwhelmed—and then desensitized. We grow accustomed to what we previously thought to be scandalous.

Furthermore, Trump's deviance has been tolerated by the Republican Party, which has helped make it acceptable to much of the Republican electorate. To be sure, many Republicans have condemned Trump's most egregious behavior. But these one-off statements are not very punitive. All but one Republican senator voted with President Trump at least 85 percent of the time during his first seven months in office. Even Senators Ben Sasse of Nebraska and Jeff Flake of Arizona, who often strongly condemned the president's norm violations, voted with him 94 percent of the time. There is no "containment" strategy for an endless stream of offensive tweets. Unwilling to pay the political price of breaking with their own president, Republicans find themselves with little alternative but to constantly redefine what is and isn't tolerable.

This will have terrible consequences for our democracy.

President Trump's assault on basic norms has expanded the bounds of acceptable political behavior. We may already be seeing some of the consequences. In May 2017, Greg Gianforte, the Republican candidate in a special election for Congress, body-slammed a reporter from *The Guardian* who was asking him about health care reform. Gianforte was charged with misdemeanor assault—but he won the election. More generally, a YouGov poll carried out for *The Economist* in mid-2017 revealed a striking level of intolerance toward the media, especially among Republicans. When asked whether or not they favored permitting the courts to shut down media outlets for presenting information that is "biased or inaccurate," 45 percent of Republicans who were polled said they favored it, whereas only 20 percent were opposed. More than 50 percent of Republicans supported the idea of imposing fines for biased or inaccurate reporting. In other words, a majority of Republican voters said they support the kind of media repression seen in recent years in Ecuador, Turkey, and Venezuela.

Two National Rifle Association recruiting videos were released in the summer of 2017. In the first video, NRA spokeswoman Dana Loesch speaks about Democrats and the use of force:

> They use their schools to teach children that their president is another Hitler. They use their movie stars and singers and comedy shows and award shows to repeat their narrative over and over again. And then they use their ex-president to endorse the "resistance." All to make them march, to make them protest, to make them scream racism and sexism and xenopho-

bia and homophobia. To smash windows, to burn cars, to burn cars, to shut down interstates and airports, bully and terrorize the law-abiding, until the only option left is for the police to do their jobs and stop the madness. And when that happens, they use it as an excuse for their outrage. The only way we stop this, the only way we save our country and our freedom, is to fight the violence of lies with the clenched fist of truth.

In the second video, Loesch issues a not-so-subtle warning of violence against the *New York Times*:

> We've had it with your pretentious . . . assertion that you are in any way truth- or fact-based journalism. Consider this the shot across your proverbial bow. . . . In short, we're coming for you.

The NRA is not a small, fringe organization. It claims five million members and is closely tied to the Republican Party— Donald Trump and Sarah Palin are lifetime members. Yet it now uses words that in the past we would have regarded as dangerously politically deviant.

Norms are the soft guardrails of democracy; as they break down, the zone of acceptable political behavior expands, giving rise to discourse and action that could imperil democracy. Behavior that was once considered unthinkable in American politics is becoming thinkable. Even if Donald Trump does not break the hard guardrails of our constitutional democracy, he has increased the likelihood that a future president will.

Saving Democracy

Writing this book has reminded us that American democracy is not as exceptional as we sometimes believe. There's nothing in our Constitution or our culture to immunize us against democratic breakdown. We have experienced political catastrophe before, when regional and partisan enmities so divided the nation that it collapsed into civil war. Our constitutional system recovered, and Republican and Democratic leaders developed new norms and practices that would undergird more than a century of political stability. But that stability came at the price of racial exclusion and authoritarian single-party rule in the South. It was only after 1965 that the United States fully democratized. And, paradoxically, that very process began a fundamental realignment of the American electorate that has once again left our parties deeply polarized. This polarization, deeper than at any time since the end of Reconstruction, has triggered the epidemic of norm breaking that now challenges our democracy.

There is a mounting perception that democracy is in retreat all over the world. Venezuela. Thailand. Turkey. Hungary. Poland. Larry Diamond, perhaps the foremost authority on democracy worldwide, believes we have entered a period of democratic recession. Might America's current crisis be part of a global wave of backsliding? We are skeptical. Prior to Donald Trump's election, claims about a global democratic recession were exaggerated. The number of democracies rose dramatically in the 1980s and 1990s, peaked around the year 2005, and has remained steady ever since. Backsliders make headlines and capture our attention, but for every Hungary, Turkey, and Venezuela there is a Colombia, Sri Lanka, or Tunisia—countries that have grown *more* democratic over the last decade. The vast majority of the world's democracies—from Argentina, Brazil, Chile, and Peru to Greece, Spain, the Czech Republic, and Romania to Ghana, India, South Korea, and South Africa—remain intact. And although European democracies face many problems, from weak economies to EU skepticism to anti-immigrant backlash, there is little evidence in any of them of the kind of fundamental erosion of norms we have seen in the United States.

But Trump's rise may itself pose a challenge to global democracy. Between the fall of the Berlin Wall and the Obama presidency, U.S. governments maintained a broadly prodemocratic foreign policy. There were numerous exceptions: Wherever America's strategic interests were at stake, as in China, Russia, and the Middle East, democracy disappeared from the agenda. But in much of Africa, Asia, Eastern Europe, and Latin America, U.S. governments used diplomatic pressure, economic assistance, and other foreign policy tools to oppose authoritarianism and press for democratization during the post–Cold War era. The 1990–2015 period was easily the most democratic quarter century in world history—partly because Western powers broadly supported democracy. That may now be changing. Under Donald Trump, the United States appears to be abandoning its role as democracy promoter for the first time since the Cold War. President Trump's is the least prodemo-cratic of any U.S. administration since Nixon's. Moreover, America is no longer a democratic model. A country whose president attacks the press, threatens to lock up his rival, and declares that he might not accept election results cannot cred-ibly defend democracy. Both existing and potential autocrats are likely to be emboldened with Trump in the White House. So even if the idea of a global democratic recession was largely a myth before 2016, the Trump presidency—together with the crisis of the EU, the rise of China, and the growing aggressive-ness of Russia—could help make it a reality.

Turning back to our own country, we see three possible futures for a post-Trump America. The first, and most optimistic, is a swift democratic recovery. In this scenario, President Trump fails politically: He either loses public support and is not re-elected or, more dramatically, is impeached or forced to resign. The implosion of Trump's presidency and the triumph of the anti-Trump resistance energize the Democrats, who then sweep back into power and reverse Trump's most egregious policies. If President Trump were to fail badly enough, public disgust could even motivate reforms that improve the quality of our democracy, as occurred in the aftermath of Richard Nixon's resignation in 1974. Republican leaders, having paid a heavy price for their association with Trump, might end their flirta-tion with extremist politics. In this future, America's reputation in the world would be quickly restored. The Trump interlude would be taught in schools, recounted in films, and recited in historical works as an era of tragic mistakes where catastrophe was avoided and American democracy saved.

This is certainly the future many of us hope for. But it is unlikely. Recall that the assault on long-standing democratic norms—and the underlying polarization driving it—began well before Donald Trump ascended to the White House. The soft guardrails of American democracy have been weakening for decades; simply removing President Trump will not miraculously restore them. Although Trump's presidency may ultimately be seen as a momentary aberration with only modest footprints on our institutions, ending it may not be enough to restore a healthy democracy.

A second, much darker future is one in which President Trump and the Republicans continue to win with a white nationalist appeal. Under this scenario, a pro-Trump GOP would retain the presidency, both houses of Congress, and the vast majority of statehouses, and it would eventually gain a solid majority in the Supreme Court. It would then use the techniques of constitutional hardball to manufacture durable white electoral majorities. This could be done through a combination of large-scale deportation, immigration restrictions, the purging of voter rolls, and the adoption of strict voter ID laws. Measures to reengineer the electorate would likely be accompanied by elimination of the filibuster and other rules that protect Senate minorities, so that Republicans could impose their agenda even with narrow majorities. These measures may appear extreme, but every one of them has been at least contemplated by the Trump administration.

Efforts to shore up the Republican Party by engineering a new white majority would, of course, be profoundly antidemocratic. Such measures would trigger resistance from a broad range of forces, including progressives, minority groups, and much of the private sector. This resistance could lead to escalating confrontation and even violent conflict, which, in turn, could bring heightened police repression and private vigilantism—in the name of "law and order." For a sense of how such a crackdown might be framed, watch recent NRA recruitment videos or listen to how Republican politicians talk about Black Lives Matter.

Such a nightmare scenario isn't likely, but it also isn't inconceivable. It is difficult to find examples of societies in which shrinking ethnic majorities gave up their dominant status without a fight. In Lebanon, the demographic decline of dominant Christian groups contributed to a fifteen-year civil war. In Israel, the demographic threat created by the de facto annexation of the West Bank is pushing the country toward a political system that two of its former prime ministers have compared to apartheid. And closer to home, in the aftermath of Reconstruction, southern Democrats responded to the threat posed by black suffrage by disenfranchising African Americans for nearly a century. Although white nationalists remain a minority within the GOP, the growing push for strict voter ID laws and the purging of voter rolls—championed by influential Republicans Attorney General Jeff Sessions and Commission on Election Integrity Co-chair Kris Kobach—suggest that electoral reengineering is on the GOP agenda.

The third, and in our view, most likely, post-Trump future is one marked by polarization, more departures from unwritten political conventions, and increasing institutional warfare—in other words, democracy without solid guardrails. President Trump and Trumpism may well fail in this scenario, but that failure would do little to narrow the divide between parties or reverse the decline in mutual toleration and forbearance.

To see what politics without guardrails might look like in the United States, consider North Carolina today. North Carolina is a classic "purple" state. With a diversified economy and an internationally recognized university system, it is wealthier, more urban, and better educated than most southern states. It is also demographically diverse, with African Americans, Asian Americans, and Latinos making up about a third of the population. All this makes North Carolina more hospitable terrain for Democrats than are the states of the Deep South. North Carolina's electorate resembles the national one: It is evenly split between Democrats and Republicans, with Democrats dominant in such urban centers as Charlotte and Raleigh-Durham and Republicans dominant in rural areas.

The state has become, in the words of Duke law professor Jedediah Purdy, a "microcosm of the country's hyper-partisan politics and growing mutual mistrust." Over the last decade, partisans have battled over Republican-imposed abortion restrictions, the Republican governor's refusal of Medicaid as part of the Affordable Care Act, a proposed constitutional amendment to ban same-sex marriage, and, most famous, the 2016 Public Facilities Privacy & Security Act (the "Bathroom Bill"), which barred local governments from allowing transgender people to use public bathrooms for the sex they identify as. All these initiatives triggered intense opposition. As one veteran Republican put it, state politics has become "more polarized and more acrimonious than I've ever seen it. . . . And I worked for Jesse Helms."

By most accounts, North Carolina's descent into all-out political warfare began after the Republicans won control of the state legislature in 2010. The following year, the legislature approved a redistricting plan that was widely viewed as "racially gerrymandered"—districts were carved out in ways that concentrated African American voters into a small number of districts, thereby diluting their electoral weight and maximizing Republican seat gains. Progressive pastor William Barber, leader of the Moral Mondays movement, described the new districts as "apartheid voting districts." The changes enabled Republicans to capture nine of the state's thirteen congressional seats in 2012—even though Democrats cast more votes statewide.

After Republican Pat McCrory's 2012 gubernatorial victory gave Republicans control of all three branches of government, the state GOP tried to lock in its dominance for the long haul. Armed with the governorship, both legislative chambers, and a majority on the state Supreme Court, Republican leaders launched an ambitious string of reforms designed to skew the political game. They began by demanding access to background data on voters across the state. With this information in hand, the legislature passed a series of electoral reforms making it harder for voters to cast their ballots. They passed a strict voter ID law, reduced opportunities for early voting, ended preregistration for sixteen- and seventeen-year-olds, eliminated same-day registration, and slashed the number of polling places in several key counties. New data allowed the Republicans to design the reforms to target African American voters, as a federal appeals court put it, with "almost surgical precision." And when an appeals court suspended the execution of the new laws, Republicans used their control of the state's election boards to implement several of them anyway.

Institutional warfare persisted after Democrat Roy Cooper narrowly defeated McCrory for the governorship in 2016. McCrory refused to concede the race for nearly a month, as Republicans made baseless accusations of voter fraud. But that was only the beginning. After McCrory finally conceded in December 2016, Republicans called a "surprise special session" of the state legislature. In a testament to how far politics had deteriorated, rumors spread of an impending "legislative coup," in which Republicans would hand the election to McCrory by exploiting a law allowing legislators to intervene when the results of a gubernatorial election are challenged.

No such coup occurred, but in what the *New York Times* described as a "brazen power grab," the special session passed several measures to reduce the power of the incoming Democratic governor. The Senate granted itself the authority to confirm gubernatorial cabinet appointments, and it empowered the sitting Republican governor to transfer temporary political appointees into permanent positions. Outgoing governor McCrory quickly granted tenure to nearly one thousand of his handpicked gubernatorial staffers—essentially "packing" the executive branch. Republicans then changed the composition of the state's election boards, which were responsible for local rules involving gerrymandering, voter registration, voter ID requirements, voting hours, and the distribution of polling places. The boards had been under the control of the sitting governor, who could award his party a majority of seats; now the GOP created a system of equal partisan representation. In another twist, the chair of the election boards would rotate between the two parties each year, with the party with the second-largest membership (the GOP) holding the chair in even years—which are election years. A few months later, the legislature voted to shrink the state court of appeals by three seats, effectively stealing three judicial appointments from Governor Cooper.

Although the racially gerrymandered districts, the 2013 voter law, and the reform of the election boards were later struck down by the courts, their passage revealed a Republican Party willing to leverage its full power to cripple its political adversaries. Congressman David Price, a Democrat from Chapel Hill, said the legislative crisis taught him that "American democracy may be more fragile than we realized."

North Carolina offers a window into what politics without guardrails looks like—and a possible glimpse into America's future. When partisan rivals become enemies, political competition descends into warfare, and our institutions turn into weapons. The result is a system hovering constantly on the brink of crisis.

This grim scenario highlights a central lesson of this book: When American democracy has worked, it has relied upon two norms that we often take for granted—mutual tolerance and institutional forbearance. Treating rivals as legitimate contenders for power and underutilizing one's institutional prerogatives in the spirit of fair play are not written into the American Constitution. Yet without them, our constitutional checks and balances will not operate as we expect them to. When French thinker Baron de Montesquieu pioneered the notion of separation of powers in his 1748 work *The Spirit of the Laws*, he worried little about what we today call norms. Montesquieu believed the hard architecture of political institutions might be enough to constrain overreaching power—that constitutional design was not unlike an engineering problem, a challenge of crafting institutions so that ambition could be used to counteract ambition, even when political leaders were flawed. Many of our founders believed this, as well.

History quickly revealed that the founders were mistaken. Without innovations such as political parties and their accompanying norms, the Constitution they so carefully constructed in Philadelphia would not have survived. Institutions were more than just formal rules; they encompassed the shared understandings of appropriate behavior that overlay them. The genius of the first generation of America's political leaders was not that they created foolproof institutions, but that, in addition to designing very good institutions, they—gradually and with difficulty—established a set of shared beliefs and practices that helped make those institutions work.

The strength of the American political system, it has often been said, rests on what Swedish Nobel Prize–winning economist Gunnar Myrdal called the American Creed: the principles of individual freedom and egalitarianism. Written into our founding documents and repeated in classrooms, speeches, and editorial pages, freedom and equality are self-justifying values. But they are not self-executing. Mutual toleration and institutional forbearance are procedural principles—they tell politicians how to behave, beyond the bounds of law, to make our institutions function. We should regard these procedural values as also sitting at the center of the American Creed—for without them, our democracy would not work.

This has important implications for how citizens oppose the Trump administration. In the wake of the 2016 election, many progressive opinion makers concluded that Democrats needed to "fight like Republicans." If Republicans were going to break the rules, the argument went, Democrats had no choice but to respond in kind. Acting with self-restraint and civility while the other side abandoned forbearance would be like a boxer entering the ring with a hand tied behind his back. When confronted with a bully who is willing to use any means necessary to win, those who play by the rules risk playing the sucker. The GOP's refusal to allow President Obama to fill a Supreme Court vacancy left Democrats feeling sucker-punched, particularly after

Trump's victory ensured that they would get away with it. Political scientist and writer David Faris typified the calls to "fight dirty":

> The Democratic negotiating position on all issues . . . should be very simple: You will give us Merrick Garland or you may go die in a fire. . . . Not only that, but they should do what they should have done the day Antonin Scalia died: Make it clear that the next time the Democrats control the Senate while the Republican Party controls the presidency. . . . there will be an extraordinarily high price to pay for what just transpired. The next Republican president facing divided government will get *nothing*. . . . Zero confirmations. No judges, not even to the lowliest district court in the country. No Cabinet heads. No laws.

Immediately after President Trump's election, some progressives called for actions to prevent him from assuming office. In an op-ed entitled "Buck Up, Democrats, and Fight Like Republicans," published a month *before* Trump's inauguration, Dahlia Lithwick and David S. Cohen lamented that Democrats were "doing little to stop him." Although there was "no shortage of legal theories that could challenge Mr. Trump's anointment," they wrote, Democrats were not pursuing them. Lithwick and Cohen argued that Democrats "should be fighting tooth and nail" to prevent Donald Trump from taking office—pushing recounts and fraud investigations in Michigan, Pennsylvania, and Wisconsin, seeking to sway the Electoral College, and even trying to overturn President Trump's victory in court.

On Inauguration Day, some Democrats questioned Donald

Trump's legitimacy as president. Representative Jerry McNerney of California boycotted the inauguration, claiming the election "lacks legitimacy" because of Russian interference; likewise, Representative John Lewis of Georgia declared that he did not view President Trump as a "legitimate president." Nearly seventy House Democrats boycotted Trump's inauguration.

After Trump was installed in the White House, some progressives called on Democrats to "take a page from the GOP playbook and obstruct everything." Markos Moulitsas, founder of the website *Daily Kos*, declared, for example, that "there is nothing that should be going through that Senate without Republicans having to fight. I don't care if it's the morning prayer. Everything should be a fight."

Some Democrats even raised the specter of an early impeachment. Less than two weeks after Trump's inauguration, Representative Maxine Waters tweeted, "my greatest desire [is] to lead @realDonaldTrump right into impeachment." Impeachment talk picked up after FBI Director James Comey was fired, reinforced by Trump's sliding popularity, which raised Democrats' hopes of winning the House majority necessary to lead an impeachment process. In a May 2017 interview, Waters declared, "Some people don't even want to mention the word. It's almost as if it's too grandiose an idea. It's too hard to do, just too much to think about. I don't see it that way."

In our view, the idea that Democrats should "fight like Republicans" is misguided. First of all, evidence from other countries suggests that such a strategy often plays directly into the hands of authoritarians. Scorched-earth tactics often erode support for the opposition by scaring off moderates. And they unify progovernment forces, as even dissidents within the incumbent party close ranks in the face of an uncompromising opposition. And when the opposition fights dirty, it provides the government with justification for cracking down.

This is what happened in Venezuela under Hugo Chávez. Although the first few years of Chávez's presidency were democratic, opponents found his populist discourse terrifying. Fearful that Chávez would steer Venezuela toward Cuban-style socialism, they tried to remove him preemptively—and by any means necessary. In April 2002, opposition leaders backed a military coup, which not only failed but destroyed their image as democrats. Undeterred, the opposition launched an indefinite general strike in December 2002, seeking to shut the country down until Chávez resigned. The strike lasted two months, costing Venezuela an estimated $4.5 billion and ultimately failing. Anti-Chávez forces then boycotted the 2005 legislative elections, but this did little more than allow the *chavistas* to gain total control over Congress. All three strategies had backfired. Not only did they fail to knock Chávez out, but they eroded the opposition's public support, allowed Chávez to tag his rivals as antidemocratic, and handed the government an excuse to purge the military, the police, and the courts, arrest or exile dissidents, and close independent media outlets. Weakened and discredited, the opposition could not stop the regime's subsequent descent into authoritarianism.

Opposition strategies in Colombia under President Álvaro Uribe were more successful. Uribe, who was elected in 2002, launched a power grab not unlike Chávez's: His administration attacked critics as subversive and terrorist, spied on opponents and journalists, tried to weaken the courts, and twice sought to modify the constitution to run for another term. In response, unlike their Venezuelan counterparts, the Colombian opposition never attempted to topple Uribe through extraconstitutional means. Instead, as political scientist Laura Gamboa shows, they focused their efforts on the congress and the courts. This made it more difficult for Uribe to question his opponents' democratic credentials or justify cracking down on them. Despite Uribe's abuses, Venezuelan-style institutional warfare did not occur, and Colombia's democratic institutions did not come under threat. In February 2010, the Constitutional Court struck down Uribe's bid for a third term as unconstitutional, forcing him to step down after two terms. The lesson is this: Where institutional channels exist, opposition groups should use them.

Even if Democrats were to succeed in weakening or removing President Trump via hardball tactics, their victory would be Pyrrhic—for they would inherit a democracy stripped of its remaining protective guardrails. If the Trump administration were brought to its knees by obstructionism, or if President Trump were impeached without a strong bipartisan consensus, the effect would be to reinforce—and perhaps hasten—the dynamics of partisan antipathy and norm erosion that helped bring Trump to power to begin with. As much as a third of the country would likely view Trump's impeachment as the machinations of a vast left-wing conspiracy—maybe even as a coup. American politics would be left dangerously unmoored.

This sort of escalation rarely ends well. If Democrats do not work to restore norms of mutual toleration and forbearance, their next president will likely confront an opposition willing to use any means necessary to defeat them. And if partisan rifts deepen and our unwritten rules continue to fray, Americans could eventually elect a president who is even more dangerous than Trump.

Opposition to the Trump administration's authoritarian behavior should be muscular, but it should seek to preserve, rather than violate, democratic rules and norms. Where possible, opposition should center on Congress, the courts, and, of course, elections. If Trump is defeated via democratic institutions, it will strengthen those institutions.

Protest should be viewed in a similar way. Public protest is a basic right and an important activity in any democracy, but its aim should be the defense of rights and institutions, rather than their disruption. In an important study of the effects of black protest in the 1960s, political scientist Omar Wasow found that black-led nonviolent protest fortified the national civil rights agenda in Washington and broadened public support for that agenda. By contrast, violent protest led to a decline in white support and may have tipped the 1968 election from Humphrey to Nixon.

We should learn from our own history. Anti-Trump forces should build a broad prodemocratic coalition. Contemporary coalition building is often a coming-together of like-minded groups: Progressive synagogues, mosques, Catholic parishes, and Presbyterian churches may form an interfaith coalition to combat poverty or racial intolerance, or Latino, faith-based, and civil liberties groups might form a coalition to defend immigrant rights. Coalitions of the like-minded are important, but they are not enough to defend democracy. The most effective coalitions are those that bring together groups with dissimilar—even opposing—views on many issues. They are built not among friends but among adversaries. An effective coalition in defense of American democracy, then, would likely require that progressives forge alliances with business executives, religious (and particularly white evangelical) leaders, and red-state Republicans. Business leaders may not be natural allies of Democratic activists, but they have good reasons to oppose an unstable and rule-breaking administration. And they can be powerful partners. Think of recent boycott movements aimed at state governments that refused to honor Martin Luther King Jr.'s birthday, continued to fly the Confederate flag, or violated gay or transgender rights. When major businesses join progressive boycotts, they often succeed.

Building coalitions that extend beyond our natural allies is difficult. It requires a willingness to set aside, for the moment, issues we care deeply about. If progressives make positions on issues such as abortion rights or single-payer health care a "litmus test" for coalition membership, the chances for building a coalition that includes evangelicals and Republican business executives will be nil. We must lengthen our time horizons, swallow hard, and make tough concessions. This does *not* mean abandoning the causes that matter to us. It means temporarily overlooking disagreements in order to find common moral ground.

A broad opposition coalition would have important benefits. For one, it would strengthen the defenders of democracy by appealing to a much wider sector of American society. Rather than confining anti-Trumpism to progressive blue-state circles, it would extend it to a wider range of America. Such broad involvement is critical to isolating and defeating authoritarian governments.

In addition, whereas a narrow (urban, secular, progressive) anti-Trump coalition would reinforce the current axes of partisan division, a broader coalition would crosscut these axes and maybe even help dampen them. A political movement that brings together—even if temporarily—Bernie Sanders supporters and businesspeople, evangelicals and secular feminists, and small-town Republicans and urban Black Lives Matter supporters, will open channels of communication across the vast chasm that has emerged between our country's two main partisan camps. And it might help foster more crosscutting allegiances in a society that has too few of them. Where a society's political divisions are crosscutting, we line up on different sides of issues with different people at different times. We may disagree with our neighbors on abortion but agree with them on health care; we may dislike another neighbor's views on immigration but agree with them on the need to raise the minimum wage. Such alliances help us build and sustain norms of mutual toleration. When we agree with our political rivals at least some of the time, we are less likely to view them as mortal enemies.

Thinking about how to resist the Trump administration's abuses is clearly important. However, the fundamental problem facing American democracy remains extreme partisan division—one fueled not just by policy differences but by deeper sources of resentment, including racial and religious differences. America's great polarization preceded the Trump presidency, and it is very likely to endure beyond it.

Political leaders have two options in the face of extreme polarization. First, they can take society's divisions as a given but try to counteract them through elite-level cooperation and compromise. This is what Chilean politicians did. As we saw in Chapter 5, intense conflict between the Socialists and the Christian Democrats helped destroy Chilean democracy in 1973. A profound distrust between the two parties persisted for years afterward, trumping their shared revulsion toward Pinochet's dictatorship. Exiled Socialist leader Ricardo Lagos, who lectured at the University of North Carolina, recalled that when former Christian Democratic president Eduardo Frei Montalva visited the university in 1975, he decided that he couldn't bear to talk to him—so he called in sick.

But eventually, politicians started talking. In 1978, Lagos returned to Chile and was invited to dinner by former Christian Democratic senator Tomás Reyes. They began to meet regularly. At around the same time, Christian Democratic leader Patricio Aylwin attended meetings of lawyers and academics from diverse partisan backgrounds, many of whom had crossed paths in courtrooms while defending political prisoners. These "Group of 24" meetings were just casual dinners in members' homes, but according to Aylwin, they "built up trust among those of us who had been adversaries." Eventually, the conversations bore fruit. In August 1985, the Christian Democrats, Socialists, and nineteen other parties gathered in Santiago's elegant Spanish Circle Club and signed the National Accord for a Transition to a Full Democracy. The pact formed the basis for the Democratic Concertation coalition. The coalition developed a practice of "consensus politics," in which key decisions were negotiated between Socialist and Christian Democratic leaders. It was successful. Not only did the Democratic Concertation topple Pinochet in a 1988 plebiscite, but it won the presidency in 1989 and held it for two decades.

The Concertation developed a governing style that broke sharply with the politics of the 1970s. Fearful that renewed conflict would threaten Chile's new democracy, leaders developed a practice of informal cooperation—which Chileans called "democracy of agreements"—in which presidents consulted the leaders of all parties before submitting legislation to congress. Pinochet's 1980 constitution had created a dominant executive with the authority to impose budgets more or less unilaterally, but President Aylwin, a Christian Democrat, consulted extensively with the Socialists and other parties before submitting his proposed budgets. And he didn't just consult his allies. Aylwin also negotiated legislation with right-wing parties that had backed the dictatorship and defended Pinochet. According to political scientist Peter Siavelis, the new norms "helped stave off potentially destabilizing conflicts both within the coalition and between the coalition and the opposition." Chile has been one of Latin America's most stable and successful democracies over the last three decades.

It is doubtful that Democrats and Republicans can follow the Chilean path. It's easy for politicians to bemoan the absence of civility and cooperation, or to wax nostalgic about the bipartisanship of a bygone era. But norm creation is a collective venture—it is only possible when a critical mass of leaders accepts and plays by new unwritten rules. This usually happens when political leaders from across the spectrum have stared into the abyss and realized that if they do not find a way of addressing polarization, democracy will die. Often, it is only when politicians suffer the trauma of violent dictatorship, as they did in Chile, or even civil war, as in Spain, that the stakes truly become clear.

The alternative to learning to cooperate despite underlying polarization is to overcome that polarization. In the United States, political scientists have proposed an array of electoral reforms—an end to gerrymandering, open primaries, obligatory voting, alternative rules for electing members of Congress, to name just a few—that might mitigate partisan enmity in America. The evidence of their effectiveness, however, is far from clear. We think it would be more valuable to focus on two underlying forces driving American polarization: racial and religious realignment and growing economic inequality. Addressing these social foundations, we believe, requires a reshuffling of what America's political parties stand for.

The Republican Party has been the main driver of the chasm between the parties. Since 2008, the GOP has at times behaved like an antisystem party in its obstructionism, partisan hostility, and extremist policy positions. Its twenty-five-year march to the right was made possible by the hollowing out of its organizational core. Over the last quarter century, the party's leadership structure has been eviscerated—first by the rise of well-funded outside groups (such as Americans for Tax Freedom, Americans for Prosperity, and many others) whose fund-raising prowess allowed them to more or less dictate the policy agenda of many GOP elected officials, but also by the mounting influence of Fox News and other right-wing media. Wealthy outside donors such as the Koch brothers and influential media personalities exert greater influence over elected Republican officials than does the GOP's own leadership. Republicans still win elections across the country, but what used to be called the Republican "establishment" has today become a phantom. This hollowing out has left the party vulnerable to takeover by extremists.

Reducing polarization requires that the Republican Party be reformed, if not refounded outright. First of all, the GOP must rebuild its own establishment. This means regaining leadership control in four key areas: finance, grassroots organization, messaging, and candidate selection. Only if the party leadership can free itself from the clutches of outside donors and right-wing media can it go about transforming itself. This entails major changes: Republicans must marginalize extremist elements; they must build a more diverse electoral constituency, such that the party no longer depends so heavily on its shrinking white Christian base; and they must find ways to win elections without appealing to white nationalism, or what Republican Arizona senator Jeff Flake calls the "sugar high of populism, nativism, and demagoguery."

A refounding of America's major center-right party is a tall

order, but there are historical precedents for such transforma-
tions—and under even more challenging circumstances. And
where it has been successful, conservative party reform has
catalyzed democracy's rebirth. A particularly dramatic case is
the democratization of West Germany after the Second World
War. At the center of this achievement was an underappreciated
development: the formation of Germany's center-right Christian Democratic Union (CDU) out of the wreckage of a discredited conservative and right-wing tradition.

Before the 1940s, Germany never had a conservative party
that was both well-organized and electorally successful, on the
one hand, and moderate and democratic on the other. German
conservatism was perennially wracked by internal division and
organizational weakness. In particular, the highly charged divide between conservative Protestants and Catholics created a
political vacuum on the center-right that extremist and authoritarian forces could exploit. This dynamic reached its nadir in
Hitler's march to power.

After 1945, Germany's center-right was refounded on a
different basis. The CDU separated itself from extremists and
authoritarians—it was founded primarily by conservative figures (such as Konrad Adenauer) with "unassailable" anti-Nazi
credentials. The party's founding statements made clear that it
was directly opposed to the prior regime and all it had stood
for. CDU leader Andreas Hermes gave a sense of the scale of
the rupture, commenting in 1945: "An old world has sunk and
we want to build a new one. . . ." The CDU offered a clear vision of a democratic future for Germany: a "Christian" society
that rejected dictatorship and embraced freedom and tolerance.

The CDU also broadened and diversified its base, by recruiting both Catholics and Protestants into the fold. This

was a challenge. But the trauma of Nazism and World War II convinced conservative Catholic and Protestant leaders to overcome the long-standing differences that had once splintered German society. As one regional CDU leader put it, "The close collaboration of Catholics and Protestants, which occurred in the prisons, dungeons, and concentration camps, brought to an end the old conflict and began to build bridges." As new Catholic and Protestant CDU leaders went door-to-door to Catholic and Protestant homes during the founding years of 1945–46, they conjured into existence a new party of the center-right that would reshape German society. The CDU became a pillar of Germany's postwar democracy.

The United States played a major role in encouraging the formation of the CDU. It is a great historical irony, then, that Americans can today learn from these successful efforts to help rescue our own democracy. To be clear: We are not equating Donald Trump or any other Republicans with German Nazis. Yet the successful rebuilding of the German center-right offers some useful lessons for the GOP. Not unlike their German counterparts, Republicans today must expel extremists from their ranks, break sharply with the Trump administration's authoritarian and white nationalist orientation, and find a way to broaden the party's base beyond white Christians. The CDU may offer a model: If the GOP were to abandon white nationalism and soften its extreme free-market ideology, a broad religious conservative appeal could allow it to build a sustainable base, for example, among Protestants and Catholics, while also potentially attracting a substantial number of minority voters.

The rebuilding of German conservatism, of course, followed a major catastrophe. The CDU had no choice but to reinvent itself. The question before Republicans today is whether such a reinvention can occur before we plunge into a deeper crisis. Can leaders muster the foresight and political courage to reorient what has become an increasingly dysfunctional political party before further damage is done, or will we need a catastrophe to inspire the change?

Although the Democratic Party has not been the principal driver of America's deepening polarization, it could nevertheless play a role in reducing it. Some Democrats have suggested the party focus on recapturing the so-called white working class, or non-college-educated white voters. This was a prominent theme in the wake of Hillary Clinton's traumatic 2016 defeat. Both Bernie Sanders and some moderates argued passionately that Democrats must win back the elusive blue-collar voters who abandoned them in the Rust Belt, Appalachia, and elsewhere. To do this, many opinion-makers argued, the Democrats needed to back away from their embrace of immigrants and so-called identity politics—a vaguely defined term that often encompasses the promotion of ethnic diversity and, more recently, anti-police-violence initiatives, such as Black Lives Matter. In a *New York Times* op-ed, Mark Penn and Andrew Stein urged Democrats to abandon "identity politics" and moderate their stance on immigration to win back white working-class votes. Though rarely voiced, the core message is this: Democrats must reduce the influence of ethnic minorities to win back the white working class.

Such a strategy might well reduce partisan polarization. If the Democratic Party were to abandon the demands of ethnic minorities or relegate them to the bottom of the agenda, it would almost certainly win back some white lower- and middle-income white voters. In effect, the party would return to what it was in the 1980s and 1990s—a party whose public face was predominantly white and in which minority constituencies were, at most, junior partners. The Democrats would—literally—begin to look more like their Republican rivals. And as they moved closer to Trumpist positions on immigration and racial equality (that is, accepting less of both), they would appear less threatening to the Republican base.

We think this is a terrible idea. Seeking to diminish minority groups' influence in the party—and we cannot emphasize this strongly enough—is the wrong way to reduce polarization. It would repeat some of our country's most shameful mistakes. The founding of the American republic left racial domination intact, which eventually led to the Civil War. When Democrats and Republicans finally reconciled in the wake of a failed Reconstruction, their conciliation was again based on racial exclusion. The reforms of the 1960s gave Americans a third chance to build a truly multiethnic democracy. It is imperative that we succeed, extraordinarily difficult though the task is. As our colleague Danielle Allen writes:

> The simple fact of the matter is that the world has never built a multiethnic democracy in which no particular ethnic group is in the majority and where political equality, social equality and economies that empower all have been achieved.

This is America's great challenge. We cannot retreat from it.

But there are other ways for Democrats to help restructure the political landscape. The intensity of partisan animosities in America today reflects the combined effect not only of growing ethnic diversity but also of slowed economic growth, stagnant wages in the bottom half of the income distribution, and rising economic inequality. Today's racially tinged partisan polarization reflects the fact that ethnic diversity surged during a period

(1975 to the present) in which economic growth slowed, especially for those at the bottom end of the income distribution. For many Americans, the economic changes of the last few decades have brought decreased job security, longer working hours, fewer prospects for upward mobility, and, consequently, a growth in social resentment. Resentment fuels polarization. One way of tackling our deepening partisan divide, then, would be to genuinely address the bread-and-butter concerns of long-neglected segments of the population—no matter their ethnicity.

Policies aimed at addressing economic inequality can be polarizing or depolarizing, depending on how they are organized. Unlike in many other advanced democracies, social policy in America has relied heavily on means tests—distributing benefits only to those who fall below an income threshold or otherwise qualify. Means-tested programs create the perception among many middle-class citizens that only poor people benefit from social policy. And because race and poverty have historically overlapped in the United States, these policies can be racially stigmatizing. Opponents of social policy have commonly used racially charged rhetoric against means-tested programs—Ronald Reagan's references to "welfare queens" or "young bucks" buying steaks with food stamps is a prime example. *Welfare* became a pejorative term in America because of a perception of recipients as undeserving.

By contrast, a social policy agenda that sets aside stiff means testing in favor of the more universalistic models found in northern Europe could have a moderating effect on our politics. Social policies that benefit everyone—Social Security and Medicare are prime examples—could help diminish resentment, build bridges across large swaths of the American electorate, and lock into place social support for more durable policies to reduce income inequality—without providing the raw materials for racially motivated backlash. Comprehensive health insurance is a prominent example. Other examples include a much more aggressive raising of the minimum wage, or a universal basic income—a policy that was once seriously considered, and even introduced into Congress, by the Nixon administration. Still another example is "family policy," or programs that provide paid leave for parents, subsidized day care for children with working parents, and prekindergarten education for nearly everyone. America's expenditures on families is currently a third of the advanced-country average, putting us on par with Mexico and Turkey. Finally, Democrats could consider more comprehensive labor market policies, such as more extensive job training, wage subsidies for employers to train and retain workers, work-study programs for high school and community-college students, and mobility allowances for displaced employees. Not only do these sorts of policies have the potential to reduce the economic inequality that fuels resentment and polarization, but they could contribute to the formation of a broad, durable coalition that realigns American politics.

Adopting policies to address social and economic inequality is, of course, politically difficult—in part because of the polarization (and resulting institutional gridlock) such policies seek to address. And we are under no illusions about the obstacles to building multiracial coalitions—those including both racial minorities *and* working-class whites. We cannot be certain that universalistic policies would provide the basis for such a coalition—only that they stand a better chance than our current means-tested programs. Difficult as it may be, however, it is imperative that Democrats address the issue of inequality. It is, after all, more than a question of social justice. The very health of our democracy hinges on it.

Comparing our current predicament to democratic crises in other parts of the world and at other moments of history, it becomes clear that America is not so different from other nations. Our constitutional system, while older and more robust than any in history, is vulnerable to the same pathologies that have killed democracy elsewhere. Ultimately, then, American democracy depends on us—the citizens of the United States. No single political leader can end a democracy; no single leader can rescue one, either. Democracy is a shared enterprise. Its fate depends on all of us.

In the darkest days of the Second World War, when America's very future was at risk, writer E. B. White was asked by the U.S. Federal Government's Writers' War Board to write a short response to the question "What is democracy?" His answer was unassuming but inspiring. He wrote:

> Surely the Board knows what democracy is. It is the line that forms on the right. It is the "don't" in don't shove. It is the hole in the stuffed shirt through which the sawdust slowly trickles; it is the dent in the high hat. Democracy is the recurrent suspicion that more than half of the people are right more than half of the time. It is the feeling of privacy in the voting booths, the feeling of communion in the libraries, the feeling of vitality everywhere. Democracy is a letter to the editor. Democracy is the score at the beginning of the ninth. It is an idea which hasn't been disproved

yet, a song the words of which have not gone bad. It's the mustard on the hot dog and the cream in the rationed coffee. Democracy is a request from a War Board, in the middle of a morning in the middle of a war, wanting to know what democracy is.

The egalitarianism, civility, sense of freedom, and shared purpose portrayed by E. B. White were the essence of mid-twentieth-century American democracy. Today that vision is under assault. To save our democracy, Americans need to restore the basic norms that once protected it. But we must do more than that. We must extend those norms through the whole of a diverse society. We must make them truly inclusive. America's democratic norms, at their core, have always been sound. But for much of our history, they were accompanied—indeed, sustained—by racial exclusion. Now those norms must be made to work in an age of racial equality and unprecedented ethnic diversity. Few societies in history have managed to be both multiracial and genuinely democratic. That is our challenge. It is also our opportunity. If we meet it, America will truly be exceptional.

Acknowledgments

We could not possibly have written this book without the collaboration of a group of extraordinary student research assistants. We are deeply grateful to Fernando Bizzarro, Kaitlyn Chriswell, Jasmine Hakimian, David Ifkovits, Shiro Kuriwaki, Martin Liby Troein, Manuel Meléndez, Brian Palmiter, Justin Pottle, Matt Reichert, Briita van Staalduinen, Aaron Watanabe, and Selena Zhao. Special thanks to David Ifkovits and Justin Pottle for their impeccable work on the blind notes. The fruits of these students' research pervade this entire book. We hope they see themselves in it.

The ideas in this book emerged from numerous conversations with friends and colleagues. We especially thank Daniel Carpenter, Ryan Enos, Gretchen Helmke, Alisha Holland, Daniel Hopkins, Jeff Kopstein, Evan Lieberman, Robert Mickey, Eric Nelson, Paul Pierson, Pia Raffler, Kenneth Roberts, Theda Skocpol, Dan Slater, Todd Washburn, and Lucan Ahmad Way for their willingness to listen to, debate, and teach us. Special thanks to Larry Diamond, Scott Mainwaring, Tarek Masoud, John Sides, and Lucan Ahmad Way for reading earlier drafts of the manuscript.

We are indebted to our agent, Jill Kneerim, for many things. Jill invented this book project and guided us through it from start to finish. She has been a source of much-needed encouragement and wise advice—and great editing to boot.

We thank our editor at Crown Publishers, Amanda Cook, for her faith in us, as well as for her patience and perseverance in coaxing a readable book out of a couple of political scientists. We are also thankful to Crown's Meghan Houser, Zach Phillips, Kathleen Quinlan, and Penny Simon for their hard work and patient support, as well as Molly Stern for the great energy she brought to the project.

Steve thanks the members of the Soccer Dads Club (Chris, Jonathan, and Todd) for their constant good humor and support (and, of course, their insights into politics).

Finally, we are deeply grateful to our families. Steve thanks Liz Mineo and Alejandra Mineo-Levitsky, the two people who matter most. Daniel thanks Suriya, Talia, and Lilah Ziblatt for their unending enthusiasm and patience. And Daniel also thanks his father, David Ziblatt, for conversation, insight, intellectual companionship, and enduring inspiration.

Endnotes

INTRODUCTION

3   **in barely visible steps:** Constitutional scholars Aziz Huq and Tom Ginsburg call this form of democratic breakdown "constitutional regression." See Aziz Huq and Tom Ginsburg, "How to Lose a Constitutional Democracy," *UCLA Law Review* 65 (2018); also Ellen Lust and David Waldner, *Unwelcome Change: Understanding, Evaluating, and Extending Theories of Democratic Backsliding* (Washington, DC: U.S. Agency for International Development, 2015).

4   **"the only antibiotic we have":** Bart Jones, *Hugo!: The Hugo Chávez Story from Mud Hut to Perpetual Revolution* (Hanover, NH: Steerforth Press, 2007), p. 225.

5   **Blatant dictatorship:** Steven Levitsky and Lucan A. Way, *Competitive Authoritarianism: Hybrid Regimes After the Cold War* (New York: Cambridge University Press, 2010); also Scott Mainwaring and Aníbal Pérez-Liñán, *Democracies and Dictatorships in Latin America: Emergence, Survival, and Fall* (New York: Cambridge University Press, 2014).

5   **by elected governments themselves:** Huq and Ginsburg, "How to Lose a Constitutional Democracy," p. 36.

6   **Many continue to believe:** Latinobarómetro, accessed March 16, 2017, http://www.latinobarometro.org/latOnline.jsp (Question: Democracy -> Scale [country] is democratic).

9   **have fueled an insidious reaction:** Robert Mickey, Steven Levitsky, and Lucan Ahmad Way, "Is America Still Safe for Democracy?," *Foreign Affairs*, May/June 2017, pp. 20–29.

CHAPTER 1: FATEFUL ALLIANCES

11   **Benito Mussolini arrived in Rome:** Simonetta Falasca-Zamponi, *Fascist Spectacle: The Aesthetics of Power in Mussolini's Italy* (Berkeley: University of California Press, 1997), p. 1.

12   **"I come from the battlefield":** Robert Paxton, *The Anatomy of Fascism* (New York: Vintage, 2004), p. 90.

12   **At the last train stop:** Falasca-Zamponi, *Fascist Spectacle*, p. 2.

12   **a new fascist epoch:** Ibid.

15   **"We've engaged him for ourselves":** Quoted in Richard Evans, *The Coming of the Third Reich* (New York: Penguin, 2003), p. 308.

15   **"fateful alliance":** Hermann Beck, *The Fateful Alliance: German Conservatives and Nazis in 1933: The Machtergreifung in a New Light* (New York: Berghahn Press, 2011). Also see Daniel Ziblatt, *Conservative Parties and the Birth of Democracy* (Cambridge: Cambridge University Press, 2017).

15   **"bourgeois bloc":** Alexander De Grand, *The Hunchback's Tailor: Giovanni Giolitti and Liberal Italy from the Challenge of Mass Politics to the Rise of Fascism* (Westport, CT: Praeger, 2001), pp. 241–42.

17   **"It is difficult to ask":** Taken from Cristina Marcano and Alberto Barrera Tyszka, *Hugo Chávez* (New York: Random House, 2004), p. 304.

18   **Caldera's departure and subsequent antiestablishment campaign:** See José E. Molina, "The Unraveling of Venezuela's Party System," in *The Unraveling of Representative Democracy in Venezuela*, eds. Jennifer L. McCoy and David J. Myers (Baltimore: Johns Hopkins University Press, 2004), p. 162.

18   **"To power":** Quoted in Jones, *Hugo!*, p. 186.

18   **he viewed Chávez as a passing fad:** Ibid., p. 189.

18   **in dropping all charges:** Marcano and Barrera Tyszka, *Hugo Chávez*, p. 107.

18   **he stood glumly:** Jones, *Hugo!*, p. 226.

19   **"Nobody thought that Mr. Chávez":** Quoted in Marcano and Barrera Tyszka, *Hugo Chávez*, p. 107.

19   **"I have just committed":** Quoted in Larry Eugene Jones, " 'The Greatest Stupidity of My Life': Alfred Hugenberg and the Formation of the Hitler Cabinet, January 1933," *Journal of Contemporary History* 27, no. 1 (1992), pp. 63–87.

20   **1998 Latinobarómetro survey:** Source: Latinobarómetro, accessed March 16, 2017, http://www.latinobarometro.org/lat Online.jsp.

21   **"litmus test":** Juan J. Linz, *The Breakdown of Democratic Regimes: Crisis, Breakdown, and Reequilibration* (Baltimore: Johns Hopkins University Press, 1978), pp. 29–30.

21   **Building on Linz's work:** See ibid., pp. 27–38.

22   **All five ended up:** Steven Levitsky and James Loxton, "Populism and Competitive Authoritarianism in the Andes," *Democratization* 20, no. 1 (2013).

24   **"distancing":** Nancy Bermeo, *Ordinary People in Extraordinary Times: The Citizenry and the Breakdown of Democracy* (Princeton, NJ: Princeton University Press, 2003), p. 238.

25   **The AVF's youth group:** Ziblatt, *Conservative Parties and the Birth of Democracy*, p. 344.

25   **The loss of 25,000 members:** Ibid.

25   **"greater affinity for extremists":** Linz, *The Breakdown of Democratic Regimes*, pp. 32–33.

26   **"join with opponents":** Ibid., p. 37.

27   **The party leadership took:** Giovanni Capoccia, *Defending Democracy: Reactions to Extremism in Interwar Europe* (Baltimore: Johns Hopkins University Press, 2005), p. 121.

28   **created the Catholic Youth Front:** Ibid., p. 120.

28   **The Catholic Party supported:** Ibid., p. 121.

28   **The choice was not easy:** Ibid., pp. 122–23.

28   **when it became evident:** Capoccia, *Defending Democracy*, p. 121.

29   **the extreme-right Lapua Movement:** Risto Alapuro and Erik Allardt, "The Lapua Movement: The Threat of Rightist Takeover in Finland, 1930–32," in *The Breakdown of Democratic Regimes: Europe*, eds. Juan J. Linz and Alfred Stepan (Baltimore: Johns Hopkins University Press, 1978), p. 130.

29   **The movement sought:** Ibid., p. 130.

29   **At first, politicians from the governing:** Bermeo, *Ordinary People in Extraordinary Times*, p. 240; Alapuro and Allardt, "The Lapua Movement," pp. 130–31.

29   **P. E. Svinhufvud, a conservative:** Alapuro and Allardt, "The Lapua Movement," pp. 130–31.

29   **the Lapua Movement continued:** Bermeo, *Ordinary People in Extraordinary Times*, p. 240.

29   **Lapua thugs abducted:** Alapuro and Allardt, "The Lapua Movement," p. 130.

29   **The Lapua Movement also organized:** Ibid., p. 133.

29   **the bulk of the Agrarian Union:** Bermeo, *Ordinary People in Extraordinary Times*, p. 240.

30   **Even the conservative president:** Ibid., p. 241.

30   **The Lapua Movement was left isolated:** Ibid., pp. 239–41.

31   **"not with passion":** "Bürgerlicher Aufruf für Van der Bellen (Citizens Appeal to Van der Bellen)," *Die Presse*, May 14, 2016, http://diepresse.com/home/innenpolitik/bpwahl/4988743/Buergerlicher-Aufruf-fuer-Van-der-Bellen.

31   **a decision that split families:** Interview with author, March 16, 2017.

CHAPTER 2: GATEKEEPING IN AMERICA

34   **extremist groups existed in the United States:** Seymour Martin Lipset and Earl Raab, *The Politics of Unreason: Right-Wing Extremism in America, 1790–1970* (New York: Harper & Row, 1970), p. 152.

34   **naming Mussolini its "Man of the Week":** Lipset and Raab, *The Politics of Unreason*, pp. 170–71.

34   **"ever to happen to radio":** Quoted in Alan Brinkley, *Voices of Protest: Huey Long, Father Coughlin & the Great Depression* (New York: Vintage Books, 1983), p. 119.

34   **He delivered speeches to packed stadiums:** Ibid., pp. 83, 175–77.

35   **lined his route to see him:** Ibid., p. 119. As late as 1938, a Gallup poll found that 27 percent of Americans approved of Father Coughlin, while 32 percent disapproved (Lipset and Raab, *The Politics of Unreason*, pp. 171–73).

35   "the great demagogue of the day": Arthur Schlesinger, *The Age of Roosevelt: The Politics of Upheaval, 1935–1936* (Boston: Houghton Mifflin, [1960] 2003), pp. viii, 68.

35   a gifted stump speaker: Richard D. White Jr., *Kingfish: The Reign of Huey P. Long* (New York: Random House, 2006), pp. 45, 99, 171; Brinkley, *Voices of Protest*, p. 69.

35   a mix of bribes and threats: Schlesinger, *The Age of Roosevelt*, p. 62; White, *Kingfish*, pp. 248–53; William Ivy Hair, *The Kingfish and His Realm: The Life and Times of Huey P. Long* (Baton Rouge: Louisiana State University Press, 1991), pp. 276–80.

35   "I'm the constitution just now": White, *Kingfish*, p. 45.

35   "the first true dictator": Quoted in ibid., p. 253.

35   Roosevelt's campaign manager: Ibid., p. 352.

35   "more mail than all other senators": Ibid., p. 198.

35   nearly eight million names: Robert E. Snyder, "Huey Long and the Presidential Election of 1936," *Louisiana History* 16, no. 2 (Spring 1975), p. 123; White, *Kingfish*, p. 198.

35   a presidential run: Brinkley, *Voices of Protest*, p. 81; Hair, *The Kingfish and His Realm*, pp. 306–7.

35   "I can take this Roosevelt": Snyder, "Huey Long and the Presidential Election of 1936," p. 128.

35   Roosevelt viewed Long as a serious threat: Lipset and Raab, *The Politics of Unreason*, pp. 209, 224.

35   Senator Joseph McCarthy: Ibid., p. 21.

36   enjoyed 40 percent: Ibid., p. 237.

36   "hate the powerful": Arthur T. Hadley, *The Invisible Primary* (Englewood Cliffs, NJ: Prentice Hall, 1976), p. 238; Jody Carlson, *George C. Wallace and the Politics of Powerlessness: The Wallace Campaigns for the Presidency, 1964–1976* (New Brunswick, NJ: Transaction Books, 1981), p. 6.

36   "What is a Constitution anyway?": Lipset and Raab, *The Politics of Unreason*, pp. 355–56.

36   blue-collar base: Dan T. Carter, *The Politics of Rage: George Wallace, the Origins of the New Conservatism, and the Transformation of American Politics*, Second Edition (Baton Rouge: Louisiana State University Press, 2000), pp. 344–52; Stephan Lesher, *George Wallace: American Populist* (Reading, MA: Addison-Wesley, 1994), pp. 276–78; Lipset and Raab, *The Politics of Unreason*, pp. 345–57.

36   **his third-party run:** Lipset and Raab, *The Politics of Unreason*, p. 21.

36   **assassination attempt:** Carlson, *George C. Wallace and the Politics of Powerlessness*, p. 149.

37   **"smoke-filled back room":** This account of the 1920 convention relies on two sources: Francis Russell, *The Shadow of Blooming Grove: Warren G. Harding in His Times* (New York: McGraw-Hill, 1968), pp. 379–81; and John Morello, *Selling the President, 1920: Albert D. Lasker, Advertising, and the Election of Warren G. Harding* (Westport, CT: Praeger, 2001), pp. 41–43.

37   **"Nobody is talking Harding":** Russell, *The Shadow of Blooming Grove*, p. 376.

39   **In parliamentary democracies:** See David Samuels and Matthew Shugart, *Presidents, Parties, and Prime Ministers: How the Separation of Powers Affects Party Organization and Behavior* (New York: Cambridge University Press, 2010).

39   **"and ending tyrants":** Alexander Hamilton, Federalist 1.

39   **built-in screening device:** James W. Ceaser, *Presidential Selection: Theory and Development* (Princeton, NJ: Princeton University Press, 1979), p. 64.

40   **"The immediate election":** Quoted in Robert Dahl, *How Democratic Is the American Constitution?*, Second Edition (New Haven, CT: Yale University Press, 2003), p. 76.

41   **"filtration":** James W. Ceaser, *Reforming the Reforms: A Critical Analysis of the Presidential Selection Process* (Cambridge, MA: Ballinger Publishing Company, 1982), pp. 84–87.

42   **They generally followed the instructions:** Ibid., pp. 19–21.

42   **Yet these brought little change:** Ibid., p. 23.

42   **the presidency's gatekeepers:** Ibid., p. 27.

43   **"peer review":** See, for example, Nelson W. Polsby, *Consequences of Party Reform* (New York: Oxford University Press, 1983), pp. 169–70.

43   **They had worked with them:** Austin Ranney, Testimony Before the Senate Committee on Rules and Administration, September 10, 1980. Quoted in Ceaser, *Reforming the Reforms*, p. 96.

43   **praise from racists worldwide:** Lipset and Raab, *The Politics of Unreason*, p. 111.

43   **mentioned with admiration by Adolf Hitler:** For more on the relationship of Henry Ford and the Nazi regime, see Neil Baldwin, *Henry Ford and the Jews: The Mass Production of Hatred* (New York: Public Affairs, 2002).

43   **Ford was also a widely admired:** See Reynold M. Wik, *Henry Ford and Grass-roots America* (Ann Arbor: University of Michigan Press, 1972).

43   **"poor farm boy who made good":** Ibid., pp. 8–10, 42, 157.

44   **"Ford Craze":** Ibid., pp. 162, 172–73.

44   **As the results rolled in:** "Ford Leads in Presidential Free-for-All," *Collier's*, May 26, 1923, p. 7; "Politics in Chaos as Ford Vote Grows," *Collier's*, June 23, 1923, p. 8.

44   **"*the* issue in American politics":** "Ford First in Final Returns," *Collier's*, July 14, 1923, p. 5.

45   **"machinery of selection":** Edward Lowry, "Dark Horses and Dim Hopes," *Collier's*, November 10, 1923, p. 12.

45   **"It is most ridiculous":** Quoted in Wik, *Henry Ford and Grass-roots America*, p. 162.

45   **"There might be a war or some crisis":** "If I Were President," *Collier's*, August 4, 1923, p. 29.

46   **isolated him from his peers:** Brinkley, *Voices of Protest*, pp. 75–77; Hair, *The Kingfish and His Realm*, pp. 268–69; White, *Kingfish*, p. 191.

46   **had little chance of winning:** Robert E. Snyder, "Huey Long and the Presidential Election of 1936," *Louisiana History* 16, no. 2 (Spring 1975), pp. 131–33.

46   **Wallace shocked the pundits:** Carlson, *George C. Wallace and the Politics of Powerlessness*, pp. 33–36.

47   **roughly 40 percent of Americans:** Lipset and Raab, *The Politics of Unreason*, p. 21.

47   **establishment would never back:** Stephen Lesher, *George Wallace: American Populist* (Reading, MA: Addison-Wesley, 1994), pp. 387–88; Carlson, *George C. Wallace and the Politics of Powerlessness*, p. 71.

47   **"racial purity":** Lynne Olson, *Those Angry Days: Roosevelt, Lindbergh, and America's Fight over World War II, 1931–1941* (New York: Random House, 2014), pp. 18–20, 72.

47 **His speeches drew large crowds:** A. Scott Berg, *Lindbergh* (New York: G. P. Putnam's Sons, 1998), p. 410.

47 **"Conventional wisdom":** Olson, *Those Angry Days*, p. 442.

47 **Idaho senator William Borah:** Berg, *Lindbergh*, p. 398.

48 **"God might have withdrawn His blessing":** Quoted in Norman Mailer, *Miami and the Siege of Chicago* (New York: Random House, 1968), p. 7.

49 **"party leaders, union bosses, and other insiders":** Marty Cohen, David Karol, Hans Noel, and John Zaller, *The Party Decides: Presidential Nominations Before and After Reform* (Chicago: University of Chicago Press, 2008), p. 1.

49 **"In the United States":** "A Look Back at the 1968 Democratic Convention," https://www.youtube.com/watch?v=aUKzSsVmnpY, accessed May 11, 2017.

50 **"The cure for the ills of democracy":** Democratic National Committee, *Mandate for Reform* (Washington, DC, Democratic National Committee, April 1970), p. 14.

50 **open up the presidential nomination process:** Quoted in James W. Ceaser, *Presidential Selection: Theory and Development* (Princeton, NJ: Princeton University Press, 1979), p. 273.

50 **"the anti-politics of the street":** Democratic National Committee, *Mandate for Reform*, p. 49.

50 **representation of women and minorities:** Ceaser, *Presidential Selection*, p. 237.

51 **"the most open political process":** Both quotes taken from David E. Price, *Bringing Back the Parties* (Washington, DC: Congressional Quarterly, 1984), pp. 149–50.

51 **volatile and divisive:** In 1972, the Democratic nomination was nearly captured by George Wallace, and the eventual nominee, George McGovern, suffered a landslide defeat at the hands of Richard Nixon. In 1976, the nomination went to Jimmy Carter, a relative outsider, and in 1980, President Carter faced a tough primary challenge from Senator Edward Kennedy.

51 **"stirring up mass hatreds":** Nelson W. Polsby and Aaron Wildavsky, *Presidential Elections* (New York: The Free Press, 1968), p. 230.

52 **Any candidate seeking:** Cohen, Karol, Noel, and Zaller, *The Party Decides*, pp. 175–79.

52 **"invisible primary"**: Arthur Hadley, *The Invisible Primary* (Englewood Cliffs, NJ: Prentice Hall, 1976).

52 **"actually selected"**: Ibid., p. xiii.

CHAPTER 3: THE GREAT REPUBLICAN ABDICATION

53 **now also open to true outsiders:** By outsiders, we mean candidates who have never previously held elective office or a cabinet post. We count all candidates who either participate in a primary or whose name is placed in contention at the convention. We thank Fernando Bizzarro for his assistance in compiling these data.

54 **skip the "invisible primary":** For a detailed explanation of why this was the case, see Cohen, Karol, Noel, and Zaller, *The Party Decides.*

55 **Las Vegas bookmakers:** James Ceaser, Andrew Busch, and John Pitney Jr., *Defying the Odds: The 2016 Elections and American Politics* (Washington, DC: Rowman & Littlefield, 2017), p. 69.

55 **"considerably less than 20 percent":** Nate Silver, "Dear Media: Stop Freaking Out About Donald Trump's Polls," *FiveThirtyEight*, November 23, 2015, http://fivethirtyeight.com/features/dear-media-stop-freaking-out-about-donald-trumps-polls/.

56 **Citizens United ruling:** Marty Cohen, David Karol, Hans Noel, and John Zaller, "Party Versus Faction in the Reformed Presidential Nominating System, *PS* (October 2016), pp. 704–5; Theda Skocpol and Alex Hertel-Fernandez, "The Koch Network and Republican Party Extremism," *Perspectives on Politics* 14, no. 3 (2016), pp. 681–99.

56 **explosion of alternative media:** Ibid., p. 705.

56 **Whereas the path to national name recognition:** Ibid., pp. 703–4.

56 **"conservative entertainment complex":** David Frum, "The Great Republican Revolt," *The Atlantic*, September 9, 2015.

56 **radicalized conservative voters:** See Matthew Levendusky, *How Partisan Media Polarize America* (Chicago: University of Chicago Press, 2013); Cass R. Sunstein, *#Republic: Divided Democracy in the Age of Social Media* (Princeton, NJ: Princeton University Press, 2017).

57 **Although many factors contributed:** See John Sides, Michael Tesler, and Lynn Vavreck, *Identity Crisis: The 2016 Presidential*

Campaign and the Battle for the Meaning of America (Princeton, NJ: Princeton University Press, 2018).

57 **more endorsements than Trump:** "The Endorsement Primary," *FiveThirtyEight*, June 7, 2016, https://projects.fivethirtyeight.com/2016-endorsement-primary/.

57 **did not yet have a single endorsement:** Ibid.

58 **When the primary season ended:** Ibid.

58 **Trump had the sympathy:** Among Republicans, more than twice as many Trump supporters as supporters of rival Republican candidates listed Breitbart News as their main news source. See Pew Research Center, "Trump, Clinton Voters Divided in Their Main Source for Election News," January 18, 2017, pp. 3, 5.

58 **new ways to use old media:** See Sides, Tesler, and Vavreck, *Identity Crisis*, Chapter 4.

58 **"uniquely tailored to the digital age":** Nathaniel Persily, "The 2016 U.S. Election: Can Democracy Survive the Internet?," *Journal of Democracy*, April 2017, p. 67.

58 **$2 billion in free media coverage:** Ibid., p. 67.

60 **"magnificent chaos":** "Why the Never Trump Movement Failed at the Republican National Convention," ABCNews.com, July 20, 2016.

61 **Levels of voter fraud:** On electoral fraud in the United States in general, see Richard L. Hasen, *The Voting Wars: From Florida 2000 to the Next Election Meltdown* (New Haven, CT: Yale University Press, 2012), and Lorraine C. Minnite, *The Myth of Voter Fraud* (Ithaca, NY: Cornell University Press, 2010). On the absence of fraud in the 2016 election, see Jessica Huseman and Scott Klein, "There's No Evidence Our Election Was Rigged," ProPublica, November 28, 2016.

61 **immigrants and dead people:** Darren Samuelsohn, "A Guide to Donald Trump's 'Rigged' Election," *Politico*, October 25, 2016.

61 **"Help Me Stop Crooked Hillary":** Ibid.

61 **"We'd better be careful":** Jeremy Diamond, "Trump: 'I'm Afraid the Election's Going to Be Rigged,'" CNN.com, August 2, 2016.

61 **"Of course there is large scale voter fraud":** "U.S. Election 2016: Trump Says Election 'Rigged at Polling Places,'" BBC.com, October 17, 2016.

61   "topple the apple cart": "Donald Trump, Slipping in Polls, Warns of 'Stolen Election,'" *New York Times*, October 14, 2016.

61   the election could be stolen: "Poll: 41 Percent of Voters Say Election Could Be Stolen from Trump," *Politico*, October 17, 2016.

62   "birther": "14 of Trump's Most Outrageous Birther Claims— Half from After 2011," CNN.com, September 16, 2016.

62   "has to go to jail": Lisa Hagen, "Trump: Clinton 'Has to Go to Jail,'" *The Hill*, October 12, 2016.

62   offered to pay the legal fees: "Donald Trump Says He May Pay Legal Fees of Accused Attacker from Rally," *New York Times*, March 13, 2016.

62   Here are a few examples: "Don't Believe Donald Trump Has Incited Violence at Rallies? Watch This Video," *Vox*, March 12, 2016, https://www.vox.com/2016/3/12/11211846/donald-trump-violence-rallies.

64   "the Second Amendment people": "Donald Trump Suggests 'Second Amendment People' Could Act Against Hillary Clinton," *New York Times*, August 9, 2016.

64   special prosecutor to investigate Hillary Clinton: "Trump: Clinton 'Has to Go to Jail,'" CNN.com, October 13, 2016.

64   "If I become president": "Donald Trump Threatens to Rewrite Libel Laws to Make It Easier to Sue the Media," *Business Insider*, February 26, 2016.

64   "open up our libel laws": Ibid.

67   "ideological collusion": This definition of "collective abdication" and the discussion that follows builds on sociologist Ivan Ermakoff's important study of interwar Germany and France, titled *Ruling Oneself Out: A Theory of Collective Abdications* (Durham, NC: Duke University Press, 2008).

67   when faced with a would-be authoritarian: Linz, *The Breakdown of Democratic Regimes*, p. 37.

68   right-wing politicians endorsed ideological rivals: For electoral data that supports this point on the French 2017 presidential election, see "French Election Results: Macron's Victory in Charts," *Financial Times*, May 9, 2017. See https://www.ft.com/content/62d782d6-31a7-11e7-9555-23ef563ecf9a.

68   Republican 1: https://www.hillaryclinton.com/briefing/updates/2016/09/29/number-of-prominent-republicans-and

-independents-backing-hillary-clinton-grows/, accessed May 20, 2017.

69   **Republican 2:** Ibid.

69   **Republican 3:** Ibid.

69   **William Pierce:** Ibid.

69   **Republicans who publicly endorsed Clinton:** "78 Republican Politicians, Donors, and Officials Who Are Supporting Hillary Clinton," *Washington Post*, November 7, 2016.

70   **In France, it is estimated that half:** "French Election Results: Macron's Victory in Charts," *Financial Times*, May 9, 2017 [see figure: "How Allegiances Shifted from the First to the Second Round of Voting in the French Presidential Election"].

71   **increasingly sorted into Republicans and Democrats:** Alan Abramowitz, *The Polarized Public? Why American Government Is So Dysfunctional* (New York: Pearson, 2012); "Partisanship and Political Animosity in 2016," Pew Research Center, June 22, 2016, http://www.people-press.org/2016/06/22/partisanship-and-political-animosity-in-2016/.

71   **predicting a close race:** John Sides, Michael Tesler, and Lynn Vavreck, "The 2016 U.S. Election: How Trump Lost and Won," *Journal of Democracy* 28, no. 2 (April 2017), pp. 36–37; Sides, Tessler, and Vavreck, *Identity Crisis*, Chapter 2.

CHAPTER 4: SUBVERTING DEMOCRACY

72   **nominated himself:** Gregory Schmidt, "Fujimori's 1990 Upset Victory in Peru: Rules, Contingencies, and Adaptive Strategies," *Comparative Politics* 28, no. 3 (1990), pp. 321–55.

72   **Short of funds:** Luis Jochamowitz, *Ciudadano Fujimori: La Construcción de un Político* (Lima: Peisa, 1993), pp. 259–63.

73   **But he had only a vague idea:** Charles Kenney, *Fujimori's Coup and the Breakdown of Democracy in Latin America* (Notre Dame, IN: University of Notre Dame Press, 2004), pp. 126–27; also Susan C. Stokes, *Mandates and Democracy: Neoliberalism by Surprise in Latin America* (New York: Cambridge University Press, 2001), pp. 69–71.

73   **Fujimori had been unsparing:** See Kenneth Roberts, "Neoliberalism and the Transformation of Populism in Latin America," *World Politics* 48, no. 1 (January 1995), pp. 82–116.

73 **Congress failed to pass any legislation:** Gregory Schmidt, "Presidential Usurpation or Congressional Preference? The Evolution of Executive Decree Authority in Peru," in *Executive Decree Authority*, eds. John M. Carey and Matthew S. Shugart (New York: Cambridge University Press, 1998), p. 124; Kenney, *Fujimori's Coup and the Breakdown of Democracy in Latin America*, pp. 131–32.

73 **he also lacked the patience:** Yusuke Murakami, *Peru en la era del Chino: La política no institucionalizada y el pueblo en busca de un salvador* (Lima: Instituto de Estudios Peruanos, 2012), p. 282; Maxwell A. Cameron, "The *Eighteenth Brumaire* of Alberto Fujimori," in *The Peruvian Labyrinth: Polity, Society, Economy*, eds. Maxwell Cameron and Philip Mauceri (University Park: Pennsylvania State University Press, 1997), pp. 54–58; Cynthia McClintock, "La Voluntad Política Presidencial y la Ruptura Constitucional," in *Los Enigmas Del Podre: Fujimori 1990–1996*, ed. Fernando Tuesta (Lima: Fundación Friedrich Ebert, 1996).

73 **"inviting the President of the Senate":** McClintock, "La Voluntad Política Presidencial y la Ruptura Constitucional," p. 65.

74 **"unproductive charlatans":** Catherine Conaghan, *Fujimori's Peru: Deception in the Public Sphere* (Pittsburgh: University of Pittsburgh Press, 2005), p. 30.

74 **"jackals" and "scoundrels":** Kenney, *Fujimori's Coup and the Breakdown of Democracy in Latin America*, p. 132.

74 **he began to bypass congress:** Schmidt, "Presidential Usurpation or Congressional Preference?," pp. 118–19.

74 **"rigid" and "confining":** Cameron, "The *Eighteenth Brumaire* of Alberto Fujimori," p. 55.

74 **"We are a country":** Conaghan, *Fujimori's Peru*, p. 30.

74 **a Japanese emperor:** McClintock, "La Voluntad Política Presidencial y la Ruptura Constitucional," p. 65.

74 **"Could Fujimori be deposed?":** Kenney, *Fujimori's Coup and the Breakdown of Democracy in Latin America*, p. 146.

75 **"the President would kill the Congress":** Cameron, "The *Eighteenth Brumaire* of Alberto Fujimori," p. 55; Kenney, *Fujimori's Coup and the Breakdown of Democracy in Latin America*, pp. 56–57, 172–76, 186.

75 **"rancid pigs" and "squalid oligarchs":** Jones, *Hugo!*, p. 1.

75 **"enemies" and "traitors":** Kirk Hawkins, *Venezuela's Chavismo and Populism in Comparative Perspective* (New York: Cambridge University Press, 2010), p. 61.

75 **judges who ruled against him as "communist":** "Silvio Berlusconi Says Communist Judges Out to Destroy Him," Reuters, October 20, 2009.

75 **called the media a "grave political enemy":** "Assaults on Media Make Ecuador an Odd Refuge," *The Age*, June 21, 2012, http://www.theage.com.au/federal-politics/political-news/assaults-on-media-make-ecuador-an-odd-refuge-20120620-20okw.html?deviceType=text.

76 **accused journalists of propagating "terrorism":** Ahmet Sik, "Journalism Under Siege," EnglishPen, 2016, https://www.englishpen.org/wp-content/uploads/2016/03/JournalismUnderSiege_FINAL.pdf.

76 **"opposition, obstruction, and provocation":** Joseph Page, *Perón* (New York: Random House, 1983), pp. 162–65.

76 **"mental incapacity":** Jones, *Hugo!*, p. 309.

79 **Orbán packed the nominally independent:** János Kornai, "Hungary's U-Turn: Retreating from Democracy," *Journal of Democracy* 26, no. 43 (July 2015), p. 35.

79 **videotaped hundreds of opposition politicians:** Maxwell A. Cameron, "Endogenous Regime Breakdown: The Vladivideo and the Fall of Peru's Fujimori," in *The Fujimori Legacy: The Rise of Electoral Authoritarianism in Peru*, ed. Julio F. Carrión (University Park: Pennsylvania State University Press, 2006).

79 **delivering monthly cash payments:** Conaghan, *Fujimori's Peru*, p. 167; and Cameron, "Endogenous Regime Breakdown," p. 180.

79 **had called him a fascist:** Page, *Perón*, p. 165.

79 **on the grounds of malfeasance:** Gretchen Helmke, *Courts Under Constraints: Judges, Generals, and Presidents in Argentina* (New York: Cambridge University Press, 2005), p. 64.

79 **Péron then appointed four loyalists:** Page, *Perón*, p. 165; Helmke, *Courts Under Constraints*, p. 64.

80 **evade constitutional term limits "unconstitutional":** Conaghan, *Fujimori's Peru*, pp. 126–31.

80　Fidesz loyalists: Bojan Bugaric and Tom Ginsburg, "The Assault on Postcommunist Courts," *Journal of Democracy* 27, no. 3 (July 2016), p. 73.

80　In a dubiously constitutional move: Ibid., pp. 73–74.

80　veto power within the tribunal: Joanna Fomina and Jacek Kucharczyk, "Populism and Protest in Poland," *Journal of Democracy* 27, no. 4 (October 2016), pp. 62–63. The Tribunal declared the repair bill unconstitutional in early 2016, but the government ignored the ruling, with Law and Justice leader Jaroslaw Kaczyński declaring that his party would "not permit anarchy in Poland, even if it is promoted by the courts." (Bugaric and Ginsburg, "The Assault on Postcommunist Courts," p. 74.)

81　Fearing for its survival: Allan R. Brewer-Carías, *Dismantling Democracy in Venezuela: The Chávez Authoritarian Experiment* (New York: Cambridge University Press, 2010), pp. 58–59; Jones, *Hugo!*, pp. 241–42.

81　"It is dead": Jones, *Hugo!*, p. 242.

81　Two months later: Brewer-Carías, *Dismantling Democracy in Venezuela*, p. 59.

81　"revolutionary" loyalists: Javier Corrales and Michael Penfold, *Dragon in the Tropics: Hugo Chávez and the Political Economy of Revolution in Venezuela* (Washington, DC: The Brookings Institution, 2011), p. 27; and Brewer-Carías, *Dismantling Democracy in Venezuela*, pp. 236–38.

81　not a single Supreme Tribunal ruling: "El chavismo nunca pierde en el Supremo Venezolano," *El País*, December 12, 2014, http://internacional.elpais.com/internacional/2014/12/12/actualidad/1418373177_159073.html; also Javier Corrales, "Autocratic Legalism in Venezuela," *Journal of Democracy* 26, no. 2 (April 2015), p. 44.

82　control over the channel's news programming: Conaghan, *Fujimori's Peru*, pp. 154–62.

82　"we plan the evening news": Ibid.

82　stay home for "personal reasons": Ibid., p. 137.

83　he stood no chance: Helmke, *Courts Under Constraints*, p. 64.

83　on sodomy charges: Dan Slater, "Iron Cage in an Iron Fist: Authoritarian Institutions and the Personalization of Power in Malaysia," *Comparative Politics* 36, no. 1 (October 2003), pp. 94–95. Anwar's conviction was overturned in 2004, a year after Mahathir Mohamad had left office.

83   **it had been "subliminal":** Corrales, "Autocratic Legalism in Venezuela," pp. 44–45; "Venezuelan Opposition Leader Leopoldo López Sentenced to Prison Over Protest," *New York Times*, September 10, 2015.

83   **chilling effect on the press:** "El Universo Verdict Bad Precedent for Free Press in America," *Committee to Protect Journalists Alert*, February 16, 2012, https://cpj.org/2012/02/el-universo-sentence-a-dark-precedent-for-free-pre.php.

84   **purchased by progovernment businessmen:** Soner Cagaptay, *The New Sultan: Erdogan and the Crisis of Modern Turkey* (London: I. B. Tauris, 2017), p. 124; also Svante E. Cornell, "As Dogan Yields, Turkish Media Freedom Plummets," *Turkey Analyst*, January 18, 2010, https://www.turkeyanalyst.org/publications/turkey-analyst-articles/item/196-as-dogan-yields-turkish-media-freedom-plummets.html.

84   **"pain in the neck":** Marshall Goldman, *PetroState: Putin, Power, and the New Russia* (Oxford: Oxford University Press, 2008), p. 102.

84   **"straight out of a bad Mafia movie":** Peter Baker and Susan Glasser, *Kremlin Rising: Vladimir Putin's Russia and the End of the Revolution*, Revised Edition (Dulles, VA: Potomac Books, 2007), p. 83.

84   **He took the deal:** Ibid., p. 482.

84   **Under intense financial pressure:** "Venden TV Venezolana Globovisón y Anuncian Nueva Linea Editorial de 'Centro,'" *El Nuevo Herald*, May 13, 2013, http://www.elnuevoherald.com/noticias/mundo/america-latina/venezuela-es/article2023054.html.

84   **Once considered a pro-opposition network:** "Media Mogul Learns to Live with Chávez," *New York Times*, July 5, 2007.

85   **only if they stayed out of politics:** Baker and Glasser, *Kremlin Rising*, pp. 86–87; Goldman, *PetroState*, p. 102.

85   **Putin had Khodorkovsky arrested:** Goldman, *PetroState*, pp. 103, 106, 113–16. Also Baker and Glasser, *Kremlin Rising*, pp. 286–92.

85 **Starved of resources:** Levitsky and Way, *Competitive Authoritarianism*, p. 198.

85 **emerged as a serious rival:** "Rakibimiz Uzan," *Sabah*, June 4, 2003, http://arsiv.sabah.com.tr/2003/06/04/p01.html.

86 **tax officials audited several Koc companies:** Svante E. Cornell, "Erdogan Versus Koc Holding: Turkey's New Witch Hunt," *Turkey Analyst*, October 9, 2013, http://www.turkeyanalyst.org/publications/turkey-analyst-articles/item/64-erdogan-vs-ko.

86 **"inspectorship of poultry and rabbits":** Edwin Williamson, *Borges: A Life* (New York: Penguin, 2004), pp. 292–95.

87 **El Sistema received increased government funding:** Gustavo Dudamel, "Why I Don't Talk Venezuelan Politics," *Los Angeles Times*, September 29, 2015.

87 **slide into dictatorship:** Gustavo Dudamel, "A Better Way for Venezuela," *New York Times*, July 19, 2017.

87 **He paid a price:** "Venezuela Cancels Gustavo Dudamel Tour After His Criticisms," *New York Times*, August 21, 2017.

88 **parliamentary districts were gerrymandered:** Harold Crouch, *Government and Society in Malaysia* (Ithaca, NY: Cornell University Press, 1996), pp. 58–59, 74.

88 **reduced the number of parliamentary seats:** William Case, "New Uncertainties for an Old Pseudo-Democracy: The Case of Malaysia," *Comparative Politics* 37, no. 1 (October 2004), p. 101.

88 **it banned campaign advertising:** Kim Lane Scheppele, "Understanding Hungary's Constitutional Revolution," in *Constitutional Crisis in the European Constitutional Area*, eds. Armin von Bogdandy and Pal Sonnevend (London: Hart/Beck, 2015), pp. 120–21; and Gabor Toka, "Constitutional Principles and Electoral Democracy in Hungary," in *Constitution Building in Consolidated Democracies: A New Beginning or Decay of a Political System?*, eds. Ellen Bos and Kálmán Pocza (Baden-Baden: Nomos-Verlag, 2014).

89 **preserve its two-thirds majority:** Cas Mudde, "The 2014 Hungarian Parliamentary Elections, or How to Craft a Constitutional Majority," *Washington Post*, April 14, 2014.

89 **emergence of authoritarian single-party regimes:** See V. O. Key Jr., *Southern Politics in State and Nation* (Knoxville: University of Tennessee Press, 1984); and Robert Mickey, *Paths out of Dixie: The Democratization of Authoritarian Enclaves in America's Deep*

South, 1944–1972 (Princeton, NJ: Princeton University Press, 2015).

89 **African Americans suddenly constituted a majority:** Key Jr., *Southern Politics in State and Nation*, p. 537; Richard Vallely, *The Two Reconstructions: The Struggle for Black Enfranchisement* (Chicago: University of Chicago Press, 2004), p. 122.

89 **Federal troops oversaw:** Mickey, *Paths out of Dixie*, p. 38.

89 **In many southern states:** Vallely, *The Two Reconstructions*, pp. 24, 33; Mickey, *Paths out of Dixie*, p. 38.

89 **estimated black turnout was 65 percent:** J. Morgan Kousser, *The Shaping of Southern Politics: Suffrage Restriction and the Establishment of the One-Party South, 1880–1910* (New Haven, CT: Yale University Press, 1974), pp. 15, 28–29.

90 **more than 40 percent:** Mickey, *Paths out of Dixie*, pp. 38, 73; Vallely, *The Two Reconstructions*, pp. 3, 78–79.

90 **to the once-dominant Democrats:** Vallely, *The Two Reconstructions*, p. 77; and Kousser, *The Shaping of Southern Politics*, p. 31.

90 **The Democrats lost power:** Kousser, *The Shaping of Southern Politics*, pp. 26–27, 41.

90 **"status of black belt whites":** Key Jr., *Southern Politics in State and Nation*, p. 8.

90 **"the Negro shall never be heard from":** Quoted in Kousser, *The Shaping of Southern Politics*, p. 209. Toombs once said he was willing to "face thirty years of war to get rid of negro suffrage in the South." Quoted in Eric Foner, *Reconstruction: America's Unfinished Revolution* (New York: HarperCollins, 1988), pp. 590–91.

90 **to disenfranchise African Americans:** Key Jr., *Southern Politics in State and Nation*, pp. 535–39; Kousser, *The Shaping of Southern Politics*; Vallely, *The Two Reconstructions*, pp. 121–48. Two non-Confederate states, Delaware and Oklahoma, also disenfranchised African Americans (Vallely, *The Two Reconstructions*, pp. 122–23).

90 **To comply with the letter of the law:** Mickey, *Paths out of Dixie*, pp. 42–43; Kousser, *The Shaping of Southern Politics*.

90 **"The overarching aim":** Alexander Keyssar, *The Right to Vote: The Contested History of Democracy in the United States* (New York: Basic Books, 2000), p. 89.

90   **"good square, honest law"**: Kousser, *The Shaping of Southern Politics*, p. 190.

90   **"Eight Box Law"**: Mickey, *Paths out of Dixie*, pp. 72–73.

91   **In 1888, Governor John Richardson declared**: Kousser, *The Shaping of Southern Politics*, p. 145.

91   **fell to just 11 percent**: Kousser, *The Shaping of Southern Politics*, p. 92.

91   **"wrecked the Republican Party"**: Mickey, *Paths out of Dixie*, p. 73. Republicans did not win the South Carolina governorship until 1974.

91   **"a sweeping Republican victory"**: Kousser, *The Shaping of Southern Politics*, pp. 103, 113. This paragraph draws on Kousser, *The Shaping of Southern Politics*, pp. 104–121.

91   **"to escape their difficulties"**: Kousser, *The Shaping of Southern Politics*, pp. 131–32.

91   **"Let me sign that bill quickly"**: Eight years later, a constitutional convention added a poll tax, literacy test, and property requirements. See Kousser, *The Shaping of Southern Politics*, p. 137.

92   **"would be almost all white"**: Kousser, *The Shaping of Southern Politics*, p. 224.

92   **Black turnout in the South**: Stephen Tuck, "The Reversal of Black Voting Rights After Reconstruction," in *Democratization in America: A Comparative-Historical Analysis*, eds. Desmond King, Robert C. Lieberman, Gretchen Ritter, and Laurence Whitehead (Baltimore: Johns Hopkins University Press, 2009), p. 140.

92   **"The whole South"**: Foner, *Reconstruction*, p. 582.

93   **an emergency to extend his rule**: William C. Rempel, *Delusions of a Dictator: The Mind of Marcos as Revealed in His Secret Diaries* (Boston: Little, Brown and Company, 1993), pp. 32, 101–3.

93   **a danger like insurrection**: A full video of Marcos's speech, September 23, 1972, ABS-CVN News, https://www.youtube.com /watch?v=bDCHIIXEXes.

93   **"rally 'round the flag"**: See John Mueller, *War, Presidents, and Public Opinion* (New York: Wiley, 1973). More recent empirical studies of the rally-'round-the-flag effect in the United States include John R. Oneal and Anna Lillian Bryan, "The Rally 'Round the Flag Effect in U.S. Foreign Policy Crises,

1950–1985," *Political Behavior* 17, no. 4 (1995), pp. 379–401; Matthew A. Baum, "The Constituent Foundations of the Rally-'Round-the-Flag Phenomenon," *International Studies Quarterly* 46 (2002), pp. 263–98; and J. Tyson Chatagnier, "The Effect of Trust in Government on Rallies 'Round the Flag," *Journal of Peace Research* 49, no. 5 (2012), pp. 631–45.

93 **the highest figure ever recorded by Gallup:** David W. Moore, "Bush Approval Rating Highest in Gallup History," *Gallup News Service*, September 21, 2001. See http://www.gallup.com /poll/4924/bush-job-approval-highest-gallup-history.aspx.

94 **fear for their own safety:** Leonie Huddy, Nadia Khatib, and Theresa Capelos, "The Polls—Trends, Reactions to the Terrorist Attacks of September 11, 2001," *Public Opinion Quarterly* 66 (2002), pp. 418–50; Darren W. Davis and Brian D. Silver, "Civil Liberties vs. Security: Public Opinion in the Context of the Terrorist Attacks on America," *American Journal of Political Science* 48, no. 1 (2004), pp. 28–46; Leonie Huddy, Stanley Feldman, and Christopher Weber, "The Political Consequences of Perceived Threat and Felt Insecurity," *The Annals of the American Academy of Political and Social Science* 614 (2007), pp. 131–53; and Adam J. Berinsky, *In Time of War: Understanding American Public Opinion from World War II to Iraq* (Chicago: University of Chicago Press, 2009), Chapter 7.

94 **In the aftermath of 9/11:** Moore, "Bush Approval Rating Highest in Gallup History."

94 **necessary to give up some civil liberties:** Sourcebook of Criminal Justice Online. Accessed at http://www.albany.edu/sourcebook /ind/TERRORISM.Public_opinion.Civil_liberties.2.html.

94 **After Pearl Harbor:** "Gallup Vault: World War II–Era Support for Japanese Internment," August 31, 2016, http://www.gallup .com/vault/195257/gallup-vault-wwii-era-support-japanese -internment.aspx.

94 **Most constitutions permit:** On "states of exception" in Latin American constitutions, see Brian Loveman, *The Constitution of Tyranny: Regimes of Exception in Spanish America* (Pittsburgh: University of Pittsburgh Press, 1994). On the U.S. Constitution, see Huq and Ginsburg, "How to Lose a Constitutional Democracy," pp. 29–31.

94 **after the coup:** Julio F. Carrion, "Public Opinion, Market Reforms, and Democracy in Fujimori's Peru," in *The Fujimori Leg-*

acy: The Rise of Electoral Authoritarianism in Peru, ed. Julio F. Carrion (University Park: Pennsylvania State University Press, 2005), p. 129.

95 **"communist menace"**: Sterling Seagrave, *The Marcos Dynasty* (New York: Harper and Row, 1988), pp. 243–44; Rempel, *Delusions of a Dictator*, pp. 52–55. In February 1970, Marcos wrote in his diary, "It has saddened me to be driven to the refuge of anti-communism" (Rempel, *Delusions of a Dictator*, p. 53).

95 **a few dozen actual insurgents**: Rempel, *Delusions of a Dictator*, pp. 61, 122, 172–73.

95 **fomented public hysteria**: Seagrave, *The Marcos Dynasty*, p. 244.

95 **Marcos wanted to declare martial law**: Rempel, *Delusions of a Dictator*, pp. 105–7.

95 **the work of government forces**: "Philippines: Marcos Gambles on Martial Law," United States Department of State Declassified Intelligence Note, Bureau of Intelligence Research, Dated October 6, 1972. Also Seagrave, *The Marcos Dynasty*, p. 242.

95 **"nowhere near the scene"**: Stanley Karnow, *In Our Image: America's Empire in the Philippines* (New York: Ballantine Books, 1989), p. 359. Also Seagrave, *The Marcos Dynasty*, p. 262.

95 **The question of whether a young Dutchman**: See account of the historiography by Richard Evans, "The Conspiracists," *London Review of Books* 36, no. 9 (2014), pp. 3–9.

96 **government's own intelligence service**: See John B. Dunlop, *The Moscow Bombings: Examinations of Russian Terrorist Attacks at the Onset of Vladimir Putin's Rule* (London: Ibidem, 2014). Also Baker and Glasser, *Kremlin Rising*, p. 55.

96 **a major boost with the bombings**: Baker and Glasser, *Kremlin Rising*, p. 55.

96 **The Russian public rallied**: Richard Sakwa, *Putin: Russia's Choice*, Second Edition (New York: Routledge, 2007), pp. 20–22; Masha Gessen, *Man Without a Face: The Unlikely Rise of Vladimir Putin* (London: Penguin, 2012), pp. 23–42; Dunlop, *The Moscow Bombings*.

96 **a series of ISIS terrorist attacks**: Cagaptay, *The New Sultan*, pp. 181–82.

96 **even two members of the Constitutional Court**: "Turkey: Events of 2016," Human Rights Watch World Report 2017,

https://www.hrw.org/world-report/2017/country-chapters/turkey. Also "Turkey Coup Attempt: Crackdown Toll Passes 50,000," BBC.com, July 20, 2016.

96 **The power grab culminated:** The reform gave the president the authority to dissolve parliament and unilaterally appoint four-fifths of the Constitutional Court. See the evaluation of the constitutional amendment by the Turkish Bar Association, available at http://anayasadegisikligi.barobirlik.org.tr/Anayasa_Degisikligi.aspx.

CHAPTER 5: THE GUARDRAILS OF DEMOCRACY

97 **a beacon of hope and possibility:** Karen Orren and Stephen Skowronek, *The Search for American Political Development* (Cambridge: Cambridge University Press, 2004), p. 36.

97 **the Constitution was the major reason:** For sources, see Guillermo O'Donnell and Laurence Whitehead, "Two Comparative Democratization Perspectives: 'Brown Areas' and 'Immanence,'" in *Democratization in America: A Comparative-Historical Perspective*, eds. Desmond King, Robert C. Lieberman, Gretchen Ritter, and Laurence Whitehead, p. 48.

98 **Adolf Hitler's usurpation of power:** Kenneth F. Ledford, "German Lawyers and the State in the Weimar Republic," *Law and History Review* 13, no. 2 (1995), pp. 317–49.

98 **near-replicas of the U.S. Constitution:** George Athan Billias, *American Constitutionalism Heard Round the World, 1776–1989* (New York: New York University Press, 2009), pp. 124–25; Zackary Elkins, Tom Ginsburg, and James Melton, *The Endurance of National Constitutions* (New York: Cambridge University Press, 2009), p. 26.

98 **Argentina's 1853 constitution:** Jonathan M. Miller, "The Authority of a Foreign Talisman: A Study of U.S. Constitutional Practice as Authority in Nineteenth Century Argentina and the Argentine Elite's Leap of Faith," *The American University Law Review* 46, no. 5 (1997), pp. 1464–572. Also Billias, *American Constitutionalism Heard Round the World*, pp. 132–35.

98 **Two-thirds of its text:** Miller, "The Authority of a Foreign Talisman," pp. 1510–11.

98 **"provided a textbook example":** Raul C. Pangalangan, "Anointing Power with Piety: People Power, Democracy, and the Rule

of Law," in *Law and Newly Restored Democracies: The Philippines Experience in Restoring Political Participation and Accountability*, ed. Raul C. Pangalangan (Tokyo: Institute of Developing Economies, 2002), p. 3.

99 **"God has never endowed"**: Benjamin Harrison, *This Country of Ours* (New York: Charles Scribner's Sons, 1897), p. ix.

100 **and even contradictory, ways**: Huq and Ginsburg, "How to Lose a Constitutional Democracy," p. 72; also William G. Howell, *Power Without Persuasion: The Politics of Direct Presidential Action* (Princeton, NJ: Princeton University Press, 2003), pp. 13–16.

100 **few constitutional safeguards against filling**: Huq and Ginsburg, "How to Lose a Constitutional Democracy," pp. 61–63; also Bruce Ackerman, *The Decline and Fall of the American Republic* (Cambridge, MA: Harvard University Press, 2010), p. 183.

100 **"thin tissue of convention"**: Huq and Ginsburg, "How to Lose a Constitutional Democracy," p. 70.

100 **does not define the limits of executive power**: Huq and Ginsburg, "How to Lose a Constitutional Democracy," pp. 29, 31. Also Howell, *Power Without Persuasion*, pp. 13–14, 183–87; and Ackerman, *The Decline and Fall of the American Republic*, pp. 67–85.

100 **"a truly antidemocratic leader"**: Huq and Ginsburg, "How to Lose a Constitutional Democracy," pp. 60, 75. Yale constitutional scholar Bruce Ackerman reaches a similar conclusion. See Ackerman, *The Decline and Fall of the American Republic*.

100 **All successful democracies rely on informal rules**: See Gretchen Helmke and Steven Levitsky, eds., *Informal Institutions and Democracy: Lessons from Latin America* (Baltimore: Johns Hopkins University Press, 2006).

100 **unwritten rules**: Princeton constitutional scholar Keith Whittington calls these "conventions." See Keith E. Whittington, "The Status of Unwritten Constitutional Conventions in the United States," *University of Illinois Law Review* 5 (2013), pp. 1847–70.

101 **reinforced by their own unwritten rules**: See Scott Mainwaring and Aníbal Pérez-Liñán, *Democracies and Dictatorships in Latin America: Emergence, Survival, and Fall* (New York: Cambridge University Press, 2013).

102 **Unwritten rules are everywhere:** For a classic account of the norms or "folkways" of the U.S. Senate, see Donald R. Matthews, *U.S. Senators and Their World* (Chapel Hill: University of North Carolina Press, 1960).

102 **As commonsensical as this idea may sound:** Richard Hofstadter, *The Idea of a Party System: The Rise of Legitimate Opposition in the United States, 1780–1840* (Berkeley: University of California Press, 1969), p. 8.

103 **the Federalists regarded them as traitors:** Joseph J. Ellis, *American Sphinx: The Character of Thomas Jefferson* (New York: Alfred A. Knopf, 1997), p. 122; Gordon S. Wood, *The Idea of America: Reflections on the Birth of the United States* (New York: Penguin Books, 2011), p. 114; Hofstadter, *The Idea of a Party System*, pp. 105, 111.

103 **plotting a British-backed monarchic restoration:** Wood, *The Idea of America*, pp. 244–45; Hofstadter, *The Idea of a Party System*, p. 94.

103 **Each side hoped to vanquish:** Wood, *The Idea of America*, p. 245.

103 **rather than destroying each other:** Hofstadter, *The Idea of a Party System*.

103 **The new left-leaning Republican government:** Gabriel Jackson, *The Spanish Republic and the Civil War, 1931–1939* (Princeton, NJ: Princeton University Press, 1965), p. 52.

104 **"bolshevizing foreign agents":** Shlomo Ben-Ami, "The Republican 'Take-Over': Prelude to Inevitable Catastrophe," in *Revolution and War in Spain, 1931–1939*, ed. Paul Preston (London: Routledge, 2001), pp. 58–60.

104 **"We have now entered the vortex":** Gerard Alexander, *The Sources of Democratic Consolidation* (Ithaca, NY: Cornell University Press, 2002), p. 111.

104 **as monarchist or fascist counterrevolutionaries:** Raymond Carr, *Spain 1808–1939* (Oxford: Oxford University Press, 1966), p. 621.

104 **willing to play the democratic game:** Michael Mann, *Fascists* (Cambridge: Cambridge University Press, 2004), p. 330.

105 **fundamentally "disloyal":** Juan J. Linz, "From Great Hopes to Civil War: The Breakdown of Democracy in Spain," in *The Breakdown of Democratic Regimes: Europe*, eds. Juan J. Linz and

Alfred Stepan (Baltimore: Johns Hopkins University Press, 1978), p. 162.

105 **a profound threat:** Jackson, *The Spanish Republic and the Civil War*, pp. 147–48.

105 **"break all solidarity with the present institutions":** Quoted in Linz, "From Great Hopes to Civil War," p. 161.

105 **brutally repressed the uprising:** As many as 2,000 workers were killed in the repression, and an estimated 20,000 leftists were imprisoned. See Hugh Thomas, *The Spanish Civil War* (London: Penguin Books, 2001), p. 136; Stanley Payne, *The Franco Regime 1936–1974* (Madison: University of Wisconsin Press, 1987), p. 43.

105 **associate the entire Republican opposition:** Jackson, *The Spanish Republic and the Civil War*, pp. 165–68.

106 **institutional forbearance:** We borrow the term *forbearance* from Alisha Holland. See Alisha Holland, "Forbearance," *American Political Science Review* 110, no. 2 (May 2016), pp. 232–46; and Holland, *Forbearance as Redistribution: The Politics of Informal Welfare in Latin America* (New York: Cambridge University Press, 2017). Also see Eric Nelson, "Are We on the Verge of the Death Spiral That Produced the English Revolution of 1642–1649?," History News Network, December 14, 2014, http://historynewsnetwork.org/article/157822.

106 **"patient self-control":** *Oxford Dictionary,* See https://en.oxford dictionaries.com/definition/forbearance.

106 **to the hilt:** Whittington, "The Status of Unwritten Constitutional Conventions in the United States," p. 106.

106 **divine-right rule:** Reinhard Bendix, *Kings or People: Power and the Mandate to Rule* (Berkeley: University of California Press, 1978), p. 7.

106 **To be "godly":** Edmund Morgan, *Inventing the People: The Rise of Popular Sovereignty in England and America* (New York: W. W. Norton, 1988), p. 21; Bendix, *Kings or People*, p. 234.

107 **"future ages groan for this foul act":** Anthony Dawson and Paul Yachnin, eds., *Richard II, The Oxford Shakespeare* (Oxford: Oxford University Press, 2011), p. 241.

107 **"a matter of royal prerogative":** Whittington, "The Status of Unwritten Constitutional Conventions in the United States," p. 107.

107   **not a law but a norm:** Julia R. Azari and Jennifer K. Smith, "Unwritten Rules: Informal Institutions in Established Democracies," *Perspectives on Politics* 10, no. 1 (March 2012); also Whittington, "The Status of Unwritten Constitutional Conventions in the United States," pp. 109–12.

108   **"I should unwillingly be":** Thomas Jefferson, Letter to the Vermont State Legislature, December 10, 1807, quoted in Thomas H. Neale, *Presidential Terms and Tenure: Perspectives and Proposals for Change* (Washington, DC: Congressional Research Service, 2004), p. 5.

108   **"departure from this time-honored custom":** Bruce Peabody, "George Washington, Presidential Term Limits, and the Problem of Reluctant Political Leadership," *Presidential Studies Quarterly* 31, no. 3, p. 402.

108   **violate an "unwritten law":** Whittington, "The Status of Unwritten Constitutional Conventions in the United States," p. 110. When Theodore Roosevelt sought a nonconsecutive third term in 1912, he failed to win the Republican nomination, and when he ran as an independent, he was shot on the campaign trail by a man who claimed to be defending the two-term limit. See Elkins, Ginsburg, and Melton, *The Endurance of National Constitutions*, p. 47.

108   **FDR's reelection in 1940:** Azari and Smith, "Unwritten Rules: Informal Institutions in Established Democracies," p. 44.

108   **especially important in presidential democracies:** See Nelson, "Are We on the Verge of the Death Spiral That Produced the English Revolution of 1642–1649?"

108   **can easily bring deadlock:** Juan J. Linz, "The Perils of Presidentialism," *Journal of Democracy* 1, no. 1 (January 1990), pp. 51–69; also see Gretchen Helmke, *Institutions on the Edge: The Origins and Consequences of Inter-Branch Crises in Latin America* (New York: Cambridge University Press, 2017).

109   **"playing for keeps":** Mark Tushnet, "Constitutional Hardball," *The John Marshall Law Review* 37 (2004), pp. 550, 523–53.

109   **"malfeasance" as grounds for impeachment:** Page, *Perón*, p. 165.

109   **authority to issue decrees:** Delia Ferreria Rubio and Matteo Gorreti, "When the President Governs Alone: The *Decretazo* in Argentina, 1989–1993," in *Executive Decree Authority*, eds. John

M. Carey and Matthew Soberg Shugart (New York: Cambridge University Press, 1998).

109 **Menem showed no such restraint:** Ferreria Rubio and Gorreti, "When the President Governs Alone," pp. 33, 50.

109 **congress passed an amnesty law:** "Venezuela's Supreme Court Consolidates President Nicolás Maduro's Power," *New York Times*, October 12, 2016; "Supremo de Venezuela declara constitucional el Decreto de Emergencia Económica," *El País*, January 21, 2016. See http://internacional.elpais.com/internacional/2016/01/21/america/1453346802_377899.html.

110 **The *chavista* court:** "Venezuela Leaps Towards Dictatorship," *The Economist*, March 31, 2017; "Maduro podrá aprobar el presupuesto a espaldas del Parlamento," *El País*, October 13, 2016. See http://internacional.elpais.com/internacional/2016/10/13/america/1476370249_347078.html; "Venezuela's Supreme Court Consolidates President Nicolás Maduro's Power," *New York Times*, October 12, 2016; "Supremo de Venezuela declara constitucional el Decreto de Emergencia Económica," *El País*, January 21, 2016. See http://internacional.elpais.com/internacional/2016/01/21/america/1453346802_377899.html.

110 **"all the laws it has approved":** "Radiografía de los chavistas que controlan el TSJ en Venezuela," *El Tiempo*, August 29, 2016. See http://www.eltiempo.com/mundo/latinoamerica/perfil-de-los-jueces-del-tribunal-supremo-de-justicia-de-venezuela-44143.

110 **few friends in congress:** Lev Marsteintredet, Mariana Llanos, and Detlef Nolte, "Paraguay and the Politics of Impeachment," *Journal of Democracy* 42, no. 4 (2013), p. 113.

110 **removed from office by the senate:** Marsteintredet, Llanos, and Nolte, "Paraguay and the Politics of Impeachment," pp. 112–14.

110 **"obvious farce":** Francisco Toro, "What's in a Coup?," *New York Times*, June 29, 2012.

110 **it was legal:** Article 225 of Paraguay's 1992 Constitution allows Congress to impeach the president for "poor performance of his duties," a "willfully vague formulation that could mean almost anything that two-thirds of sitting senators want it to mean." See Toro, "What's in a Coup?"

110 **"The Crazy One":** Aníbal Pérez-Liñán, *Presidential Impeachment and the New Political Instability in Latin America* (New York: Cambridge University Press, 2007), p. 26.

111 **milk named after himself:** Carlos De la Torre, *Populist Seduction in Latin America*, Second Edition (Athens, OH: Ohio University Press, 2010), p. 106; Pérez-Liñán, *Presidential Impeachment and the New Political Instability in Latin America*, p. 155.

111 **In a clear violation:** See De la Torre, *Populist Seduction in Latin America*, p. 102; Ximena Sosa, "Populism in Ecuador: From José M. Velasco to Rafael Correa," in *Populism in Latin America*, Second Edition, ed. Michael L. Conniff (Tuscaloosa, AL: University of Alabama Press, 2012), pp. 172–73; and Pérez-Liñán, *Presidential Impeachment and the New Political Instability in Latin America*, p. 26.

111 **"in a perfectly legal way":** Kousser, *The Shaping of Southern Politics,* pp. 134–36.

112 **"cycle of escalating constitutional brinksmanship":** Nelson, "Are We on the Verge of the Death Spiral That Produced the English Revolution of 1642–1649?" Also Linz, "The Perils of Presidentialism," and Helmke, *Institutions on the Edge.*

113 **"spiral of legislative obstruction":** Nelson, "Are We on the Verge of the Death Spiral That Produced the English Revolution of 1642–1649?"

113 **vibrant democratic norms:** See Arturo Valenzuela, *The Breakdown of Democratic Regimes: Chile* (Baltimore: Johns Hopkins University Press, 1978), pp. 13–20.

113 **"culture of compromise":** Pamela Constable and Arturo Valenzuela, *A Nation of Enemies: Chile Under Pinochet* (New York: W. W. Norton, 1991), pp. 21–22. Also Luis Maira, "The Strategy and Tactics of the Chilean Counterrevolution in the Area of Political Institutions," in *Chile at the Turning Point: Lessons of the Socialist Years, 1970–1973*, eds. Federico Gil, Ricardo Lagos, and Henry Landsberger (Philadelphia: Institute for the Study of Human Issues, 1979), p. 247.

113 **"There was no argument":** Constable and Valenzuela, *A Nation of Enemies*, p. 21.

113 **strained by Cold War polarization:** Valenzuela, *The Breakdown of Democratic Regimes*, pp. 22–39.

113 **bourgeois anachronism:** Constable and Valenzuela, *A Nation of Enemies*, p. 25.

113 **into another Cuba:** Youssef Cohen, *Radicals, Reformers, and Reactionaries: The Prisoner's Dilemma and the Collapse of Democracy*

in Latin America (Chicago: University of Chicago Press, 1994), p. 100.

114 **"gigantic campaign of hatred"**: Rodrigo Tomic, "Christian Democracy and the Government of the Unidad Popular," in *Chile at the Turning Point: Lessons of the Socialist Years, 1970–1973*, eds. Federico Gil, Ricardo Lagos, and Henry Landsberger, p. 232.

114 **committed to democracy**: Paul Sigmund, *The Overthrow of Allende and the Politics of Chile, 1964–1976* (Pittsburgh: University of Pittsburgh Press, 1977), p. 18; Valenzuela, *The Breakdown of Democratic Regimes*, p. 45.

114 **by any means necessary**: Julio Faúndez, *Marxism and Democracy in Chile: From 1932 to the Fall of Allende* (New Haven, CT: Yale University Press, 1988), p. 181.

114 **Abandoning forbearance**: Valenzuela, *The Breakdown of Democratic Regimes*, p. 48; Sigmund, *The Overthrow of Allende*, p. 111.

114 **Statute of Guarantees**: Sigmund, *The Overthrow of Allende*, pp. 118–20; Faúndez, *Marxism and Democracy in Chile*, pp. 188–90.

114 **"breakdown in mutual understanding"**: Valenzuela, *The Breakdown of Democratic Regimes*, p. 49.

114 **Lacking a legislative majority**: Valenzuela, *The Breakdown of Democratic Regimes*, pp. 50–60, 81; Ricardo Israel, *Politics and Ideology in Allende's Chile* (Tempe: Arizona State University Center for Latin American Studies, 1989), pp. 210–16.

114 **"legal loopholes"**: Sigmund, *The Overthrow of Allende*, p. 133; Cohen, *Radicals, Reformers, and Reactionaries*, pp. 104–5.

115 **"institutional checkmate"**: Maira, "The Strategy and Tactics of the Chilean Counterrevolution," pp. 249–56.

115 **it would be a weapon**: Maira, "The Strategy and Tactics of the Chilean Counterrevolution," pp. 249–56; Israel, *Politics and Ideology in Allende's Chile*, p. 216.

115 **Allende responded by reappointing**: Sigmund, *The Overthrow of Allende*, p. 164.

115 **His leftist allies**: Valenzuela, *The Breakdown of Democratic Regimes*, p. 67; Constable and Valenzuela, *A Nation of Enemies*, p. 28.

115 **"opening the door to fascism"**: Valenzuela, *The Breakdown of Democratic Regimes*, pp. 67–77.

115 **"not let Allende score a single goal"**: Israel, *Politics and Ideology in Allende's Chile*, p. 80.

116 **"constitutional overthrow"**: Jorge Tapia Videla, "The Difficult Road to Socialism: The Chilean Case from a Historical Perspective," in *Chile at the Turning Point: Lessons of the Socialist Years, 1970–1973*, eds. Federico Gil, Ricardo Lagos, and Henry Landsberger, p. 56; Sigmund, *The Overthrow of Allende*, p. 282; Valenzuela, *The Breakdown of Democratic Regimes*, pp. 83–85.

116 **"an illegitimate head of state"**: Valenzuela, *The Breakdown of Democratic Regimes*, pp. 89–94.

117 **the government was unconstitutional**: Cohen, *Radicals, Reformers, and Reactionaries*, p. 117.

CHAPTER 6: THE UNWRITTEN RULES OF AMERICAN POLITICS

118 **"I shall ask the Congress"**: Franklin Roosevelt, First Inaugural Address, March 4, 1933, The Avalon Project: Documents in Law, History, and Diplomacy, Yale Law School, http://avalon.law.yale.edu/20th_century/froos1.asp.

118 **The Court found large portions**: Samuel Eliot Morison and Henry Steele Commager, *The Growth of the American Republic* (New York: Oxford University Press, 1953), pp. 615–16.

119 **Roosevelt's proposal**: Sidney Milkis and Michael Nelson, *The American Presidency: Origins and Development, 1776–2014*, Seventh Edition (Washington, DC: Congressional Quarterly Press, 2016), pp. 378–79.

119 **Roosevelt's court-packing plan**: Noah Feldman, *Scorpions: The Battles and Triumphs of FDR's Great Supreme Court Justices* (New York: Twelve, 2010), p. 108.

120 **the Federalists passed**: Hofstadter, *The Idea of a Party System*, p. 107.

120 **The act was used**: Matthew Crenson and Benjamin Ginsberg, *Presidential Power: Unchecked and Unbalanced* (New York: W. W. Norton, 2007), pp. 49–50; Hofstadter, *The Idea of a Party System*, pp. 107–11.

120 **"legal and constitutional step"**: Hofstadter, *The Idea of a Party System*, pp. 136, 140; Wood, *The Idea of America*, p. 246.

121 **"typified the spirit"**: Ibid., p. 216.

121 **"many opponents"**: Donald B. Cole, *Martin Van Buren and the American Political System* (Princeton, NJ: Princeton University Press, 1984), pp. 39, 430.

121 **Van Buren's generation**: See Hofstadter, *The Idea of a Party System*, pp. 216–31.

121 **"emotional intensity"**: Donald Fehrenbacher, *The South and the Three Sectional Crises* (Baton Rouge: Louisiana State University Press, 1980), p. 27.

121 **"raised above the whites"**: Quoted in John Niven, *John C. Calhoun and the Price of Union: A Biography* (Baton Rouge: Louisiana State University Press, 1988), p. 325.

122 **"traitors to the Constitution"**: Representative Henry M. Shaw, U.S. House of Representatives, April 20, 1858. See https://archive.org/details/kansasquestionsp00shaw; Ulrich Bonnell Phillips, *The Life of Robert Toombs* (New York: The MacMillan Company, 1913), p. 183.

122 **Antislavery politicians**: Representative Thaddeus Stevens, U.S. House of Representatives, February 20, 1850. See https://catalog.hathitrust.org/Record/009570624.

122 **Yale historian Joanne Freeman**: Joanne B. Freeman, "Violence Against Members of Congress Has a Long, and Ominous, History," *Washington Post*, June 15, 2017. Also see Joanne B. Freeman, *The Field of Blood: Congressional Violence and the Road to Civil War* (New York: Farrar, Straus and Giroux, 2018).

122 **President Lincoln famously suspended**: Milkis and Nelson, *The American Presidency*, pp. 212–13.

122 **The sheer destruction**: Louis Menand, *The Metaphysical Club: A Story of Ideas in America* (New York: Farrar, Straus and Giroux, 2001), p. 61.

122 **then–political science professor Woodrow Wilson**: Woodrow Wilson, *Congressional Government: A Study in American Politics* (Boston: Houghton Mifflin Company, 1885).

123 **"Every man that tried"**: Robert Green Ingersoll, *Fifty Great Selections, Lectures, Tributes, After Dinner Speeches* (New York: C. P. Farrell, 1920), pp. 157–58.

123 **the Republican Congress reduced**: Horwill, *The Usages of the American Constitution*, p. 188.

124 **"high misdemeanor"**: Keith Whittington, "Bill Clinton Was No Andrew Johnson: Comparing Two Impeachments," *University of*

Pennsylvania Journal of Constitutional Law 2 no. 2 (May 2000), pp. 438–39.

124 **"fold up the bloody shirt":** Charles Calhoun, *From Bloody Shirt to Full Dinner Pail: The Transformation of Politics and Governance in the Gilded Age* (New York: Hill and Wang, 2010), p. 88.

124 **The pact effectively ended:** C. Vann Woodward, *Reunion and Reaction: The Compromise of 1877 and the End of Reconstruction* (Boston: Little, Brown and Company), 1966.

125 **polarization gradually declined:** Nolan McCarty, Keith Poole, and Howard Rosenthal, *Polarized America: The Dance of Ideology and Unequal Riches* (Cambridge, MA: MIT Press, 2008), p. 10.

125 **Bipartisan cooperation enabled:** Kimberly Morgan and Monica Prasad, "The Origins of Tax Systems: A French American Comparison," *American Journal of Sociology* 114, no. 5 (2009), p. 1366.

125 **In his two-volume masterpiece:** James Bryce, *The American Commonwealth*, vol. 1 (New York: Macmillan and Company, 1896), pp. 393–94.

127 **It is virtually silent:** Howell, *Power Without Persuasion*, pp. 13–14.

127 **the executive branch has built up:** Arthur Schlesinger, *The Imperial Presidency* (Boston: Houghton Mifflin, [1973] 2004); Crenson and Ginsberg, *Presidential Power*; Ackerman, *The Decline and Fall of the American Republic*; Milkis and Nelson, *The American Presidency*; Chris Edelson, *Power Without Constraint: The Post-9/11 Presidency and National Security* (Madison: University of Wisconsin Press, 2016).

128 **"constitutional battering ram":** Ackerman, *The Decline and Fall of the American Republic*, pp. 87–119; Crenson and Ginsberg, *Presidential Power*, pp. 180–351; Edelson, *Power Without Constraint*.

128 **Presidents who find their agenda stalled:** William Howell, "Unitary Powers: A Brief Overview," *Presidential Studies Quarterly* 35, no. 3 (2005), p. 417.

128 **presidents can circumvent the judiciary:** See James F. Simon, *Lincoln and Chief Justice Taney: Slavery, Secession, and the President's War Powers* (New York: Simon & Schuster, 2007).

128 **"naturally inspire scrupulousness and caution":** Alexander Hamilton, Federalist 74.

128 **"I walk on untrodden ground"**: Quoted in Fred Greenstein, *Inventing the Job of President: Leadership Style from George Washington to Andrew Jackson* (Princeton, NJ: Princeton University Press, 2009), p. 9.

129 **He energetically defended**: Milkis and Nelson, *The American Presidency*, p. 91.

129 **He limited his use**: Ibid., p. 82.

129 **"signed many bills"**: Quoted in ibid., p. 82.

129 **Washington was also reluctant**: Gerhard Peters and John T. Woolley, "Executive Orders," The American Presidency Project, eds. John T. Woolley and Gerhard Peters, Santa Barbara, CA, 1999–2017. Available at http://www.presidency.ucsb.edu/data/orders.php.

129 **"gained power from his readiness"**: Gary Wills, *Cincinnatus: George Washington and the Enlightenment* (Garden City, NY: Doubleday, 1984), p. 23.

129 **"If any single person"**: Gordon Wood, *Revolutionary Characters: What Made the Founders Different* (New York: Penguin, 2006), pp. 30–31. Also see Seymour Martin Lipset, "George Washington and the Founding of Democracy," *Journal of Democracy* 9, no. 4 (October 1998), pp. 24–36.

129 **stewardship theory**: Stephen Skowronek, *The Politics Presidents Make: Leadership from John Adams to Bill Clinton* (Cambridge, MA: Harvard University Press, 1993), pp. 243–44.

129 **"boundless energy and ambition"**: Quoted in Milkis and Nelson, *The American Presidency*, pp. 125–27.

129 **"Don't you realize"**: Quoted in ibid., p. 125.

129 **Roosevelt acted with surprising restraint**: Ibid., p. 128.

130 **He took great care**: Sidney Milkis and Michael Nelson, *The American Presidency: Origins and Development, 1776–2007*, Fifth Edition (Washington, DC: Congressional Quarterly Press, 2008), p. 217.

130 **Roosevelt operated well within**: Ibid., pp. 289–90.

130 **presidents abided by established norms**: Crenson and Ginsberg, *Presidential Power*, p. 211; Ackerman, *The Decline and Fall of the American Republic*, p. 87.

130 **They never used pardons**: Lauren Schorr, "Breaking the Pardon Power: Congress and the Office of the Pardon Attorney," *American Criminal Law Review* 46 (2009), pp. 1535–62.

131   **"ardent Federalist"**: Alexander Pope Humphrey, "The Impeachment of Samuel Chase," *The Virginia Law Register* 5, no. 5 (September 1889), pp. 283–89.

131   **Jefferson pushed for his impeachment**: Ellis, *American Sphinx*, p. 225.

131   **"political persecution from beginning to end"**: Humphrey, "The Impeachment of Samuel Chase," p. 289. Historian Richard Hofstadter describes Chase's impeachment as an "act of partisan warfare, pure and simple" (Hofstadter, *The Idea of a Party System,* p. 163).

131   **The Senate acquitted Chase:** Lee Epstein and Jeffrey A. Segal, *Advice and Consent: The Politics of Judicial Appointment* (New York: Oxford University Press, 2005), p. 31.

131   **Beginning with the Federalists' move:** The seven instances are these: 1) In 1800, when the lame-duck Federalist Congress reduced the Court from 6 to 5 to limit Jefferson's ability to shape the judiciary; 2) In 1801, when the newly installed Jeffersonian Congress restored the Court's size from 5 to 6; 3) In 1807, when Congress expanded the Court to 7 to give Jefferson an additional appointment; 4) In 1837, when Congress expanded the Court to 9 to give Andrew Jackson two additional appointments; 5) In 1863, when Congress expanded the Court to 10 to grant Lincoln an additional antislavery justice; 6) In 1866, when the Republican-dominated Congress reduced the Court to 7 to limit Democratic President Andrew Johnson's ability to shape the Court; 7) In 1869, when the Congress expanded the Court to 9 to give newly elected Republican President Ulysses S. Grant two additional appointments. See Jean Edward Smith, "Stacking the Court," *New York Times*, July 26, 2007.

131   **"such outrages"**: Woodrow Wilson, *An Old Master and Other Political Essays* (New York: Charles Scribner's Sons, 1893), p. 151.

131   **"is very tempting to partisans"**: Benjamin Harrison, *This Country of Ours* (New York: Charles Scribner's Sons, 1897), p. 317.

131   **"strong enough to prohibit"**: Horwill, *The Usages of the American Constitution*, p. 190.

132   **"extraordinary in its hubris"**: Lee Epstein and Jeffrey A. Segal, *Advice and Consent: The Politics of Judicial Appointment* (New York: Oxford University Press, 2005), p. 46.

132   "open declaration of war": Quoted in H. W. Brands, *Traitor to His Class: The Privileged Life and Radical Presidency of Franklin Delano Roosevelt* (New York: Doubleday, 2008), pp. 470–71.

132   "a step toward making himself dictator": Quoted in Feldman, *Scorpions*, p. 108.

132   "change the meaning": Brands, *Traitor to His Class*, p. 472.

132   "The whole mess smells of Machiavelli": Gene Gressley, "Joseph C. O'Mahoney, FDR, and the Supreme Court," *Pacific Historical Review* 40, no. 2 (1971), p. 191.

133   "masterly retreat": Morison and Commager, *The Growth of the American Republic*, p. 618.

133   It developed a range of tools: Gregory Koger, *Filibustering: A Political History of Obstruction in the House and Senate* (Chicago: University of Chicago Press, 2010); Gregory J. Wawro and Eric Schickler, *Filibuster: Obstruction and Lawmaking in the U.S. Senate* (Princeton, NJ: Princeton University Press, 2006).

133   the Senate lacked any rules: Wawro and Schickler, *Filibuster*, p. 6.

134   "[Each senator] has vast power": Matthews, *U.S. Senators and Their World*, p. 100.

134   such dysfunction did not occur: Ibid., p. 101; Wawro and Schickler, *Filibuster*, p. 41.

134   "exist as a potential threat": Matthews, *U.S. Senators and Their World*, p. 101.

134   Matthews's seminal study: Ibid.; also Donald Matthews, "The Folkways of the United States Senate: Conformity to Group Norms and Legislative Effectiveness," *American Political Science Review* 53, no. 4 (December 1959), pp. 1064–89.

134   Courtesy meant: Matthews, *U.S. Senators and Their World*, pp. 98–99.

134   "it is hard": Quoted in Matthews, "Folkways," 1959, p. 1069.

134   "your enemies on one issue": Matthews, *U.S. Senators and Their World*, p. 98.

134   "dictates at least a semblance": Ibid., p. 99.

134   "If a senator does push": Matthews, "Folkways," p. 1072.

135   "It's not a matter of friendship": Quoted in Matthews, *U.S. Senators and Their World*, p. 100.

135 **No institutional tool:** On the origins and evolution of the Senate filibuster, see Sarah Binder and Steven Smith, *Politics or Principle? Filibustering in the United States Senate* (Washington, DC: Brookings Institution Press, 1997); Wawro and Schickler, *Filibuster*; and Koger, *Filibustering*.

135 **Yet this rarely happened:** Wawro and Schickler, *Filibuster*, pp. 25–28.

135 **"procedural weapon of last resort":** Binder and Smith, *Politics or Principle?*, p. 114.

135 **only twenty-three manifest filibusters:** Ibid., p. 11.

135 **A modest increase in filibuster use:** Wawro and Schickler, *Filibuster*, p. 41.

135 **Sarah Binder and Steven Smith:** Binder and Smith, *Politics or Principle?*, p. 60.

135 **Filibuster use remained low:** Ibid., p. 9.

135 **"advice and consent":** Horwill, *The Usages of the American Constitution*, pp. 126–28; Lee Epstein and Jeffrey A. Segal, *Advice and Consent: The Politics of Judicial Appointments* (New York: Oxford University Press, 2007); Robin Bradley Kar and Jason Mazzone, "The Garland Affair: What History and the Constitution *Really* Say About President Obama's Powers to Appoint a Replacement for Justice Scalia," *New York University Law Review* 91 (May 2016), pp. 58–61.

135 **This has not happened:** Horwill, *The Usages of the American Constitution*, pp. 137–38; Kar and Mazzone, "The Garland Affair," pp. 59–60.

135 **Only nine presidential cabinet nominations:** Epstein and Segal, *Advice and Consent*, p. 21.

136 **"unbroken practice of three generations":** Horwill, *The Usages of the American Constitution*, pp. 137–38.

136 **more than 90 percent:** Based on Kar and Mazzone, "The Garland Affair," pp. 107–14.

136 **Highly qualified nominees:** Epstein and Segal, *Advice and Consent*, p. 106.

136 **The ultraconservative Antonin Scalia:** Ibid., p. 107.

136 **And on all seventy-four occasions:** Based on Kar and Mazzone, "The Garland Affair," pp. 107–14.

136 **"the heaviest piece of artillery":** James Bryce, *American Commonwealth* (New York: Macmillan and Company, [1888] 1896), p. 211.

137 **"partisan tool for undermining electoral officials":** Keith Whittington, "An Impeachment Should Not Be a Partisan Affair," *Lawfare*, May 16, 2017.

137 **The legal barriers to impeachment:** Ibid.

137 **"The House of Representatives should not":** Tushnet, "Constitutional Hardball," p. 528.

138 **His use of executive orders:** Data from Gerhard Peters and John T. Woolley, "The American Presidency Project" (2017), http://www.presidency.ucsb.edu/executive_orders.php?year=2017.

138 **His decision to seek:** Constitutional scholar Noah Feldman describes the court-packing scheme as "one of the most remarkable pieces of constitutional one-upsmanship ever tried." See Feldman, *Scorpions*, p. 108.

139 **The advent of the Cold War:** Edward Shils, *The Torment of Secrecy* (Glencoe: Free Press, 1956), p. 140.

139 **McCarthy took the national stage:** Richard Fried, *Nightmare in Red: The McCarthy Era in Perspective* (Oxford: Oxford University Press, 1990), p. 122.

139 **"I have here in my hand":** Quoted in ibid., p. 123.

139 **Moderate Republicans were alarmed:** Ibid., p. 125.

139 **"Keep talking":** Quoted in ibid., p. 125.

139 **"Pick up your phone":** Quoted in Robert Griffith, *The Politics of Fear: Joseph McCarthy and the Senate* (Amherst: University of Massachusetts Press, 1970), pp. 53–54.

140 **"Pink Lady":** Iwan Morgan, *Nixon* (London: Arnold Publishers, 2002), p. 19.

140 **"Red Pepper":** Matthews, *U.S. Senators and Their World*, p. 70.

140 **McCarthy repeatedly impugned:** Fried, *Nightmare in Red*, p. 22.

140 **Eisenhower initially resisted:** David Nichols, *Ike and McCarthy: Dwight Eisenhower's Secret Campaign Against Joseph McCarthy* (New York: Basic Books, 2017), pp. 12–15.

141 **Even Nixon:** Morgan, *Nixon*, p. 53.

141   "was at pains": Ibid., p. 57.

141   "kept the McCarthyist spirit alive": Geoffrey Kabaservice, *Rule and Ruin: The Downfall of Moderation and the Destruction of the Republican Party, from Eisenhower to the Tea Party* (New York: Oxford University Press, 2012), p. 126.

141   press as enemies: Morgan, *Nixon*, pp. 158–59; Keith W. Olson, *Watergate: The Presidential Scandal That Shook America* (Lawrence: University Press of Kansas, 2003). p. 2.

141   anarchists and communists: Jonathan Schell, "The Time of Illusion," *The New Yorker*, June 2, 1975; Olson, *Watergate*, p. 30.

141   "We're up against an enemy": Morgan, *Nixon*, p. 24.

141   "at war, internally": Rick Perlstein, *Nixonland: The Rise of a President and the Fracturing of America* (New York: Scribner, 2008), p. 667.

141   The Nixon administration's path: Morgan, *Nixon*, pp. 160, 179; Olson, *Watergate*, p. 12; Perlstein, *Nixonland*, pp. 517, 676.

142   "dozens of Democrats": Morgan, *Nixon*, p. 24.

142   The administration also deployed: Perlstein, *Nixonland*, p. 413.

142   Nixon's criminal assault on democratic institutions: Olson, *Watergate*, pp. 35–42.

142   "bipartisan search for the unvarnished truth": Quoted in ibid., p. 90.

142   nearly a dozen Republican senators: Ibid., pp. 76–82.

142   Cox requested that Nixon: Ibid., p. 102.

142   Rodino had sufficient Republican support: Ibid., p. 155.

142   Nixon held out hope: Morgan, *Nixon*, pp. 186–87.

143   "Ten at most, maybe less": Olson, *Watergate*, p. 164.

143   America's full democratization: Eric Schickler, *Racial Realignment: The Transformation of American Liberalism, 1932–1965* (Princeton, NJ: Princeton University Press, 2016).

144   the greatest challenge to established forms: Also see Mickey, Levitsky, and Way, "Is America Still Safe for Democracy?," pp. 20–29.

CHAPTER 7: THE UNRAVELING

145   "If Scalia has actually passed away": This reconstruction below of the social media response to Scalia's death is based on two

sources: Jonathan Chait, "Will the Supreme Court Just Disappear?," *New York Magazine*, February 21, 2016, and "Supreme Court Justice Antonin Scalia Dies: Legal and Political Worlds React," *The Guardian*, February 14, 2016.

145 **"What is less than zero?":** Ibid.

145 **the first time in American history:** Kar and Mazzone, "The Garland Affair," pp. 53–111. According to Kar and Mazzone, there are six occasions in American history—all prior to the twentieth century—in which the Senate has refused to vote on a president's Supreme Court nominee. In all six cases, the legitimacy of the appointment was open to question because the nomination was made after the election of the president's successor or because the president himself had not been elected but had succeeded to office via the vice presidency (during the nineteenth century, there was a constitutional debate over whether vice presidents who succeeded to office were truly presidents or merely acting presidents).

146 **every time a president:** Based on Kar and Mazzone, "The Garland Affair," pp. 107–14.

147 **"Boy Scout words":** Text of speech reprinted in "To College Republicans: Text of Gingrich Speech," *West Georgia News*. Reprinted: http://www.pbs.org/wgbh/pages/frontline/newt/newt78 speech.html.

147 **House Minority Leader Bob Michel:** Ike Brannon, "Bob Michel, House GOP Statesman Across Five Decades, Dies at Age 93," *Weekly Standard*, February 17, 2017.

147 **Winning a Republican majority:** Ronald Brownstein, *The Second Civil War: How Extreme Partisanship Has Paralyzed Washington and Polarized America* (New York: Penguin, 2007), pp. 137, 144; Thomas E. Mann and Norman J. Ornstein, *The Broken Branch: How Congress Is Failing America and How to Get It Back on Track* (Oxford: Oxford University Press, 2008), p. 65.

147 **Gingrich launched an insurgency:** Matt Grossman and David A. Hopkins, *Asymmetric Politics: Ideological Republicans and Interest Group Democrats* (New York: Oxford University Press, 2016), p. 285.

148 **"used adjectives like rocks":** Brownstein, *The Second Civil War*, p. 142.

148 **He questioned his Democratic rivals' patriotism:** Thomas E. Mann and Norman J. Ornstein, *It's Even Worse Than It Looks:*

How the American Constitutional System Collided with the New Politics of Extremism (New York: Basic Books, 2016), p. 35.

148 **"destroy our country"**: Quoted in James Salzer, "Gingrich's Language Set New Course," *Atlanta Journal-Constitution*, January 29, 2012.

148 **"the things that came out of Gingrich's mouth"**: Quoted in Salzer, "Gingrich's Language Set New Course."

148 **Gingrich's former press secretary Tony Blankley**: Gail Sheehy, "The Inner Quest of Newt Gingrich," *Vanity Fair*, January 12, 2012.

148 **Gingrich and his team distributed memos**: Mann and Ornstein, *It's Even Worse Than It Looks*, p. 39; James Salzer, "Gingrich's Language Set New Course."

149 **"Gingrich Senators"**: Sean Theriault, *The Gingrich Senators: The Roots of Partisan Warfare in Congress* (Oxford: Oxford University Press, 2013).

149 **"transformed American politics"**: Quoted in Salzer, "Gingrich's Language Set New Course."

149 **Senate Minority Leader Robert Dole**: Michael Wines, "G.O.P. Filibuster Stalls Passage of Clinton $16 Billion Jobs Bill," *New York Times*, April 2, 1993.

149 **Filibuster use**: Binder and Smith, *Politics or Principle?*, pp. 10–11; Mann and Ornstein, *The Broken Branch*, pp. 107–8.

149 **"epidemic" levels**: Former senator Charles Mathias, quoted in Binder and Smith, *Politics or Principle?*, p. 6.

149 **the annual number of cloture motions**: Data from United States Senate. See https://www.senate.gov/pagelayout/reference/cloture_motions/clotureCounts.htm.

150 **House Republicans refused to compromise**: Mann and Ornstein, *The Broken Branch*, pp. 109–10; Grossman and Hopkins, *Asymmetric Politics*, p. 293.

150 **"on a technicality"**: Whittington, "Bill Clinton Was No Andrew Johnson," p. 459.

150 **In an act without precedent**: The 1868 impeachment of Andrew Johnson was a far more serious affair, involving a high-stakes dispute over the constitutional authority of the president. See Whittington, "Bill Clinton Was No Andrew Johnson."

151 **"just another weapon in the partisan wars"**: Mann and Ornstein, *The Broken Branch*, p. 122.

151 **He demonstrated this**: Jacob Hacker and Paul Pierson, *Winner Take All Politics* (New York: Simon & Schuster, 2010), p. 207.

151 **"If it wasn't illegal, do it"**: Quoted in John Ydstie, "The K Street Project and Tom DeLay," NPR, January 14, 2006.

151 **"Time and time again"**: Sam Tanenhaus, "Tom DeLay's Hard Drive," *Vanity Fair*, July 2004.

151 **"because it has been a home"**: Brownstein, *The Second Civil War*, p. 227.

152 **"We don't work with Democrats"**: Tanenhaus, "Tom DeLay's Hard Drive."

152 **President Bush governed hard to the right**: Brownstein, *The Second Civil War*, pp. 263–323.

152 **Harry Reid and other Senate leaders**: Ibid., pp. 339–40.

152 **Senate Democrats also began to stray**: Todd F. Gaziano, "A Diminished Judiciary: Causes and Effects of the Sustained High Vacancy Rates in the Federal Courts," The Heritage Foundation, October 10, 2002; Mann and Ornstein, *The Broken Branch*, pp. 164–65.

152 **the New York Times quoted**: Neil Lewis, "Washington Talk: Democrats Readying for a Judicial Fight," *New York Times*, May 1, 2001.

152 **the Democrats turned to filibusters**: Tushnet, "Constitutional Hardball," pp. 524–25; Epstein and Segal, *Advice and Consent*, p. 99.

153 **"one of the great traditions"**: Quoted in Mann and Ornstein, *The Broken Branch*, p. 167.

153 **the number of filibusters reached**: Data from United States Senate. See https://www.senate.gov/pagelayout/reference/cloture_motions/clotureCounts.htm.

153 **the informal practice of "regular order"**: Mann and Ornstein, *It's Even Worse Than It Looks*, pp. 7, 50.

153 **The share of bills introduced**: Mann and Ornstein, *The Broken Branch*, p. 172.

153 **"long-standing norms of conduct in the House"**: Mann and Ornstein, *The Broken Branch*, p. xi.

153   **140 hours of sworn testimony:** Brownstein, *The Second Civil War*, pp. 274–75.

153   **The congressional watchdog:** Ibid., pp. 274–75.

154   **widely shared norm:** Tushnet, "Constitutional Hardball," p. 526.

154   **In 2003, Texas Republicans:** Steve Bickerstaff, *Lines in the Sand: Congressional Redistricting in Texas and the Downfall of Tom DeLay* (Austin: University of Texas Press, 2007), pp. 132, 171.

154   **Texas Republicans drew up:** Ibid., pp. 84–108.

154   **The new map left:** Ibid., pp. 102–4.

154   **"was as partisan":** Quoted in ibid., p. 108.

155   **They remained there:** Ibid., pp. 220, 228.

155   **DeLay flew in from Washington:** Ibid., pp. 251–53.

155   **"the most aggressive map":** Quoted in ibid., pp. 251–53.

155   **"taking up arms for Al Qaeda":** "First Democrat Issue: Terrorist Rights," *The Rush Limbaugh Show*, January 10, 2006. See https://origin-www.rushlimbaugh.com/daily/2006/01/10/first _democrat_issue_terrorist_rights/.

156   **defends Joseph McCarthy:** Ann Coulter, *Treason: Liberal Treachery from the Cold War to the War on Terrorism* (New York: Three Rivers Press, 2003).

156   **"intrinsic to [liberals'] entire worldview":** Coulter, *Treason*, pp. 292, 16.

156   **"There are millions of suspects here":** "Coulter Right on Rape, Wrong on Treason," CoulterWatch, December 11, 2014. See https://coulterwatch.wordpress.com/2014/12/11/coulter-right -on-rape-wrong-on-treason/#_edn3.

156   **Democratic presidential candidate Barack Obama:** For a summary of these attacks, see Martin A. Parlett, *Demonizing a President: The "Foreignization" of Barack Obama* (Santa Barbara, CA: Praeger, 2014).

156   **The Fox News program *Hannity & Colmes*:** Grossman and Hopkins, *Asymmetric Politics*, pp. 129–30.

157   **"unless Obama proves me wrong":** Parlett, *Demonizing a President*, p. 164.

157   **"totalitarian dictatorship":** "Rep. Steve King: Obama Will Make America a 'Totalitarian Dictatorship,'" *ThinkProgress*, October 28, 2008.

157 "palling around with terrorists": Grossman and Hopkins, *Asymmetric Politics*, p. 130.

157 "launched his political career": Dana Milibank, "Unleashed, Palin Makes a Pit Bull Look Tame," *Washington Post*, October 7, 2008.

157 Her racially coded speeches: Frank Rich, "The Terrorist Barack Hussein Obama," *New York Times*, October 11, 2008.

158 its opposition to Obama: See Christopher S. Parker and Matt A. Barreto, *Change They Can't Believe In: The Tea Party and Reactionary Politics in America* (Princeton, NJ: Princeton University Press, 2013); also see Theda Skocpol and Vanessa Williamson, *The Tea Party and the Remaking of American Conservatism* (New York: Oxford University Press, 2013).

158 Georgia congressman Paul Broun: "Georgia Congressman Calls Obama Marxist, Warns of Dictatorship," *Politico*, November 11, 2008.

158 "you don't believe in the Constitution": "Broun Is Asked, Who'll 'Shoot Obama,' " *Politico*, February 25, 2011.

158 "has become a dictator": Mann and Ornstein, *It's Even Worse Than It Looks*, p. 214.

158 followers stressed repeatedly: See Parker and Barreto, *Change They Can't Believe In*.

159 "This was not a shift": Quoted in Parker and Barreto, *Change They Can't Believe In*, p. 2.

159 *"THIS WILL CURDLE YOUR BLOOD!!!"*: Quoted in Jonathan Alter, *The Center Holds: Obama and His Enemies* (New York: Simon & Schuster, 2013), p. 36.

159 "I do not believe Barack Obama": Quoted in Parker and Barreto, *Change They Can't Believe In*, p. 200.

159 "the first anti-American president": "Newt Gingrich: Obama 'First Anti-American President,' " *Newsmax*, March 23, 2016; and "Gingrich: Obama's Worldview Shaped by Kenya," *Newsmax*, September 12, 2010.

159 "I do not believe, and I know": Darren Samuelson, "Giuliani: Obama Doesn't Love America," *Politico*, February 18, 2015.

160 "I do not know": "Mike Coffman Says Obama 'Not an American' at Heart, Then Apologizes," *Denver Post*, May 16, 2012.

160 "birther enablers": Gabriel Winant, "The Birthers in Congress," *Salon*, July 28, 2009.

160   **U.S. Senators Roy Blunt:** Ibid.

160   **"I have people":** "What Donald Trump Has Said Through the Years About Where President Obama Was Born," *Los Angeles Times*, December 16, 2016.

160   **his high-profile questioning:** Parker and Barreto, *Change They Can't Believe In*, p. 210.

161   **37 percent of Republicans:** "Fox News Poll: 24 Percent Believe Obama Not Born in the U.S.," FoxNews.com, April 7, 2011.

161   **Forty-three percent of Republicans:** "Poll: 43 Percent of Republicans Believe Obama is a Muslim," *The Hill*, September 13, 2015.

161   **a *Newsweek* poll found:** Daniel Stone, "Newsweek Poll: Democrats May Not Be Headed for a Bloodbath," *Newsweek,* August 27, 2010.

161   **"absorb as much of the Tea Party":** Quoted in Abramowitz, *The Polarized Public?*, p. 101.

161   **Well-funded organizations:** Skocpol and Williamson, *The Tea Party and the Remaking of American Conservatism*, pp. 83–120.

161   **Tea Party–backed candidates:** "How the Tea Party Fared," *New York Times*, November 4, 2010. Also Michael Tesler, *Post-Racial or Most-Racial? Race and Politics in the Obama Era* (Chicago: University of Chicago Press, 2016), pp. 122–23.

161   **the House Tea Party Caucus:** "Who Is in the Tea Party Caucus in the House?," CNN.com (*Political Ticker*), July 29, 2011.

162   **"threat to the rule of law":** "Ted Cruz Calls Obama 'The Most Lawless President in the History of This Country,'" Tu94.9FM. See http://tu949fm.iheart.com/articles/national-news-104668/listen-ted-cruz-calls-barack-obama-14518575/.

162   **a group of young House members:** See reporting by Michael Grunwald, *The New New Deal: The Hidden Story of Change in the Obama Era* (New York: Simon & Schuster, 2013), pp. 140–42.

162   **"Young Guns":** Ibid., pp. 140–42.

162   **"single most important thing":** Quoted in Abramowitz, *The Polarized Public?*, p. 122.

163   **the Republicans filibustered it:** The bill eventually passed. See Joshua Green, "Strict Obstructionist," *The Atlantic*, January/February 2011.

163 **Senate obstructionism spiked after 2008:** Mann and Ornstein, *It's Even Worse Than It Looks*, pp. 87–89.

163 **"indefinite or permanent vetoes":** Ibid., p. 85.

163 **A stunning 385 filibusters:** Milkis and Nelson, *The American Presidency*, p. 490.

163 **The confirmation rate:** Mann and Ornstein, *It's Even Worse Than It Looks*, pp. 92–94.

163 **"nuclear option":** "Reid, Democrats Trigger 'Nuclear' Option; Eliminate Most Filibusters on Nominees," *Washington Post*, November 21, 2013.

163 **"raw exercise of political power":** Quoted in ibid.

163 **"We can't wait":** Quoted in Jonathan Turley, "How Obama's Power Plays Set the Stage for Trump," *Washington Post*, December 10, 2015.

163 **Obama began to use executive authority:** See Nelson, "Are We on the Verge of the Death Spiral That Produced the English Revolution of 1642–1649?"

164 **"executive memorandum":** "Obama Mandates Rules to Raise Fuel Standards," *New York Times*, May 21, 2010.

164 **he announced an executive action:** "Obama to Permit Young Migrants to Remain in U.S.," *New York Times*, June 15, 2012.

164 **President Obama responded to Congress's refusal:** "Obama Orders Cuts in Federal Greenhouse Gas Emissions," *New York Times*, March 19, 2015.

164 **Mitch McConnell urged states:** "McConnell Urges U.S. States to Defy U.S. Plan to Cut Greenhouse Gases," *New York Times*, March 4, 2015.

164 **"John Calhoun's Secessionist screed":** "A New Phase in Anti-Obama Attacks," *New York Times*, April 11, 2015.

165 **Raising the debt limit:** Mann and Ornstein, *It's Even Worse Than It Looks*, p. 5.

165 **leaders of both parties knew:** Mann and Ornstein, *It's Even Worse Than It Looks*, pp. 6–7.

165 **willing to use the debt limit:** Grossman and Hopkins, *Asymmetric Politics*, pp. 295–96; Mann and Ornstein, *It's Even Worse Than It Looks*, pp. 7–10.

165 **"bring the whole system crashing down"**: Mann and Ornstein, *It's Even Worse Than It Looks*, pp. 25–26.

165 **Tea Party–backed Senators**: Ibid., pp. 7–8, 26–27.

165 **"We weren't kidding"**: Ibid., p. 26.

166 **Senate Republicans intervened**: As former George W. Bush speechwriter Michael Gerson put it, "The Senate simply has no business conducting foreign policy with a foreign government, especially an adversarial one. . . . The Cotton letter creates the impression that Senate Republicans are rooting for negotiations to fail." Michael Gerson, "The True Scandal of the GOP Senators' Letter to Iran," *Washington Post*, March 12, 2015.

166 **"I couldn't help but reflect"**: Quoted in Susan Milligan, "Disrespecting the Oval Office," *U.S. News & World Report*, March 16, 2015.

166 **Cotton and his allies**: The *New York Daily News* blazed the word *Traitors* on its front cover the following day.

166 **not once since Reconstruction**: Kar and Mazzone, "The Garland Affair."

166 **several Republican senators**: "Republican Senators Vow to Block Any Clinton Supreme Court Nominee Forever," *The Guardian*, November 2, 2006.

166 **"if Hillary Clinton becomes president"**: Ibid.

166 **"historical precedent"**: Quoted in ibid.

167 **Their voters are now deeply divided**: Marc J. Hetherington and Jonathan D. Weiler, *Authoritarianism and Polarization in American Politics* (New York: Cambridge University Press, 2009); Abramowitz, *The Polarized Public?*

167 **"way of life"**: Bill Bishop with Robert G. Cushing, *The Big Sort: Why the Clustering of Like-Minded America Is Tearing Us Apart* (Boston: Houghton Mifflin, 2008), p. 23.

167 **"somewhat or very unhappy"**: Shanto Iyengar, Gaurav Sood, and Yphtach Lelkes, "Affect, Not Ideology: A Social Identity Perspective on Polarization," *Public Opinion Quarterly* 76, no. 3 (2012), pp. 417–18.

168 **Being a Democrat or a Republican**: Ibid.

168 **the numbers are even higher**: Pew Research Center, "Partisanship and Political Animosity in 2016," June 22, 2016, http://www.people-press.org/2016/06/22/partisanship-and-political-animosity-in-2016/.

168   **The Democrats represented:** See James L. Sundquist, *Dynamics of the Party System: Alignment and Re-Alignment of Political Parties in the United States* (Washington, DC: The Brookings Institution, 1983), pp. 214–27; Alan I. Abramowitz, *The Disappearing Center: Engaged Citizens, Polarization, and American Democracy* (New Haven, CT: Yale University Press, 2010), pp. 54–56.

168   **Evangelical Christians:** Geoffrey Layman, *The Great Divide: Religious and Cultural Conflict in American Party Politics* (New York: Columbia University Press, 2001), p. 171.

168   **the parties overlapped:** Schickler, *Racial Realignment*, p. 179; Edward G. Carmines and James A. Stimson, *Issue Evolution: Race and the Transformation of American Politics* (Princeton, NJ: Princeton University Press, 1989), Chapter 3.

168   **southern Democrats' opposition and strategic control:** Ibid., p. 119.

169   **"conservative coalition":** Binder and Smith, *Politics or Principle?*, p. 88.

169   **democratize the South:** See Mickey, *Paths out of Dixie*.

169   **Nixon's "Southern Strategy":** Abramowitz, *The Disappearing Center*, pp. 66–73; Tesler, *Post-Racial or Most-Racial?*, pp. 11–13.

169   **what had long been:** Earl Black and Merle Black, *The Rise of Southern Republicans* (Cambridge, MA: Harvard University Press, 2002); Abramowitz, *The Disappearing Center*, pp. 66–73.

169   **southern blacks:** Carmines and Stimson, *Issue Evolution*.

169   **The post-1965 realignment:** Matthew Levendusky, *The Partisan Sort: How Liberals Became Democrats and Conservatives Became Republicans* (Chicago: University of Chicago Press, 2009).

169   **partisanship and ideology converged:** Ibid.; Abramowitz, *The Disappearing Center*, pp. 63–73.

170   **the ideological differences between the parties:** See Pew Research Center, *Political Polarization in the American Public* (Washington, DC: Pew Foundation), June 12, 2014.

170   **The social, ethnic, and cultural bases:** This section draws on Hetherington and Weiler, *Authoritarianism and Polarization in American Politics*; Abramowitz, *The Disappearing Center*; Abramowitz, *The Polarized Public?*; and Alan I. Abramowitz and Steven Webster, "The Rise of Negative Partisanship and the Nationalization of U.S. Elections in the 21st Century," *Electoral Studies* 41 (2016), pp. 12–22.

170 **they constituted 38 percent:** "It's Official: The U.S. Is Becoming a Majority-Minority Nation," *U.S. News & World Report*, July 6, 2015.

170 **the U.S. Census Bureau projects:** Sandra L. Colby and Jennifer M. Ortman, "Projections of the Size and Composition of the U.S. Population: 2014–2060," *United States Census Bureau Current Population Reports*, March 2015. See https://www.census.gov/content/dam/Census/library/publications/2015/demo/p25-1143.pdf.

171 **The nonwhite share of the Democratic vote:** Tesler, *Post-Racial or Most-Racial?*, p. 166; Abramowitz, *The Polarized Public?*, p. 29.

171 **Republican voters:** Tesler, *Post-Racial or Most-Racial?*, pp. 166–68.

171 **the GOP embraced the Christian Right:** Geoffrey C. Layman, *The Great Divide: Religious and Cultural Conflict in American Party Politics* (New York: Columbia University Press, 2001); Abramowitz, *The Polarized Public?*, pp. 69–77.

171 **76 percent of white evangelicals:** "The Parties on the Eve of the 2016 Election: Two Coalitions, Moving Further Apart," *Pew Research Center*, September 13, 2016, http://www.people-press.org/2016/09/13/2-party-affiliation-among-voters-1992-2016/.

171 **The percentage of white Democrats:** Abramowitz, *The Polarized Public?*, p.67.

171 **married white Christians:** Abramowitz, *The Disappearing Center*, p. 129.

171 **By the 2000s:** Ibid., p. 129.

171 **the two parties are now divided:** Hetherington and Weiler, *Authoritarianism and Polarization in American Politics*, pp. 27–28, 63–83.

172 **most of the norm breaking:** Grossman and Hopkins, *Asymmetric Politics*; Mann and Ornstein, *It's Even Worse Than It Looks*.

172 **Republican voters rely more heavily:** Levendusky, *How Partisan Media Polarize America*, pp. 14–16; Grossman and Hopkins, *Asymmetric Politics*, pp. 149–64.

172 **69 percent of Republican voters:** Levendusky, *How Partisan Media Polarize America*, p. 14.

172 **popular radio talk-show hosts:** Grossman and Hopkins, *Asymmetric Politics*, pp. 170–74.

172   The rise of right-wing media: Theda Skocpol and Alexander Hertel-Fernandez, "The Koch Network and Republican Party Extremism," *Perspectives on Politics* 16, no. 3 (2016), pp. 681–99.

172   "no compromise" position: Levendusky, *How Partisan Media Polarize America*, p. 152.

172   California Republican representative Darrell Issa: Levendusky, *How Partisan Media Polarize America*, p. 152.

172   "If you stray the slightest": Quoted in Grossman and Hopkins, *Asymmetric Politics*, p. 177.

172   Hard-line positions were reinforced: Skocpol and Hertel-Fernandez, "The Koch Network," pp. 681–99.

172   Grover Norquist's Americans for Tax Reform: Elizabeth Drew, *Whatever It Takes: The Real Struggle for Power in America* (New York: Viking Press, 1997), p. 65.

173   outside groups such as Americans for Prosperity: Skocpol and Hertel-Fernandez, "The Koch Network," p. 683.

173   the Koch family was responsible: Ibid., p. 684.

173   the GOP has remained culturally homogeneous: Grossman and Hopkins, *Asymmetric Politics,* pp. 43–46, 118–23.

173   white Protestants are a minority: Abramowitz, *The Disappearing Center*, p. 129.

174   "overheated, oversuspicious, overaggressive": Richard Hoftstadter, *The Paranoid Style in American Politics and Other Essays* (New York: Vintage, 1967), p. 4.

174   "slipping away": Parker and Barreto, *Change They Can't Believe In*, pp. 3, 157.

174   "strangers in their own land": Arlie Russell Hochschild, *Strangers in Their Own Land: Anger and Mourning on the American Right* (New York: The New Press, 2016).

174   "real Americans": Based on an analysis of national survey results, Elizabeth Theiss-Morse found that those who most strongly identify as Americans tend to view "real Americans" as 1) native-born, 2) English-speaking, 3) white, and 4) Christian. See Elizabeth Theiss Morse, *Who Counts as an American: The Boundaries of National Identity* (New York: Cambridge University Press, 2009), pp. 63–94.

174   "The American electorate isn't moving": Ann Coulter, *Adios America! The Left's Plan to Turn Our Country into a Third World Hellhole* (Washington, DC: Regnery Publishing, 2015), p. 19.

174 **"Take Our Country Back":** Parker and Barreto, *Change They Can't Believe In*.

CHAPTER 8: TRUMP AGAINST THE GUARDRAILS

176 **A study by the Shorenstein Center:** Thomas E. Patterson, "News Coverage of Donald Trump's First 100 Days," Shorenstein Center on Media, Politics, and Public Policy, May 18, 2017, https://shorensteincenter.org/news-coverage-donald-trumps-first-100-days. The news outlets covered in the study were the *New York Times*, *Wall Street Journal*, and *Washington Post*, as well as CNN, CBS, CNN, Fox News, NBC, and two European media outlets.

176 **Trump administration officials were feeling besieged:** See Glenn Thrush and Maggie Haberman, "At a Besieged White House, Tempers Flare and Confusion Swirls," *New York Times*, May 16, 2017.

176 **press coverage:** Patterson, "News Coverage of Donald Trump's First 100 Days."

177 **"no politician in history":** "Trump Says No President Has Been Treated More Unfairly," *Washington Post*, May 17, 2017.

177 **He later reportedly pressured:** "Comey Memo Says Trump Asked Him to End Flynn Investigation," *New York Times*, May 16, 2017; "Top Intelligence Official Told Associates Trump Asked Him If He Could Intervene with Comey on FBI Russia Probe," *Washington Post*, June 6, 2017.

178 **he dismissed Comey:** Josh Gerstein, "Trump Shocks with Ouster of FBI's Comey," *Politico*, May 9, 2017; and "Trump Said He Was Thinking of Russia Controversy When He Decided to Fire Comey," *Washington Post*, May 11, 2017.

178 **Only once in the FBI's eighty-two-year history:** Philip Bump, "Here's How Unusual It Is for an FBI Director to Be Fired," *Washington Post*, May 9, 2017; "FBI Director Firing in Early '90s Had Some Similarities to Comey Ouster," *U.S. News & World Report*, May 10, 2017.

178 **Trump had attempted to establish:** Tina Nguyen, "Did Trump's Personal Lawyer Get Preet Bharara Fired?," *Vanity Fair*, June 13, 2017; "Mueller Expands Probe into Trump Business Transactions," *Bloomberg*, July 20, 2017.

178 **the president removed him:** "Mueller Expands Probe into Trump Business Transactions."

178 **Trump publicly shamed Sessions:** Nolan McCaskill and Louis Nelson, "Trump Coy on Sessions's Future: 'Time Will Tell,'" *Politico*, July 25, 2017; Chris Cilizza, "Donald Trump Doesn't Want to Fire Jeff Sessions. He Wants Sessions to Quit," CNN .com, July 24, 2017.

178 **launched an effort to dig up dirt:** Michael S. Schmidt, Maggie Haberman, and Matt Apuzzo, "Trump's Lawyers, Seeking Leverage, Investigate Mueller's Investigators," *New York Times*, July 20, 2017.

179 **the government's dubiously elected Constituent Assembly:** "Venezuela's Chief Prosecutor Luisa Ortega Rejects Dismissal," BBC.com, August 6, 2017.

179 **"the opinion of this so-called judge":** "Trump Criticizes 'So-Called Judge' Who Lifted Travel Ban," *Wall Street Journal*, February 5, 2017.

179 **"unelected judge":** White House Office of the Press Secretary, "Statement on Sanctuary Cities Ruling," April 25, 2017. See https:// www.whitehouse.gov/the-press-office/2017/04/25/statement -sanctuary-cities-ruling.

179 **Trump himself responded:** "President Trump Is 'Absolutely' Considering Breaking Up the Ninth Circuit Court," *Time*, April 26, 2017.

179 **the pardon was clearly political:** A few nights earlier, Trump had said to loud applause at a political rally, "Do the people in this room like Sheriff Joe?" He rhetorically asked, "So was Sheriff Joe convicted for doing his job?" See "Trump Hints at Pardon for Ex-Sheriff Joe Arpaio," CNN.com, August 23, 2017.

179 **The move reinforced fears:** "Trump's Lawyers Are Exploring His Pardoning Powers to Hedge Against the Russia Investigation," *Business Insider*, July 20, 2017.

180 **"If the president can immunize his agents":** Martin Redish, "A Pardon for Arpaio Would Put Trump in Uncharted Territory," *New York Times*, August 27, 2017.

180 **The Trump administration also trampled:** Ryan Lizza, "How Trump Broke the Office of Government Ethics," *The New Yorker*, July 14, 2017.

180 **House Oversight Chair Jason Chaffetz:** Richard Painter, an ethics lawyer in the George W. Bush administration, described Chaffetz's action as "strong-arming" and "political retaliation." "GOP Lawmaker Hints at Investigating Ethics Chief Critical of Trump," *New York Times*, January 13, 2017.

180 **administration officials tried to force the OGE:** "White House Moves to Block Ethics Inquiry into Ex-Lobbyists on Payroll," *New York Times*, May 22, 2017.

180 **"broken" OGE:** Lizza, "How Trump Broke the Office of Government Ethics."

180 **Trump did not replace Comey:** "Trump Faces Tough Choices in FBI Pick," *The Hill*, May 15, 2017. Trump's eventual appointee, Christopher Wray, was widely expected to maintain the FBI's independence.

180 **Senate Republicans resisted Trump's efforts:** "Trump Is Reportedly Considering Bringing Rudy Giuliani on as Attorney General amid Troubles with Jeff Sessions," *Business Insider*, July 24, 2017.

181 **"enemy of the American people":** "Trump Calls the News Media the 'Enemy of the American People,'" *New York Times*, February 17, 2017.

181 **"I love the First Amendment":** "Remarks by President Trump at the Conservative Political Action Committee," White House Office of the Press Secretary, February 24, 2017. See https://www.whitehouse.gov/the-press-office/2017/02/24/remarks-president-trump-conservative-political-action-conference.

181 **"disgraced the media world":** See https://twitter.com/realdonaldtrump/status/847455180912181249.

181 **"I think that's something we've looked at":** Jonathan Turley, "Trump's Quest to Stop Bad Media Coverage Threatens Our Constitution," *The Hill*, May 2, 2017.

182 **multimillion-dollar defamation suits:** "Confrontation, Repression in Correa's Ecuador," Committee to Protect Journalists, September 1, 2011, https://cpj.org/reports/2011/09/confrontation-repression-correa-ecuador.php.

182 **"If I become president":** Conor Gaffey, "Donald Trump Versus Amazon: All the Times the President and Jeff Bezos Have Called Each Other Out," *Newsweek*, July 25, 2017.

182 **He also threatened to block:** Philip Bump, "Would the Trump Administration Block a Merger Just to Punish CNN?," *Washington Post*, July 6, 2017.

182 **President Trump signed an executive order:** "President Trump Vows to Take Aggressive Steps on Immigration," *Boston Globe*, January 25, 2017.

182 **"If we have to":** "Judge Blocks Trump Effort to Withhold Money from Sanctuary Cities," *New York Times*, April 25, 2017.

182 **The plan was reminiscent:** "Venezuela Lawmakers Strip Power from Caracas Mayor," Reuters, April 7, 2009.

182 **President Trump was blocked by the courts:** "Judge Blocks Trump Effort to Withhold Money from Sanctuary Cities." *New York Times*, April 25, 2017.

183 **he called for changes:** Aaron Blake, "Trump Wants More Power and Fewer Checks and Balances—Again," *Washington Post*, May 2, 2017. Also https://twitter.com/realdonaldtrump/status/869553853750013953.

183 **Senate Republicans did eliminate the filibuster:** Aaron Blake, "Trump Asks for More Power. Here's Why the Senate GOP Will Resist," *Washington Post*, May 30, 2017.

183 **some Republican leaders:** See Hasen, *The Voting Wars*; Ari Berman, *Give Us the Ballot: The Modern Struggle for Voting Rights in America* (New York: Picador, 2015).

183 **strict voter identification laws:** Berman, *Give Us the Ballot*; Benjamin Highton, "Voter Identification Laws and Turnout in the United States," *Annual Review of Political Science* 20, no. 1 (2017), pp. 49–67.

184 **The push for voter ID laws:** Justin Levitt, "The Truth About Voter Fraud," New York University School of Law Brenner Center for Justice (2007). See https://www.brennancenter.org/publication/truth-about-voter-fraud; also Minnite, *The Myth of Voter Fraud*; Hasen, *The Voting Wars*, pp. 41–73; Sharad Goel, Marc Meredith, Michael Morse, David Rothschild, and Houshmand Shirani-Mehr, "One Person, One Vote: Estimating the Prevalence of Double-Voting in U.S. Presidential Elections," unpublished manuscript, January 2017.

184 **All reputable studies:** See, for example, Levitt, "The Truth About Voter Fraud"; Minnite, *The Myth of Voter Fraud*.

184 "modern day poll tax": Quoted in Berman, *Give Us the Ballot*, p. 223.

184 An estimated 300,000 Georgia voters: Ibid., p. 223.

184 "a not-too-thinly veiled attempt": Quoted in ibid., p. 254.

184 Bills were introduced: Ibid., pp. 260–61.

184 fifteen states had adopted such laws: Highton, "Voter Identification Laws and Turnout in the United States," pp. 152–53.

184 a disproportionate impact: Charles Stewart III, "Voter ID: Who Has Them? Who Shows Them?" *Oklahoma Law Review* 66 (2013).

184 reported not possessing a valid driver's license: Ibid., pp. 41–42.

184 A study by the Brennan Center for Justice: Berman, *Give Us the Ballot*, p. 254.

185 seven adopted stricter voter ID laws: Ibid., p. 264.

185 Scholars have just begun: Highton, "Voter Identification Laws and Turnout in the United States," p. 153.

185 "premier advocate of vote suppression": Peter Waldman, "Why We Should Be Very Afraid of Trump's Vote Suppression Commission," *Washington Post*, June 30, 2017.

185 Kobach helped push through: See Ari Berman, "The Man Behind Trump's Voter-Fraud Obsession," *New York Times Magazine*, June 13, 2017.

185 "won the popular vote": See https://twitter.com/realdonald trump/status/80297294453220966?lang=en.

185 He repeated this point: "Without Evidence, Trump Tells Lawmakers 3 Million to 5 Million Illegal Ballots Cost Him the Popular Vote," *Washington Post*, January 23, 2017. Trump's statement appears to have been based on claims made by noted conspiracy theorist Alex Jones on his website Infowars. See Jessica Huseman and Scott Klein, "There's No Evidence Our Election Was Rigged," ProPublica, November 28, 2016.

185 national vote-monitoring project: Huseman and Klein, "There's No Evidence Our Election Was Rigged."

185 *Washington Post* reporter Philip Bump: "There Have Been Just Four Documented Cases of Voter Fraud in the 2016 Election," *Washington Post*, December 1, 2016.

185 "absolutely correct": Berman, "The Man Behind Trump's Voter-Fraud Obsession."

185   **"we will probably never know":** Max Greenwood and Ben Kamisar, "Kobach: 'We May Never Know' If Clinton Won Popular Vote," *The Hill*, July 17, 2019.

186   **The Commission has already sought:** Waldman, "Why We Should Be Very Afraid of Trump's Vote Suppression Commission."

186   **the number of mistakes:** Goel, Meredith, Morse, Rothschild, and Houshmand, "One Person, One Vote."

186   **Trump's Commission on Election Integrity:** In July 2017, it was reported that forty-four states had refused to share voter information with the Commission. See "Forty-Four States and DC Have Refused to Give Certain Voter Information to Trump Commission," CNN.com, July 5, 2017.

189   **the Law and Justice Party:** "Poland's President Vetoes 2 Laws That Limited Courts' Independence," *New York Times*, July 24, 2017.

189   **Active loyalists:** Representative Duncan Hunter of California, for example, publicly defended Trump even after the release of the *Access Hollywood* tape during the 2016 campaign. See "Trump's 10 Biggest Allies in Congress," *The Hill*, December 25, 2016.

190   **A few of them pushed quietly:** "Special Counsel Appointment Gets Bipartisan Praise," *The Hill*, May 17, 2017.

190   **important Republican senators:** "Republicans to Trump: Hands off Mueller," *Politico*, June 12, 2017.

190   **Senate Judiciary Committee Chair Chuck Grassley:** Ibid.

190   **Graham, McCain, and Corker:** See https://projects.fivethirty eight.com/congress-trump-score/?ex_cid=rrpromo.

191   **"found their own red line":** "Senators Unveil Two Proposals to Protect Mueller's Russia Probe," *Washington Post*, August 3, 2017; Tracy, "As Mueller Closes In, Republicans Turn away from Trump."

191   **President Trump's approval rating:** Jeffrey M. Jones, "Trump Has Averaged 50% or Higher Job Approval in 17 States," Gallup News Service, July 24, 2017. See http://www.gallup.com /poll/214349/trump-averaged-higher-job-approval-states.aspx.

191   **Democratic senator Joe Manchin:** See https://projects.fivethirty eight.com/congress-trump-score/?ex_cid=rrpromo.

191 *The Hill* listed Manchin: "Trump's 10 Biggest Allies in Congress."

192 "Have we not heard enough": "In West Virginia, Trump Hails Conservatism and a New GOP Governor," *New York Times*, August 3, 2017.

192 they increase support for the government: See again Mueller, *War, Presidents, and Public Opinion* and more recent empirical studies of the rally-'round-the-flag effect in the United States, including Oneal and Bryan, "The Rally 'Round the Flag Effect in U.S. Foreign Policy Crises, 1950–1985," Baum, "The Constituent Foundations of the Rally-Round-the-Flag Phenomenon," and Chatagnier, "The Effect of Trust in Government on Rallies 'Round the Flag."

192 Citizens become more likely to tolerate: Huddy, Khatib, and Capelos, "The Polls—Trends," pp. 418–50; Darren W. Davis and Brian D. Silver, "Civil Liberties vs. Security: Public Opinion in the Context of the Terrorist Attacks on America," *American Journal of Political Science* 48, no. 1 (2004), pp. 28–46; Huddy, Feldman, and Weber, "The Political Consequences of Perceived Threat and Felt Insecurity," pp. 131–53; and Adam J. Berinsky, *In Time of War: Understanding American Public Opinion from World War II to Iraq* (Chicago: University of Chicago Press, 2009), Chapter 7.

192 Judges are notoriously reluctant: Howell, *Power Without Persuasion*; Ackerman, *The Decline and Fall of the American Republic*, pp. 67–85.

192 institutional constraints: Howell, *Power Without Persuasion*, p. 184.

193 President Trump's foreign policy ineptitude: During the 2016 campaign, fifty Republican foreign policy experts, many of them former Bush administration officials, wrote a letter warning that Trump's ignorance and recklessness would "put at risk our nation's national security." See "50 G.O.P. Officials Warn Donald Trump Would Put Nation's Security 'At Risk,'" *New York Times*, August 8, 2016.

193 "smashed through the behavior standards": David Brooks, "Getting Trump out of My Brain," *New York Times*, August 8, 2017.

194   "closed and armored limousine": James Wieghart and Paul Healy, "Jimmy Carter Breaks Protocol at Inauguration," *New York Daily News*, January 21, 1977.

194   "an informal custom": Christine Hauser, "The Inaugural Parade, and the Presidents Who Walked It," *New York Times*, January 19, 2017.

194   **William Henry Harrison broke tradition:** Paul F. Boller, *Presidential Campaigns: From George Washington to George W. Bush* (Oxford: Oxford University Press, 2004), p. 70

194   **"Booker T. Washington of Tuskegee, Alabama":** The following account draws on Clarence Lusane, *The Black History of the White House* (San Francisco: City Lights Books, 2011), pp. 219–78.

194   **"the prevailing social etiquette":** Ibid.

195   **President Trump broke:** "President Trump Breaks a 150-Year Tradition of Pets in the White House," AOL.com, July 28, 2017.

195   **"American carnage":** Yashar Ali, "What George W. Bush Really Thought of Donald Trump's Inauguration," *New York Magazine*, March 29, 2017.

195   **not technically required:** As Walter Shaub, the former head of the Office of Government Ethics, put it, "You could seriously be the Secretary of the Department of Energy and hold Chevron, Exxon, and B.P. [shares] and not be violating the law, as long as you were willing to go to work every day, put your feet up on your desk, and read the newspaper and do nothing else." See Lizza, "How Trump Broke the Office of Government Ethics."

196   **President Trump exercised no such forbearance:** Trump maintained a number of potential conflicts of interest stemming from his international business dealings and his extensive links to the Trump Organization. Within weeks of the election, the Sunlight Foundation had created a list of "red flag" conflicts, posting thirty-two of them in November 2016. By July 2017, the list had grown to more than six hundred potential conflicts of interest. Many of Trump's cabinet and advisory appointees—drawn from the worlds of energy, finance, and lobbying—also faced potential conflicts of interest. See data: http://www.sunlightfoundation.com.

196   **The Office of Government Ethics:** "As Trump Inquiries Flood Ethics Office, Director Looks to House for Action," NPR.com,

April 17, 2017. Trump's legal team pointed to former Vice President Nelson Rockefeller as an example of an executive official who didn't fully divest from his family fortune. However, Vice President Rockefeller was subjected to four months of hearings over potential conflicts. See "Conflicts of Interest: Donald Trump 2017 vs. Nelson Rockefeller 1974," CBSNews.com, January 13, 2017.

196 **President Trump also violated:** See https://twitter.com/real donaldtrump/status/802972944532209664?lang=en.

196 **"millions" of illegal voters:** "California Official Says Trump's Claim of Voter Fraud Is 'Absurd,'" *New York Times*, November 28, 2016; "Voter Fraud in New Hampshire? Trump Has No Proof and Many Skeptics," *New York Times*, February 13, 2017; "Trump's Baseless Assertions of Voter Fraud Called 'Stunning,'" *Politico*, November 27, 2016.

196 **A poll taken prior:** "Un Tercio de los Mexicans Cree Que Hubo Fraude en las Elecciones de 2006," *El Pais*, July 3, 2008. See https://elpais.com/internacional/2008/07/03/actualidad /1215036002_850215.html; Emir Olivares Alonso, "Considera 71% de los Mexicanos que Puede Haber Fraude Electoral," *La Jornada*, June 29, 2012. See http://www.jornada.unam .mx/2012/06/29/politica/003n1pol.

197 **"meaningful amount" of fraud:** Sam Corbett-Davies, Tobias Konitzer, and David Rothschild, "Poll: 60% of Republicans Believe Illegal Immigrants Vote; 43% Believe People Vote Using Dead People's Names," *Washington Post*, October 24, 2016.

197 **47 percent of Republicans:** "Many Republicans Doubt Clinton Won Popular Vote," *Morning Consult*, July 27, 2017.

197 **Fifty-two percent of Republicans:** Ariel Malka and Yphtach Lelkes, "In a New Poll, Half of Republicans Say They Would Support Postponing the 2020 Election If Trump Proposed It," *Washington Post*, August 10, 2017.

197 **"Terrible! Just found out":** https://twitter.com/realdonaldtrump /status/837996746236182529; also see www.politifact.com /truth-o-meter/article/2017/mar/21/timeline-donald-trumps -false-wiretapping-charge%2F.

198 **"never deny the undeniable":** "Many Politicians Lie, but Trump Has Elevated the Art of Fabrication," *New York Times*, August 8, 2017.

198   *PolitiFact* classified: *PolitiFact.* See http://www.politifact.com
       /personalities/donald-trump/.

198   "achieved something remarkable": David Leonhardt and Stu-
       art Thompson, "Trump's Lies," *New York Times*, https://www
       .nytimes.com/interactive/2017/06/23/opinion/trumps-lies
       .html?mcubz=1.

198   President Trump claimed: Rebecca Savransky, "Trump Falsely
       Claims He Got Biggest Electoral College Win Since Reagan,"
       The Hill, February 16, 2017; Tom Kertscher, "Donald Trump
       Not Close in Claiming He Has Signed More Bills in First Six
       Months Than Any President," *PolitiFact Wisconsin,* July 20,
       2017, http://www.politifact.com/wisconsin/statements/2017/jul
       /20/donald-trump/donald-trump-not-close-claiming-he-has
       -signed-more/.

198   "the greatest speech ever": Ella Nilsen, "Trump: Boy Scouts
       Thought My Speech Was 'Greatest Ever Made to Them.' Boy
       Scouts: No," *Vox*, August 2, 2017.

198   view him as dishonest: Surveys from mid-2017 showed that
       57 percent of Americans believed the president was not hon-
       est. See Quinnipiac University Poll, "Trump Gets Small Bump
       from American Voters," January 10, 2017 (https://poll.qu.edu
       /national/release-detail?ReleaseID=2415); "U.S. Voters Send
       Trump Approval to Near Record Low," May 10, 2017 (https://
       poll.qu.edu/national/release-detail?ReleaseID=2456); "Trump
       Gets Small Bump from American Voters," June 29, 2017 (https://
       poll.qu.edu/national/release-detail?ReleaseID=2471).

198   Citizens have a basic right: See Robert Dahl, *Polyarchy: Partici-
       pation and Opposition* (New Haven, CT: Yale University Press,
       1971).

199   "among the most dishonest human beings": "With False
       Claims, Trump Attacks Media on Turnout and Intelligence
       Rift," *New York Times*, January 21, 2017. See also http://video
       .foxnews.com/v/5335781902001/?#sp=show-clips.

200   "I heard poorly rated @Morning_Joe": https://twitter.com
       /realdonaldtrump/status/880408582310776832, https://twitter
       .com/realdonaldtrump/status/880410114456465411.

200   Press Secretary Sean Spicer: "CNN, *New York Times,* Other
       Media Barred from White House Briefing," *Washington Post*,
       February 24, 2017.

200 **The only modern precedent:** "Trump Not the Only President to Ban Media Outlets from the White House," ABC10.com, February 24, 2017.

200 **Humans have a limited ability to cope:** Daniel Patrick Moynihan, "Defining Deviancy Down: How We've Become Accustomed to Alarming Levels of Crime and Destructive Behavior," *The American Scholar* 62, no. 1 (Winter 1993), pp. 17–30.

201 **All but one Republican senator:** Susan Collins of Maine voted with Trump 79 percent of the time. See https://projects.fivethirty eight.com/congress-trump-score/?ex_cid=rrpromo.

201 **Even Senators Ben Sasse:** See https://projects.fivethirtyeight .com/congress-trump-score/?ex_cid=rrpromo.

202 **Greg Gianforte, the Republican candidate:** "GOP Candidate in Montana Race Charged with Misdemeanor Assault After Allegedly Body-Slamming Reporter," *Washington Post*, May 24, 2017.

202 **"biased or inaccurate":** "Attitudes Toward the Mainstream Media Take an Unconstitutional Turn," *The Economist*, August 2, 2017; https://www.economist.com/blogs/graphicdetail /2017/08/daily-chart-0.

202 **"They use their schools":** "Why Join the National Rifle Association? To Defeat Liberal Enemies, Apparently," *The Guardian*, July 1, 2017.

203 **"We've had it":** "'We're Coming for You': NRA Attacks *New York Times* in Provocative Video," *The Guardian,* August 5, 2017.

CHAPTER 9: SAVING DEMOCRACY

204 **It was only after 1965:** Mickey, *Paths out of Dixie.*

204 **fundamental realignment:** Mickey, Levitsky, and Way, "Is America Still Safe for Democracy?," pp. 20–29.

204 **There is a mounting perception:** See Larry Diamond, "Facing Up to the Democratic Recession," *Journal of Democracy* 26, no. 1 (January 2015), pp. 141–55; and Roberto Stefan Foa and Yascha Mounk, "The Democratic Disconnect," *Journal of Democracy* 27, no. 3 (July 2016), pp. 5–17.

204 **Larry Diamond:** Diamond, "Facing Up to the Democratic Recession."

205 **claims about a global democratic recession:** Steven Levitsky and Lucan A. Way, "The Myth of Democratic Recession," *Journal of Democracy* 26, no. 1 (January 2015), pp. 45–58.

205 **U.S. governments used diplomatic pressure:** Levitsky and Way, *Competitive Authoritarianism*; Mainwaring and Pérez-Liñan, *Democracies and Dictatorships in Latin America*.

207 **a pro-Trump GOP:** Republican control over the various branches of government would be made possible by the concentration of the Democratic vote in urban centers. This has allowed the Republicans—who dominate the small-town and rural vote—to become nearly unbeatable in much of the national territory, giving them an edge in the Electoral College and particularly in the Senate.

209 **It is also demographically diverse:** See https://www.census.gov /quickfacts/NC.

209 **"microcosm of the country's hyper-partisan politics":** Jedediah Purdy, "North Carolina's Partisan Crisis," *The New Yorker*, December 20, 2016.

209 **partisans have battled:** "North Carolina Governor Signs Controversial Transgender Bill," CNN.com, March 24, 2016.

209 **"more polarized and more acrimonious":** Quoted in Mark Joseph Stern, "North Carolina Republicans' Legislative Coup Is an Attack on Democracy," *Slate*, December 15, 2016.

210 **The changes enabled Republicans:** Max Blau, "Drawing the Line on the Most Gerrymandered District in America," *The Guardian*, October 19, 2016.

210 **They began by demanding access:** See: http://pdfserver .amlaw.com/nlj/7-29-16%204th%20Circuit%20NAACP%20 v%20NC.pdf, pp. 10, 13.

210 **They passed a strict voter ID law:** "North Carolina Governor Signs Extensive Voter ID Law," *Washington Post*, August 12, 2013; and "Critics Say North Carolina Is Curbing the Black Vote. Again," *New York Times*, August 30, 2016.

210 **"almost surgical precision":** "Justices Reject Two Gerrymandered North Carolina Districts, Citing Racial Bias," *New York Times*, May 27, 2017.

210 **Republicans used their control:** "Critics Say North Carolina Is Curbing the Black Vote. Again."

210 **McCrory refused to concede:** "North Carolina Governor Alleges Voter Fraud in Bid to Hang On," *Politico*, November 21,

2016; and "North Carolina Gov. Pat McCrory Files for Recount as Challenger's Lead Grows," NBCNews.com, November 22, 2016.

210 **"surprise special session"**: "Democrats Protest as GOP Calls Surprise Special Session," WRAL.com, December 14, 1016.

211 **"legislative coup"**: "NC Is in the Hot National Spotlight Yet Again as Media Focus on General Assembly, Cooper," *Charlotte Observer*, December 16, 2016; Stern, "North Carolina Republicans' Legislative Coup Is an Attack on Democracy."

211 **"brazen power grab"**: "A Brazen Power Grab in North Carolina," *New York Times*, December 15, 2016.

211 **The Senate granted itself the authority**: "Proposed Cuts to Gov.-Elect Roy Cooper's Appointment Powers Passes NC House in 70–36 Vote," *News & Observer*, December 15, 2016; and see "Bill Would Curb Cooper's Appointment Powers," WRAL.com, December 14, 2016.

211 **Outgoing governor McCrory**: "Before Leaving Office, McCrory Protected 908 State Jobs from Political Firings," *News & Observer*, February 23, 2017.

211 **Republicans then changed the composition**: "Senate Passes Controversial Merger of Ethics, Elections Boards," WRAL.com, December 15, 2016.

211 **responsible for local rules**: See https://www.ncsbe.gov/about-us.

211 **The boards had been under**: Purdy, "North Carolina's Partisan Crisis."

211 **the chair of the election boards**: "Proposed Cuts to Gov.-Elect Roy Cooper's Appointment Powers Passes NC House in 70–36 Vote."

211 **the legislature voted to shrink**: "Rebuked Twice by Supreme Court, North Carolina Republicans Are Unabashed," *New York Times*, May 27, 2017.

212 **"American democracy"**: Quoted in Purdy, "North Carolina's Partisan Crisis."

212 **Baron de Montesquieu pioneered**: Baron von Montesquieu, *The Spirit of the Laws* (Cambridge: Cambridge University Press, 1989).

213 **American Creed**: Gunnar Myrdal, *An American Dilemma: The Negro Problem and American Democracy* (New York: Harper and Brothers, 1944), pp. 3–4.

214 **"The Democratic negotiating position"**: David Faris, "It's Time for Democrats to Fight Dirty," *The Week*, December 1, 2016.

214 **"doing little to stop him"**: Dahlia Lithwick and David S. Cohen, "Buck Up, Democrats, and Fight Like Republicans," *New York Times*, December 14, 2016.

215 **"lacks legitimacy"**: Quoted in Daniella Diaz and Eugene Scott, "These Democrats Aren't Attending Trump's Inauguration," CNN.com, January 17, 2017.

215 **"legitimate president"**: Quoted in Theodore Schleifer, "John Lewis: Trump Is Not a 'Legitimate' President," CNN.com, January 14, 2017.

215 **Nearly seventy House Democrats**: Michelle Goldberg, "Democrats Are Finally Learning How to Fight Like Republicans," *Slate*, January 19, 2017.

215 **"take a page"**: Faris, "It's Time for Democrats to Fight Dirty." Also Graham Vyse, "Democrats Should Stop Talking About Bipartisanship and Start Fighting," *The New Republic*, December 15, 2016.

215 **"Everything should be a fight"**: Michelle Goldberg, "The End Is Nigh," *Slate*, May 16, 2017.

215 **"my greatest desire"**: Daniella Diaz, "Rep. Maxine Waters: Trump's Actions 'Leading Himself' to Impeachment," CNN.com, February 6, 2017.

215 **Impeachment talk picked up**: Goldberg, "The End Is Nigh."

215 **"I don't see it that way"**: Ibid.

216 **when the opposition fights dirty**: See Laura Gamboa, "Opposition at the Margins: Strategies Against the Erosion of Democracy in Colombia and Venezuela," *Comparative Politics* 49, no. 4 (July 2017), pp. 457–77.

216 **The strike lasted two months**: Ibid., p. 466.

216 **All three strategies had backfired**: Laura Gamboa, "Opposition at the Margins: The Erosion of Democracy in Latin America," PhD Dissertation, Department of Political Science, University of Notre Dame (2016), pp. 129–51.

216 **they eroded the opposition's public support**: Ibid., pp. 102–7.

216 **Opposition strategies in Colombia**: Ibid.

216 **a power grab not unlike Chávez's**: Gamboa, "Opposition at the Margins: Strategies Against the Erosion of Democracy in Colombia and Venezuela," pp. 464–68.

217   **This made it more difficult:** Ibid., pp. 468–72.

218   **black-led nonviolent protest:** Omar Wasow, "Do Protests Matter? Evidence from the 1960s Black Insurgency," unpublished manuscript, Princeton University, February 2, 2017.

220   **A profound distrust:** "Interview with President Ricardo Lagos," in *Democratic Transitions: Conversations with World Leaders*, eds. Sergio Bitar and Abraham F. Lowenthal (Baltimore: Johns Hopkins University Press, 2015), p. 85.

220   **Exiled Socialist leader Ricardo Lagos:** Ibid., p. 74.

221   **They began to meet regularly:** Ibid.

221   **Christian Democratic leader Patricio Aylwin:** "Interview with President Patricio Aylwin," in Bitar and Lowenthal, *Democratic Transitions*, pp. 61–62.

221   **"Group of 24":** Ibid.

221   **National Accord:** Constable and Valenzuela, *A Nation of Enemies*, pp. 271–72.

221   **The pact formed the basis:** "Interview with President Ricardo Lagos," p. 83.

221   **"consensus politics":** Ibid.

221   **leaders developed a practice:** Peter Siavelis, "Accommodating Informal Institutions and Chilean Democracy," in *Informal Institutions and Democracy: Lessons from Latin America,* eds. Gretchen Helmke and Steven Levitsky (Baltimore: Johns Hopkins University Press, 2006) pp. 40–48.

221   **Pinochet's 1980 constitution:** Ibid., p. 49.

221   **Aylwin also negotiated:** Ibid., pp. 48–49.

222   **"helped stave off":** Ibid., p. 50.

222   **political scientists have proposed:** See, for example, Nathaniel Persily, ed., *Solutions to Political Polarization in America* (New York: Cambridge University Press, 2015).

222   **The Republican Party:** Jacob Hacker and Paul Pierson, *Off Center: The Republican Revolution and the Erosion of American Democracy* (New Haven, CT: Yale University Press, 2006); Mann and Ornstein, *It's Even Worse Than It Looks*; Grossman and Hopkins, *Asymmetric Politics*; Michael Barber and Nolan McCarty, "Causes and Consequences of Polarization," in Persily, *Solutions to Political Polarization in America.*

223 **This hollowing out:** Nathaniel Persily, "Stronger Parties as a Solution to Polarization," in Persily, *Solutions to Political Polarization in America*, p. 123.

223 **"sugar high of populism":** Jeff Flake, *Conscience of a Conservative: A Rejection of Destructive Politics and a Return to Principle* (New York: Random House, 2017), p. 8.

224 **conservative party reform:** Daniel Ziblatt, *Conservative Parties and the Birth of Democracy* (Cambridge: Cambridge University Press, 2017).

224 **Christian Democratic Union:** Charles Maier, "The Two Postwar Eras and the Conditions for Stability in Twentieth-Century Western Europe," *American Historical Review* 86, no. 2, pp. 327–52.

224 **German conservatism:** Ziblatt, *Conservative Parties and the Birth of Democracy*, pp. 172–333.

224 **"unassailable" anti-Nazi credentials:** Jeffrey Herf, *Divided Memory: The Nazi Past in the Two Germanys* (Cambridge, MA: Harvard University Press, 1997), p. 270. Some figures in the party's early years had links to the Nazi regime, leaving the party always the subject of criticism on this front.

224 **"An old world has sunk":** Noel Cary, *The Path to Christian Democracy: German Catholics and the Party System from Windthorst to Adenauer* (Cambridge, MA: Harvard University Press, 1996), p. 147.

224 **The CDU offered a clear vision:** Geoffrey Pridham, *Christian Democracy in Western Germany* (London: Croom Helm, 1977), pp. 21–66.

224 **a "Christian" society:** Ibid., p. 32.

225 **"The close collaboration":** Quoted in ibid., pp. 26–28.

226 **Both Bernie Sanders and some moderates:** Mark Penn and Andrew Stein, "Back to the Center, Democrats," *New York Times*, July 6, 2017; Bernie Sanders, "How Democrats Can Stop Losing Elections," *New York Times*, June 13, 2017; also see Mark Lilla, "The End of Identity Liberalism," *New York Times*, November 18, 2016.

226 **Mark Penn and Andrew Stein:** Penn and Stein, "Back to the Center, Democrats." Also Mark Lilla, "The End of Identity Liberalism."

227 **"The simple fact of the matter":** Danielle Allen, "Charlottesville Is Not the Continuation of an Old Fight. It Is Something New," *Washington Post*, August 13, 2017.

227 **The intensity of partisan animosities:** Thomas Piketty, *Capital in the Twenty-First Century* (Cambridge, MA: Harvard University Press, 2013).

227 **Today's racially tinged partisan polarization:** Robert Gordon, *The Rise and Fall of American Growth: The U.S. Standard of Living Since the Civil War* (Princeton, NJ: Princeton University Press, 2016), p. 613.

228 **economic changes of the last few decades:** Katherine Kramer, *The Politics of Resentment: Rural Consciousness in Wisconsin and the Rise of Scott Walker* (Chicago: University of Chicago Press, 2016), p. 3.

228 **"welfare queens":** Ian Haney Lopez, *Dog Whistle Politics* (Oxford: Oxford University Press, 2013).

228 **a social policy agenda:** Gosta Esping-Andersen, *The Three Worlds of Welfare Capitalism* (Princeton, NJ: Princeton University Press, 1990).

229 **"family policy":** Paul Krugman, "What's Next for Progressives?," *New York Times*, August 8, 2017.

229 **America's expenditures on families:** Ibid.

229 **Democrats could consider:** Harold Wilensky, *American Political Economy in Global Perspective* (Cambridge: Cambridge University Press, 2012), p. 225.

229 **we are under no illusions:** For an example of when this has worked, see the revisionist account of the New Deal coalition by Eric Schickler, *Racial Realignment*.

230 **Surely the Board knows what democracy is:** E. B. White, "The Meaning of Democracy," *The New Yorker*, July 3, 1943.

Index

Page numbers in *italics* refer to tables.